LIVES
OF THE
PRESIDENTS

By

JULIAN DE VRIES

THE WORLD PUBLISHING CO.

CLEVELAND, OHIO NEW YORK, N. Y.

Tower Book Editions

1st printing, January, 1941
2nd printing, March, 1941
3rd printing, July, 1941

PRINTED IN THE UNITED STATES OF AMERICA

CONTENTS

LIVES OF THE PRESIDENTS

GEORGE WASHINGTON

PERHAPS no figure in American history has been the subject of so much anecdote as George Washington. Abraham Lincoln is probably the only exception. Many of the stories that have grown up around the boy and the man who was later to become the first president of the new-born democracy have since been discounted by research as legend although some of them might have had their roots in actual truth.

Suffice it to say, however, that had some inkling of his later greatness been apparent in his youth and young manhood, he might have had his Boswell who would have preserved for us much that is now forever lost.

Everyone now knows the date of the birthday which appears in red on almost every calendar in the United States. George Washington was born on the winter morning of February 22, 1732 in the small home on Bridge's Creek where the two immense chimneys at either end of the house must have given a queer appearance to the story and a half high structure.

His early boyhood must have been a healthy, happy one, crowded with hearty, robust activities and sports in the outdoor world that lay so fair and vast about him; the dark, solemn wildernesses stretching away to unknown horizons, while the great snow-daisied meadow which formed the scene of his childish sports sloped down to the swift-flowing waters of the Rappahannock.

When the boy reached his eleventh year death crossed the threshold. At that time his father died. Through all his busy, crowded life George Washington's memory must often have reverted to the day when his mother sat a widow among her group of young children, and looked on him, her first-born, through her tear-dimmed eyes. He must have felt then—the boy always grave and thoughtful beyond his years—a sudden access of responsibility. His father's mantle had, in some way, fallen on his young shoulders.

George had two half brothers—the father having been twice married. Laurence, the elder, wedded the young daughter of the Fairfaxes. This brought the boy of eleven into family relations with all that was most refined and elegant in the old colonial society of Virginia.

The eldest of Augustine Washington's sons inherited the fine qualities of his race; he had the cultivated tastes and habits acquired at Oxford, where, after the fashion of the time, he had been sent as the eldest son to complete his education. He was fourteen years the senior of George, who adored his splendid elder brother, accomplished by study, travel, and foreign society. Laurence appears to have been worthy of this admiration, and the young brother sought to form his own life and character after the example constantly before him.

Laurence inherited from his father, who left large landed estates, a noble domain on the banks of the Potomac. It was called Hunting Creek; but Laurence, in honor of the admiral under whom he had served in the West Indies, changed the name to Mount Vernon.

At Belvoir, only a few miles distant, the Fairfaxes had their home, which, in its luxurious appointments, as well as in its domestic and social habits, must have greatly resembled an English country-seat of that day. The house was filled with gay young Fairfaxes, and George, closely connected with their elder sister, made frequent visits to Belvoir as well as to Mount Vernon. He lived awhile, too, with Augustine, the younger of the halfbrothers, and attended Mr. Williams' school. This was, no doubt, an improvement on the one to which he had been first sent, kept by the sexton, where he had learned to read and write, and had studied the rudiments of arithmetic.

George Washington was intended by his family for a Virginia planter; his education was conducted with sole reference to this fact. It was of the most practical kind. Nobody appears to have thought of sending the eldest son of the second wife of Augustine Washington to Oxford, to follow in the steps of his halfbrother. George learned early to draw up all varieties of business documents. In this work he showed remarkable skill and thoroughness. His exercise books, written in a large, bold hand, still remain, and are models of their kind. What is more remarkable, and more precious still, as furnishing a keynote to his character and temperament, are the hundred and ten rules on morals and manners which the exercise book contains.

Some of these rules are of the most minute and painstaking kind. They show a deep conscientiousness, and a patience, thoroughness, and scrupulous regard for details, most unusual in a boy of the writer's age. His rigid training was no doubt partly responsible for this.

There was a good deal of the stuff of a Roman matron in that Virginia widow who was bringing up her young family on the banks of the Rappahannock. The domestic manners were formal and ceremonious, and would appear to our free-and-easy life burdensome and absurd; but beneath all the formality, beautiful and sterling virtues flourished vigorously.

Augustine Washington, the father of George, had given the highest proof of his confidence in his wife's character and abilities, by appointing her guardian of their children.

George Washington was, in his early teens, a large-limbed, powerful young fellow, with a grave, thoughtful face, with blue eyes and brown hair. He was singularly quiet, shy, and keenly observant. He had no brilliant conversational gifts, though he had a quiet sense of humor. The thing about him most likely to strike an observer was his immense enjoyment of all outdoor sports and games. He was a splendid athlete and he showed to much better advantage on the field than he did in the gay drawing room at Belvoir, where his native shyness often made the tall, grave, handsome youth silent and awkward.

Those who knew him best were quite aware that under the silence and shyness were a strong will and a swift temper; and whatever confidence they may have had in his word, they were not likely to regard him as a youthful saint. He had the makings of a soldier.

But Mrs. Washington cherished other than military ambitions for her son. The dearest wish of her heart was that he should follow in the steps of his father, become the head of the household, and a Virginia planter.

This desire once briefly and reluctantly yielded to her son's wishes, backed, no doubt, by Laurence's influence. The latter inherited the martial spirit of his race. English naval officers, with whom he had served in the West Indies, were frequent guests at Mount Vernon. Here the talk could not fail to run much upon military affairs. George, thrown at his impressible age into this society, must have been greatly stirred by it. His soul took fire. At fourteen—it must always be borne in mind that he looked and seemed older than his birthdays—a passion to enter the navy took possession of him. This was a cruel frustration of all the mother's hopes. Everybody knows the story of the consent won from her unwilling lips, and how, at the last moment, when the midshipman's warrant had been procured, and the trunk was on board the ship of war, her heart failed her. She withdrew her consent. It must have been a cruel blow to a boy of fourteen, his soul on fire with dreams of future honor and glory to be won in his new career. But he does not appear to have rebelled; he was made of the same stuff as his mother; he returned to school; he studied surveying; he took great delight in it, and soon became an admirable scholar in this department.

When George Washington was sixteen a new figure came into the foreground of his life, the figure of one destined to have a commanding influence on all the years of that opening manhood. This was Lord Thomas Fairfax. He was a man of singular character and history. He came to America to visit his cousins at Belvoir, and to look over the immense landed estates which he had inherited from his mother, and which were under the care of his cousin, William Fairfax, Laurence Washington's father-in-law.

The advent of the shrewd, eccentric old nobleman at Belvoir, with his knowledge of courts, of the army, of the world, must have created a profound sensation. It could not have been long before he and George Washington met. Lord Fairfax soon discovered that the tall, shy youth of sixteen had some traits in common with his own. Each had the same delight in the wide, free life of the fields and woods; each had a passion, too, for hunting the game to cover.

These common sympathies brought the polished English nobleman and the shy Westmoreland youth much together. Out of this friendship grew an event of vast consequence to young Washington's future.

Immense tracts of Lord Fairfax's estate lay in the Shenandoah Valley, beyond the great walls of the Blue Ridge. Nobody knew their extent; very few cared about it. Pioneers from the northern colonies, especially from Pennsylvania, attracted by the beauty and fertility of the land, established themselves wherever they chose, in utter disregard of the owner's title.

Lord Fairfax at length resolved to have his estates surveyed. He actually proposed that the boy of sixteen, with whom he had hunted in the Virginia woods, should undertake this immense task.

In March 1748 the little party set out on its perilous journey into the primeval wildernesses.

If the trip was full of perils and hardships, it had also immense fascinations for youth and health and courage. Washington now had his first taste of that frontier life of which he was to have so varied an experience. He learned what keen pleasure it was "to sleep on the hard ground, lying well wrapped before a blazing fire, with no roof but the skies."

The small party which accompanied Washington did good work at the surveying, in which he appears to have taken the lead. His diligent study served him well now. Some days, we read, he earned twenty dollars—immense wages at that time for a youth of sixteen.

When he returned to Lord Fairfax, George Washington's school days were over. He had performed his task so well that he soon afterward received a commission from the governor as public surveyor.

While Washington was busy with his government surveys, the events which were to form so thrilling a chapter in American history were coming to the front.

Two nations had long been bent on obtaining supremacy in America. The English had planted their colonies along the Atlantic coast and "guarded the front door of the American continent." The French had held steadily to their plans of building forts in the interior. They meant the chain should be secure—not a link missing from Canada to Louisiana.

Of course each nation had followed the bent of its own genius in laying the foundations for its supremacy in America. The English planted their farms and built their towns; the French raised forts and established trading posts. Every year the English pushed deeper into the lonely forests and stretched their clearings farther to the west. One almost seems to catch from that faraway time the ringing of the axe in the wilderness, the hum of busy industry, and the old songs with which the brave pioneers set to their work, resolved, with Anglo-Saxon grit, that the fair land beyond the Alleghenies should be theirs and their children's forever.

But another race, with all its old Gallic courage and shrewdness, was there too. It had pre-empted the land, and it had come to stay. It perceived with alarm and wrath that each year the English clearings drew nearer to the French posts, over which the Bourbon lilies waved in the great interior, west of the Appalachian Range.

Then there were the Indians—a foe that English and French must alike count with. The savages regarded both the white races with jealousy and rage that often flamed up in terrible vengeance.

The palefaces were to the tribes the foreign and hated foe who had seized their ancient hunting grounds. But the Indians sided sometimes with the French, sometimes with the English, as interest or caprice dictated; while frequent and bloody wars between the tribes weakened their numbers and wasted their strength.

Meanwhile, the great aim of each race was to secure possession of the Ohio Valley. Each, as we have seen, set about achieving its purpose by characteristic methods. The French steadily added to the number of their forts in the interior; the English organized the Ohio Company. Laurence Washington was the head of this company. Events were marching rapidly. It was evident that the immense area of the Ohio Valley was to be the scene of a fierce struggle for dominion.

The colonies now took the alarm. There was talk of war on every side. Military drills suddenly became the fashion in the quiet old Virginia towns. It was significant that at this time George Washington began to study military treatises and take lessons in sword exercise.

But all this was brought to a sudden close by the alarming condition of Laurence Washington's health, impaired by his life in the West Indies. He was forced at this juncture to leave his young wife and daughter and go to Barbadoes for the winter. His brother accompanied him.

This was the only time in which George Washington ever set foot on any soil but his native one. During this absence he had two experiences, widely unlike. He fell ill with smallpox, and always retained slight marks of it, and he visited the theater for the first time.

But the invalid's health did not permanently rally; he barely reached Mount Vernon to die there in July, 1752.

George Washington's heart and hands must have been full at this time. The youth of twenty was appointed one of the executors of Laurence's estate, and, in case the young daughter died, Mount Vernon was to revert to the brother, between whom and her father had existed so close an affection. Washington now went to live at Mount Vernon. It was to be home to him for the rest of his life.

A lowering May morning of 1754 forms an important date in American history and in the life of George Washington. At that time the first gun was fired in the long contest between the English and French for possession of the Ohio Valley. Washington was in that battle. Young Jumonville, the French commander, was killed. The Americans won the victory, and sent twenty-one prisoners to the colony.

"I heard the bullets whistle, and, believe me, there is something charming in the sound," Washington is reported to have written to his brother. The words do not sound like him, but he was only twenty-two, and in the flush of his first victory.

He must have smiled grimly to himself when, on the following 4th of July, he led his defeated and draggled little army from Great Meadows. During these months he had seen another side of war than the swift whistling of bullets. His fiery temper had been tried by all sorts of vexations and disappointments. These were largely the result of the incompetency, jealousy, and obstinacy of the colonial government. He was at last reduced to extremities; his supplies had failed; his troops were starving.

The draggled little army marched bravely away—drums beating and colors flying—from an enemy whose numbers made it impossible to prolong the contest. George Washington's heart must have been very heavy on that 4th of July. How little he could dream that date would yet be illuminated with undying glory for himself and his country!

Twenty-two years from that time he was to draw his sword under the old Cambridge elm in another and longer contest.

There came an hour which must have seemed, in the completeness of his triumph, to reward him for all his wrongs and toils and sufferings. That hour fell on November 25, 1758, when the young

Virginia colonel marched with the advanced guard into Fort Duquesne, and planted the English colors where the French had waved so long. The enemy, reduced to extremities, had blown up the magazines, set fire to the fort, and departed the night before.

The long struggle between the two peoples for the land whose eastern wall was the Alleghenies, had ended in victory for the race which had begun its career in America by tilling farms and planting towns on the Atlantic seaboard.

A few months later George Washington was settled at Mount Vernon. He had inherited this noble domain at the death of Laurence's daughter. It was to be the dearest spot on earth to him for the rest of his life.

Everybody knows how unexpectedly he met the beautiful Martha Custis—how her charms fascinated him on the first interview, and what an impression the young officer's handsome presence and stately bearing made on her—how his wooing prospered, and how their wedding took place in the January which followed the close of the campaign.

The next sixteen years of George Washington's life were spent at Mount Vernon.

The old passion for the chase always revived with the hunting season. Then the busy, dignified master of Mount Vernon put aside all business to go out with the hounds. He and his neighbors had merry mornings in the woods. On these hunts he must have felt himself very much the boy he had been when he and Lord Fairfax chased the game to cover.

The bright sixteen years went their smooth, swift course, and then the clouds gathered slowly but surely.

Washington's love of country was the deepest feeling of that strong, reserved nature. When the test came, every other affection, every other interest had to yield to this supreme one.

Yet the prospect of rebellion when he first forced himself to look it in the face must have been terrible to him. He had nothing to gain, he had much to lose, even in the case of a successful issue, to a strife begun under such immense disadvantages for the colonies.

All the military ambitions of his youth had long been laid to rest. His temperament, education, surroundings, made him conservative. His early associations, the long military service of his youth, had strengthened his attachment to the mother country, and his pride in the ties that bound the colonies to their old home.

Washington's hope that England would be wise and relent in time yielded very slowly. He saw one high-handed measure follow another, whose purpose could only be to crush the liberties and ruin the prosperity of his country. The air around him shook with the dangerous wrath of freemen.

During all this trying time Washington maintained his calmness of speech and bearing. Yet under these the fire burned bright and steady. He was not silent when the time came to speak, nor idle when it came to work. In every assembly where Virginia freemen met to protest against the tyranny of England, or to assert the rights and liberties of British colonies, one man was, if possible, in their midst; one man's strong, brief sentences had the ring of unfaltering patriotism, of undying courage.

Perhaps George Washington was never himself conscious of the precise hour when he made up his mind where the war—if it came to one—between England and the colonies would find him. Yet, what tremendous issues for his country, for the world, were to hang on the decision of that unknown hour!

Another hour, which in reality was George Washington's summons to the field, and which every schoolboy knows, struck in the pleasant April morning, when "the shot was fired that was heard around the world."

On the twentieth of the following June the Continental Congress at Philadelphia appointed George Washington commander in chief of the American army. The next day he set out for the camp.

On July 3, 1775 he took command of the forces assembled at Cambridge. The General was now in the prime of manhood, forty-three years of age. His tall, stately figure, his noble face, his dignified presence—all the ideal of a soldier—made a profound impression on the people who had crowded into Cambridge to see the new commander.

Under the old elm, among whose green leaves the winds still play softly as they did on that historic summer morning, Washington wheeled his horse and drew the sword, which he then ardently hoped to lay down in the next autumn, but which he was destined to bear for the next eight years.

The close of the war of the Revolution is followed by one scene after another of thrilling interest, in which Washington is the central figure. Not the least of these scenes is that solemn, pathetic one, where he met his officers for the last time, and parted with them in New York.

Nineteen days after that event Washington, with a simple, characteristic speech, resigned his commission before a large audience assembled at Annapolis, and craved leave of Congress to retire from the service of his country.

On the following night—it was Christmas eve—he was at Mount Vernon.

He returned to the old life and habits with the old zest. His highest ambition, to repeat his own grandly simple words, was "to be a farmer and live an honest man."

But his country could not leave him to the privacy of his home, to dear domestic ties, to the old enjoyments and activities of his domestic life.

The Confederacy, from which so much had been hoped for America and for humanity, proved, in its practical workings, a failure.

After three years at Mount Vernon, years whose domestic happiness had been shadowed by anxieties for his country, the Convention assembled at Philadelphia framed the Constitution, and George Washington was, in the following spring, unanimously elected first President of the United States.

The great soldier might well be appalled by the new duties and responsibilities which confronted him on every side. These were of a nature which demanded the highest qualities of statesmanship. There were no precedents, no traditions to guide him. The young nation had been impoverished by the long war of the Revolution. Its domestic affairs were in utmost confusion. Its foreign relations were ill-defined, unsatisfactory, and might, at any moment, become so dangerous as to threaten its existence.

All eyes were fastened on the brave figure which stood at the helm of the ship of state, as she moved out on unknown, perilous seas.

The fortunes of the nation seemed to hang on the skill, energy, and wisdom of one man.

The history of his administration is a record of the sound judgment, courage, and devotion with which he guided the ship of state for the next eight years over the stormy waters. Washington had proved himself a great soldier; he showed now the instinct of the wise, conscientious, far-sighted statesman.

It is only fair to say something here of the part Mrs. Washington played at this time. The wife of the President of the United States must always be an object of interest to her countrywomen. She is, for the time, the representative of American womanhood to her nation—to the world. That her character and bearing should lend grace and dignity to her high position, must be desired by every woman who cares for the honor of her country. Martha Washington came, like her husband, to bear a new name, to fill a new place. The social duties which it involved proved at once a burdensome tax on the President's precious time. His wife exerted herself to relieve him. She was accustomed to the accomplished circles of the old commonwealth. As lady of the nation she presided with an ease and dignity which had become her second nature.

But it was not as the gracious, affable wife of our first President that Martha Washington shows her finest quality. Many women of her day could, no doubt, have played her role there with equal satisfaction. But not *all* women would have left the elegant seclusion of Mount Vernon to share the hardships and privations of the army's winter quarters. Martha Washington was not daunted even by the miseries and sufferings of Valley Forge.

She seems to have been remarkably well adapted to a man of her husband's character and habits. She was not a woman, however, of marked mental gifts. She did not possess the strong intellectual tastes, the delight in books, the sensitive imagination, of the woman, who in 1764, married her husband's successor as chief executive of the new nation.

But Martha Washington showed, through all adverse fates, the heart and temper of a true woman, and proved herself worthy of the immortal name she bears.

On March 4, 1797 George Washington, to his unspeakable relief and happiness, closed his administration. It is touching to see how tired he had grown, how he looked forward to his release from the weight of public affairs, as the prisoner looks forward to the first hour of his freedom.

He returned as soon as possible to Mount Vernon and resumed

the old life with the old energy and activity. Washington superintended his workmen, planned his improvements, attended to all the details of his affairs, precisely as in his youth. Yet his hair was getting white; he was growing, as he said of himself long before to his soldiers, "an old man."

His time was much consumed by the guests who crowded to that quiet home. His hospitalities taxed the resources which had suffered heavily during his long public service. He soon discovered that every distinguished foreigner who set foot on the western shores was eager to meet America's most illustrious citizen.

But he carried his cares and his years bravely, and his splendid health and tireless activity were the source of constant satisfaction to his friends.

He had no children of his own, but his family relations and those of his wife brought a good deal of gay young life to Mount Vernon at this time.

Washington was fond of reading, but his opportunities for study had always been of the most meager kind. Under any circumstances he would not, probably, have made a scholar in the technical sense of the word. The bent of his genius was eminently practical. He had a passion for horses, for trees, for the wide, green, pleasant earth, for the fields and the forests.

The peace of Mount Vernon was rudely broken once more. The war clouds again loomed threatening above the horizon. They showed themselves this time in a quarter where they would have been last looked for. The French Directory, angry and resentful at what it regarded its grievances, and accustomed to deal with nations in the most high-handed fashion, passed measures which struck a deadly blow at American commerce.

This was received with a storm of indignation which swept through the country. War with our ancient ally seemed for awhile inevitable. There was only one man whom the nation would place at the head of that army. The commission which appointed Washington commander in chief was promptly carried to Mount Vernon.

It was a most unwelcome honor. But the gray-haired soldier could not bring himself to refuse the last of his life to the country to whom he had given the strength of his youth, the prime of his manhood. He soon found himself compelled to leave Mount Vernon again. He took up the old wearisome burden of military cares. He organized the new army, appointed its officers, and attended to infinite details which must have told heavily on his waning vigor.

The arrogant Directory was not prepared for the storm which it had aroused in America. When France was satisfied that her ancient ally really meant, if things came to the worst, to go to war with her, she retreated from her first position.

America gladly responded to the new advances, and the difficulties between the two nations were happily adjusted.

Washington returned once more to Mount Vernon. He was never to leave it again.

Days followed full of restful quiet and content. In the early mornings a stately figure, which had long moved at the head of armies, might have been seen riding about Mount Vernon, the thin gray hair shining about the calm, fine face.

George Washington's life and that of the century in which he had done his work, were drawing to a close. He was nearing his sixty-eighth birthday.

The Washington breed was not a long-lived one, but it seemed as though the greatest of the stock might enjoy a hale old age. As that last autumn of the century passed into winter, Washington appeared to those about him in perfect health and vigor. He was leading a busy but tranquil life; he was still alert with interest on all that concerned his country; he was, with all his old energy, projecting improvements and supervising affairs at Mount Vernon.

One morning he took a ride around his grounds in the rough December weather. When he returned to the house, snowflakes glistened in his white hair. He had spent too much of his youth in wilderness and camp to have any fear about the weather, and went to dinner in his damp garments.

But the next morning he complained of a sore throat, while the snow, continuing to fall, prevented his taking his usual ride. In the afternoon, however, when the weather cleared, he went out, and marked some trees which he wished cut down. When he returned to the house that afternoon he had taken his last walk around Mount Vernon.

That night the trouble in his throat increased, and by the next morning it was evident to the household that he was seriously ill.

Doctors were summoned, who endeavored to relieve the sufferer after the bungling methods of their time. But all their efforts were in vain.

The old courage and calmness ring through George Washington's last utterances, though these were few, for his disease—acute laryngitis—made speech extremely painful to him.

The death he had faced so often on the battlefield had stolen upon him unawares in the peace and security of home; but it found him ready.

The illness lasted forty-eight hours. At last the agonized breathing grew easier. "Washington withdrew his hand from his secretary's, and felt his own pulse." This act showed the clearness of his mind, as well as the habit of the soldier. Then a change crept over his features.

The life that had begun a few miles away, in the home on Bridge's Creek, one winter's morning when the century was still in its youth, ended when that century had only a fortnight's more lease of life.

George Washington died on the morning of December 17, 1799.

JOHN ADAMS

SOMEWHERE among the closing days of the summer of 1774, in the old colonial town of Philadelphia, a man still young, for he had not yet reached his thirty-ninth birthday, was eagerly reading a letter which contained these words:

"I have taken a very great fondness for reading Rollin's Ancient History since you left me. I am determined to go through with it, if possible, in these my days of solitude. I find great pleasure and entertainment from it, and I have persuaded Johnny to read me a page or two every day, and hope he will, from his desire to oblige me, entertain a fondness for it."

At that time Boston, ten miles distant, lay prostrate under the iron heel of the blockade. The Port Bill had been carried out with merciless rigor. The British army was on the common; the British fleet was in the harbor. The fight at Concord took place just eight months after the date of the letter. In those hard days, in all the harder ones of the years that followed, the wives and mothers of the Revolution did their part with noble constancy and self-sacrifice; yet it may be doubted whether, in all the American colonies, there was another wife who fortified her heart and solaced her loneliness, by turning resolutely to the pages of the prolix old history; whether there was another boy of seven on all the American seaboard in that famous year of 1774 who found more pleasure in a page of "Rollin" than he did in his games and his playground.

John Adams, who was reading his wife's letter in the closing days of the summer, was one of the five Massachusetts delegates to the First Continental Congress which met in Philadelphia. "He was born October 19, 1735 (O. S.*), in Braintree on the S. shore of Boston harbor." His father was one of the small farmers of those days who managed to wrest a living out of the rugged New England soil, and who was foresighted enough to send his eldest son to Harvard, where he graduated in 1755.

The young man of twenty immediately took charge of a grammar school at Worcester. His ardent, intense nature found school teach-

* Old Style Calendar.

ing a slow business at best. In some of his moods he was heartily sick of it; he felt the stir of larger ambitions; he thirsted for a wider sphere of action.

The long war with France for the possession of the country beyond the Allegheny Range was, at this period, a matter of supreme interest with the Colonies, and it aroused all the patriotic instincts of the grammar school teacher. He had now, too, serious debates with himself as to his choice of a profession. At one time he inclined toward the ministry. But the ecclesiastical councils and the rigid Calvinism of the day repelled him, and he finally decided in favor of the law. But he was not satisfied; he had longings for a soldier's life. This was quite natural to one of his age and temperament. He was eager to command "a company of foot, a troop of horse." But the outlook on this side was hopeless to "one who lacked interest and patronage." It was probably John Adams' good fortune that he was not, at this time, drawn into a military career. The laurels fate held in store for him were to be won on other and more congenial battlefields. He was restless, moody, dejected at times; but at last he made up his mind to study for the law, and set about it with characteristic pluck and energy.

November 6, 1758 was a memorable date in young Adams' life, for at that time he "was recommended to the court for the oath, and shook hands with the bar."

He at once began the practice of law in Suffolk County.

John Adams settled himself to his life work, as he then regarded it. He soon found clients, and in the years that followed they steadily increased. He brought the intellectual and moral qualities to his profession, which always, in the long run, insure success. But the fees were small, and his material fortunes did not make rapid progress.

He was just twenty-nine years old when on October 25, 1764 he wedded Abigail Smith, the young daughter of a Weymouth clergyman.

The year that followed the marriage saw the passage of the Stamp Act. We know what kind of reception it met with in America. The young lawyer was, from the beginning, one of its most outspoken and insistent opponents. He was a New Englander, and he cast in his lot promptly and absolutely with the patriots. No fears could shake, no temptations swerve him. From this time to the end of his life he was devoted heart and soul to the service of his country. Men might talk of his faults and foibles, but nobody ever detected a flaw in his patriotism.

The storm which had been roused in the colonies quieted with the repeal of the Stamp Act. But that fatal measure had a lasting influence on the old traditional sentiment of loyalty to Great Britain. The current of popular feeling never quite set again in the old channels. A watchful, suspicious temper had been aroused, which the home government and those who represented it in America took little pains to allay.

During the half dozen years which preceded the Revolution John Adams probably led as happy a life as any man in New England. His success in his profession proved his wisdom in choosing it. He was a man of ardent family feelings, and his domestic relations were of a peculiarly delightful character. As the years went on, children—three boys and a girl—came to gladden his home. He removed from Braintree to Boston, and back again as his health or circumstances made the change desirable. But there was one shadow on all these bright prospects. John Adams was too sincere a patriot to feel at ease about his country. He seems through all these busy, prosperous years to have had some prescience of the dark days ahead. It must have been a bitter sight to him when he saw the two regiments of redcoats which England sent to awe the turbulent little province march proudly through Boston town, "the drums beating, the fifes playing, with charged muskets and fixed bayonets."

About this time efforts were made to detach him from the patriotic side. The lucrative post which the government offered him "in the Court of Admiralty" was a flattering testimony to his character and influence. But John Adams was not deceived. This offer from the government, with all that it promised, was in the nature of a bribe, and was promptly declined.

In the midst of his professional cares he found time to contribute various political articles to the papers. Some of these were of such marked force and ability that they were afterward republished in London.

During this period Mr. Adams was much in the thick of public affairs. This involved great personal sacrifices. He did not choose his side without fully counting the cost. If he grew moody and despondent at times, if his heart and his hope failed him occasionally, his central purpose never did.

During these years he was chosen representative at the General Court, and his defense of Captain Preston and the soldiers after the Boston massacre was one of the bravest deeds of his life.

The destruction of the tea chests, the Boston Port Bill, brought the crisis. On June 17, 1774 the Provincial Assembly voted behind its closed doors to send five Massachusetts delegates to the Continental Congress to be held in Philadelphia. Probably nobody was surprised that one of the delegates was John Adams.

A little later he made the long journey on which such great issues were to depend.

If the history of that First Continental Congress had been amply reported, there would be no space to linger upon it here. When it broke up late in the autumn, it appeared to Mr. Adams, as no doubt it did to most of his constituents, that very little had been done. Commercial nonintercourse seemed a pitiful outcome for all those long secret deliberations of a body which represented the wisest heads, the most patriotic hearts, in America. Had the Colonies sent at this momentous period their wisest statesmen to Congress? Had the whole country waited eager and breathless for months for so meager a result?

All over the land men must have been asking this question, resentful and disappointed in the lessening days of the autumn of 1774.

But they made a mistake. The Congress had done its work. It was everything to the Colonies at this juncture that their best material had been brought together; that their real statesmen and leaders had met, and parted, and understood each other.

On John Adams's return to his home he found plenty to do. Braintree at once sent him as a delegate to the Provincial Assembly. His immense activity and patriotic fervor found a fresh field for work in the famous newspaper controversy, in which he maintained the people's side with masterly reasoning. So the winter passed into spring, and then the strife took another form than that of newspaper articles. Mr. Adams could lay down his pen. The day of Lexington and Concord had come!

He was appointed a delegate to the Second Continental Congress, and arrived there on May 10. He had been seriously ill, and was only partially recovered. When he left home Mrs. Adams writes of that second separation, fraught in many respects with more perils and fears than the first:

"I felt very anxious about you, though I endeavored to be very insensible and heroic, yet my heart felt like a heart of lead."

A few hours earlier he had written to her:

"In case of real danger, of which you cannot fail to have previous intimations, fly to the woods with our children."

This was not advice suggested by overcautious affection. Only a few days before the Yankee farmers in their homespun had confronted the redcoats for the first time. The air was still full of the excitement of the fight. It had taken place only a few miles from the farmhouse where Mr. Adams had been compelled to leave his wife and her young children. A little way off rode his Majesty's ships of war. It was by no means impossible that the English sailors would swoop down on the unguarded coast and spread wide havoc among the quiet country homes to wreak revenge on the rebels that 19th of April.

A few days later Mrs. Adams watched on one of the Braintree hills, with her eldest boy—the John Quincy with whom she had been reading Rollin's *History*—the burning of Charlestown; the distant Battle of Bunker Hill.

Meanwhile John Adams, keenly anxious for his family, full of wrath and grief over the sufferings of that "beloved town," as he called Boston, was doing his work with passionate energy and zeal. It exasperated his fiery temper almost beyond endurance, that others could not keep pace with his strong virile step. It was not in his fiery, dauntless nature to adopt half measures, to cling to futile hopes that Great Britain might yet relent and come to terms with her colonies. He believed the day for arguments and appeals was past. He saw clearer than many of his colleagues that America's only salvation was in independence, and that she would have to fight for this.

It was not strange that the prospect of a war, waged by the scant colonies at such tremendous odds, with the great conquering military and naval power of the world, should have struck terror to the soul of many a true patriot. But John Adams's dauntless, impetuous nature felt an impatient scorn for those who paused to count the costs where all that was dear to freemen was at stake. He was inflamed with rage when a motion for a second memorial to George III was carried in Congress. He felt that the day for appeals had passed; the time for action had come.

But to his infinite satisfaction the Congress at last took a step from which there was no retreat, and advised Massachusetts Bay, which in its prevailing confusion and disorder had applied for counsel, to "establish a government of its own."

Mr. Adams's sagacious mind perceived clearly all that was involved in this advice to organize a rebel government. But important as this measure was, there was still another and higher stake to be won.

The Massachusetts delegate, with clear, patriotic forecast, perceived that all local struggles, like those of Concord and Lexington, would in the end be futile, unless Congress assumed responsibility for the army which was now besieging Boston. The war for American liberties must be a war in which every colony must take her part and fight for her life, or it was foredoomed to failure. The struggle with England would be unequal enough when the Colonies presented a united front to the foe.

John Adams proposed before the astonished members that Congress should adopt the army before Boston, and appoint Colonel Washington its commander.

A breathless silence must have followed the motion. No wonder that Washington himself, always modest, was startled out of his habitual self-control, and the proposed commander in chief, covered with confusion, "darted into the library." But the work had been done in that critical moment. Where the leader had planted himself, the others slowly gathered and fell into line. A few days later George Washington was unanimously chosen commander in chief of the American army. The irrevocable step was taken now. There could be no retreats, no more looking back—no more appeals to George III.

George Washington was now in the camp of the American army, and his reception at Cambridge had more than fulfilled John Adams's wishes.

In December of that year John Adams again made one of his brief visits home. He returned to Congress in company with Elbridge Gerry. On that long journey, in the bitter weather, the two New England delegates acquired a strong liking for each other. This bore fruit long afterward when both had gained high distinction in the world.

The change from the passionately patriotic atmosphere of Massachusetts to the colder one of Philadelphia, was always certain, at first, to dispirit John Adams. But a little later his mood had changed so far, that he was writing to his wife about "marching in the rank and file if possibly a contingency should happen to make doing it proper. I will not fail to march if it should," he adds, in his positive way.

A little later, he had startling news from home. His wife's letter of March 2, 1776 was interrupted "by the roar of cannon, which shook the house." Washington's strategy was justified at last. The long inactivity in which the American lines had lain before Boston, was broken one Saturday evening by "a cannonade and bombardment, which, with intervals, was continued through the night." This was a feint to deceive the enemy; but on Tuesday morning the American troops held possession of Dorchester Hill. A little later the British evacuated Boston town, and the sufferings of the blockaded little seaport, which thus far had borne the brunt of the war, were ended.

With the relief of Boston, John Adams turned to the great work which was absorbing his heart and brain at this period.

It was nothing less than the Declaration of Independence. All that spring and early summer of 1776 the Massachusetts delegate had been moving heaven and earth to bring Congress to the point. He called the measure, in his own strong, incisive words, "the end of his creation."

The history of that time and of Mr. Adams's herculean labors, cannot be written here. It was Thomas Jefferson who was the author of the Declaration of Independence; it was John Adams who, in the debate before Congress as to its adoption, carried that body with him. He did this by a speech of thrilling earnestness, of splendid eloquence. In that great hour, as his audience afterward affirmed, "the man seemed lifted out of himself." He appeared to have no idea of the grandeur of his effort. He was only conscious of the issues which hung upon the moment. When he ceased, "his praise was in everybody's mouth."

In November of the following year John Adams was appointed commissioner to the court of France.

At the time when this new field of activity so unexpectedly opened to him he had been forced by the condition of his health, much broken by long and engrossing services, to resign his position in Congress and return home, where he had barely resumed his professional labors. These intervening months had been immensely important to America. Yet they had formed a period of such varied disasters to her armies that the hearts of the stanchest patriots had sunk with the defeat on Long Island, the evacuation of New York, the retreat through the Jerseys, and the abandonment of Philadelphia. Mr. Adams, like every American, had, in those days, moods of despondency, and he expressed these in his trenchant style. But his patriotism was never long in recovering its old, resolute, hopeful temper.

After the Declaration of Independence he had continued to devote himself unsparingly to the service of Congress. He had done his part in forming the "League which held the Thirteen States" together, and, although it was a slight, imperfect bond, it still served its purpose, and was as strong a union as popular sentiment then permitted.

He had been placed at the head of the War Department. The position had involved enormous labors and responsibilities. In the work of army organization he had, of course, to encounter a world of military pride, red tape, and jealousy. The earnestness, sincerity, and devotion of the civilian exercised a controlling influence over all who had relations with him while he was in this office.

The foreign appointment must have taken him by surprise. It opened to the New Englander, who had laid down the armor of public service, a new and untried field for his energies.

If the French appointment was an honor, it was also a most perilous one. This was proved by the suggestion that accompanied it, "that he should have his dispatch bags sufficiently weighted to sink them instantly in case of capture."

He sailed in the waning winter, in the frigate *Boston.* His son, John Quincy Adams, the boy who, in the Bunker Hill days, had read Rollin's *History* to his mother, accompanied him.

The two had been out less than a week when an English warship gave chase to the frigate. "Adams urged the crew to fight desperately." It was better to die on board the *Boston,* better to sink in the sea, than be taken prisoner.

Fortunately the frigate escaped. "On March 31, 1778 she was riding safely at anchor in the harbor at Bordeaux."

Mr. Adams's first foreign mission occupied nearly a year and a half, yet it did not afford any large field of activity to his abounding energies. The famous alliance with France had already been consummated.

Dr. Franklin was then having his career of unparalleled popularity in France. The shrewd, simple American had captivated the polished, critical Parisians. He, of course, threw the other commissioners much into the background. Mr. Adams was not a man to enjoy remaining there, and he recommended that the commission should be entrusted to one person, though this would exclude himself. It was a foregone conclusion that Dr. Franklin would receive the appointment. Mr. Adams's advice was followed, and he was left with nothing to do but enjoy the brilliant Paris world around him. Idleness was most distasteful to him.

"I cannot eat pensions and sinecures; they would stick in my throat," he characteristically wrote to his wife.

He returned in the same ship with the first minister France ever sent to America. John Quincy Adams, who accompanied his father, had been making the most of his time, seeing with his grave young eyes the wonderful French world about him, and drawing his own conclusions. On the long voyage the boy of eleven gave the French minister and his secretary lessons in English, and proved an inexorable teacher.

On reaching home Mr. Adams was soon in the thick of affairs. He had a leading part in framing the new constitution for Massachusetts. The work was hardly done before he was summoned to a wider arena.

In 1779 he sailed again in the French frigate which had brought him home. This time he was appointed "Minister to treat with Great Britain for peace and commerce."

Having arrived in France, Mr. Adams's first experiences were not encouraging. He was at once brought into critical relations with the Comte de Vergennes, who was at the head of the foreign affairs of France.

The keen, polished, autocratic, and dangerous French diplomat—who cared only for the affairs of France, who hated only England—and the outspoken, independent, resolute American did not get on well together.

The story cannot be dwelt on here. Mr. Adams made serious

mistakes at first. His lack of tact, his insistence, his blunt directness, all astonished and offended the cool, brilliant, crafty nobleman, trained in the wiles and subterfuges of the diplomatic school of his day.

But though the two matched their strength on many an important field which required the exercise of the highest, most farsighted statesmanship, the American did not in the end come worsted from the encounter.

Indeed, Mr. Adams, though conspicuously lacking in the traditions and qualities of a finished diplomat, proved himself "precisely the man for the place and the duty."

It was unfortunate that, at this period, a strong ill feeling developed itself between himself and Dr. Franklin. No doubt the differences in their mental and moral constitutions had much to do with their deep alienation.

Between Vergennes and Dr. Franklin Mr. Adams's position could not have been a very comfortable one, and he always lacked the tact to conciliate an enemy.

Perhaps his position at the French Court had much to do with his journey to Holland in July, 1780, though he was revolving in his mind the chances of negotiating a Dutch loan for his impoverished country.

Mr. Adams now had the field to himself, and he worked with untiring energy. The Dutch at that time knew little about America. He made it his aim to enlighten them, both in his conversation and in a series of letters which he published.

But the sky was suddenly overcast. Great Britain declared war against Holland. Laurens, a negotiator sent by Congress to the Dutch, had been captured, and with him some letters which the English Government chose to regard as a breach of Holland's engagements. In this state of affairs Mr. Adams was summoned to France by Vergennes. The Comte, alarmed at the exhausted condition of the French treasury, was now desirous of concluding a peace. He did not intend that American interests should stand in the way.

Before Mr. Adams left he had been appointed minister to Holland in place of Laurens, who was now immured in the Tower of London.

But when Mr. Adams arrived in France, the prospects for peace were not flattering. England, arrogant and exasperated, could not bring herself to the point of negotiating on equal terms with her former colonies. Mr. Adams was extremely suspicious of Vergennes, and having little to do in France soon returned to Holland, where he inspired much friendly feeling toward America "among the merchants and the popular party."

The existence of this feeling was due largely to Mr. Adams's own exertions; but anger with Great Britain, as well as the capture of Lord Cornwallis and his army, had much to do with Dutch sentiment toward America.

Mr. Adams now showed another instance of that splendid audacity which had served him so well when he proposed George Washington as commander in chief of the American armies. He presented a formal demand to the States-General that he should be recognized as the minister of an independent nation.

It is impossible at the present day to form any conception of the boldness of this demand. It was made in defiance of all the traditions and habits of diplomacy. Behind the man who stood before the States-General with this high claim for recognition was a company of small impoverished provinces, loosely bound together, the whole country still in arms for that independence their representative boldly asserted they had won.

It is not difficult to see that Mr. Adams's attitude might easily have become one of supreme ridiculousness. But his sublime audacity carried the day. There were delays, of course. In such an unprecedented affair delegates must revert to constituents for instructions. But on April 19, 1782 the high stake was won. At that date the recognition of Mr. Adams took place, and he was installed American minister at the Hague.

Before the end of the year the new minister succeeded in obtaining a loan of two million dollars from the shrewd Dutch bankers. This loan proved of incalculable service to his distressed country.

When the year 1782 opened there were plentiful signs that the ministry of Lord North was approaching its end. A little later it fell.

This narrative now approaches a point in Mr. Adams's life which brings the reader to the most momentous event in American history. It is the signing of the Treaty of Peace between the United States and England.

Familiar as the ground is it tempts one to linger on it. The long negotiation had episodes of intense dramatic interest. The two ancient nations and the young one engaged in negotiating the treaty had affairs at stake that often clashed. The commissioners could not look to Vergennes for support. He was at heart concerned only for the welfare of France.

Mr. Adams, coming from Holland, appeared in Paris at a critical moment. His unflinching courage braced his colleagues, Dr. Franklin and Mr. Jay. He came upon a scene of endless debates, arguments, bickerings. The English Cabinet yielded slowly to American demands. The negotiations reached a point many times when it looked as though they must be broken off. But Mr. Adams's moral courage never flinched. Mr. Jay, with all his resolution, could not have held his ground without the aid of his bold, determined colleague. The Boundaries, the Fisheries, the Navigation of the Mississippi—all vital questions—were settled at last. The Americans had, with good reason, lost confidence in Vergennes. They carried on their most important negotiations without consulting him. When the amazed count learned this, it was too late for him to interfere, but he loudly complained that the Americans had not kept faith with him.

The only charge, however, which could be brought against them was "a disregard of diplomatic formalities." They kept their word with their ancient ally; they made no separate peace. On the day that England signed her treaty with the United States, she signed her treaty also with France. The date was September 3, 1783.

Adams sent in his resignation as soon as he felt the Treaty of Peace assured, and declared in his positive fashion that if the acceptance did not duly arrive "he would come back without it." But, despite his utmost efforts, he could not leave the field of his present activity. Not long after the signing of the Treaty of Peace he, with Dr. Franklin and Mr. Jay, was commissioned to negotiate a treaty of commerce with Great Britain. This was a matter he had much at heart. He felt that if the two nations could agree to forget the past, and enter into a generous commercial alliance, it would undoubtedly be for the advantage of both. An opportunity seemed suddenly afforded him to promote a large and generous policy. He would not desert his post.

But he now wrote his wife to join him with his daughter.

The long strain told on him at last. During this memorable autumn he was prostrated by a "fever of great severity." When he partially recovered he visited London.

A little later Mr. Adams, still an invalid, was forced to undertake a long winter journey to Holland. His object was to negotiate a fresh loan with the Dutch bankers, already appalled by the drafts which the States had made on them. He actually succeeded in obtaining fresh funds from these shrewd moneylenders. The Fates seem to have ordained that Mr. Adams should succeed in all that he attempted in Holland.

Meanwhile a fresh commission arrived from Congress and included Dr. Franklin and Mr. Jefferson. The three men were empowered to negotiate commercial treaties with European powers. The new government was taking its place "in the stately march of the nations."

The summer of 1784 brought Mr. Adams a great happiness. His wife and daughter joined him. The entire family were now abroad. They set up housekeeping in Auteuil, near Paris. He now enjoyed a season of quiet, domestic life, amid public labors that were not burdensome. But Congress had not exhausted the honors it had heaped on him. The last was the crowning one. On February 24, 1785 he was appointed minister to Great Britain. Even the cool Comte de Vergennes was impressed by all the circumstances of this new embassy, and said to Mr. Adams, "It is a mark."

But the position of the first minister which America sent to England was necessarily a delicate and trying one.

Mr. Adams's first presentation was private. The interview between the monarch of the House of Brunswick and the Braintree lawyer was, in some of its aspects, one of the most momentous scenes which ever occurred in the lives of the two men.

But though things went smoothly at that first presentation, Mr. Adams's position at the English Court was not an agreeable one. He was in a critical and hostile atmosphere, and his salary was totally insufficient to the demands of the place. The first minister which America had sent to England had cherished high hopes of establishing cordial relations between the two countries. He was doomed to disappointment. England did not forgive America for her victory in the field; and jealous of commercial rivalry, she was bent on crippling the foreign trade of the United States.

When Mr. Adams was convinced that he could not serve his country by remaining in England, he sent in his resignation.

He sailed for home April 20, 1788. He never again set foot on a foreign shore.

John Adams returned to America one of its greatest men. He

was now to enter an untried political field. The Constitution, created amid vast labors and compromises, was at this juncture to undergo its first trial.

Washington was elected first President. It was thought fitting that New England should be represented by the Vice-Presidency. Mr. Adams's eminent services and high character entitled him to the election.

The long, bitter feud between himself and Alexander Hamilton appears to have had its beginnings in events connected with the election.

Alexander Hamilton, usually generous and magnanimous, entertained one of those inveterate prejudices against Mr. Adams, which men of strong, autocratic nature often exhibit toward those whom they cannot influence. Pliancy was not in the Adams fiber. The Vice-President was as thorough and outspoken in his enmities as he was in everything else.

Mr. Adams's first term as Vice-President proved a comparatively smooth one. In all the constructive measures before Congress he gave Hamilton valuable assistance by voting with the Federalists.

Mr. Adams was re-elected. The second term of his office was the period of the French Revolution. That mighty upheaval shook the United States. The passionate feeling of the time carried everything before it. Even Washington's great name and vast services could not save him from the fiercest attacks of calumny. The Vice-President seems to have mostly escaped at this time.

When Washington retired, John Adams took his place. The summit of his ambitions was reached. But Hamilton had covertly used his great influence to prevent a unanimous election. It was carried by a narrow majority. Mr. Adams felt this strongly. When he learned the facts he was naturally filled with resentment. The acrimony between these two distinguished men became at last "the most bitter feud in American history."

It was certainly unfortunate for Mr. Adams that he had during his Presidency so powerful, and, in this instance, so vindictive a foe.

The relations between the United States and France became now greatly strained. The Directory, inflated with its success, and carrying everything before it, actually refused to receive the new minister the United States had sent to France.

This intolerable insult was followed by a shameful decree against

American commerce. It had its origin in the angry disappointment with which the Directory learned of Mr. Adams's election. They had confidently hoped to see their favorite, Jefferson, President of the United States.

Greatly as Mr. Adams resented these indignities, he kept his fiery temper under admirable control. He desired, if possible, to avoid a collision with France. But the party which had elected him was strongly Anglican in its sympathies, and this made the President's position a delicate and perplexing one.

A second mission was, however, sent to France. This time the envoys were received. The French treasury was impoverished. Secret attempts were soon set in train to frighten or cajole the Americans into purchasing a peace by the payment of large sums. They indignantly rejected these base proposals. The consequence was a fresh decree against American commerce.

When these facts became known in America, a wave of popular indignation swept over the land. There was a universal cry for war. The President suddenly rose into great popularity. He acted with characteristic promptness and energy. The heart of the nation was with him. Washington was persuaded to leave his retirement at his beloved Mount Vernon, and organize the new army, of which he was to be commander in chief.

The bold attitude of the United States took France by surprise. Absorbed in European politics and ambitions, she had no wish to expend her resources in a remote war on American battlefields.

Talleyrand, greatly chagrined that his attempts to corrupt the envoys had become known in America, sought with infinite tact and audacity to smooth over matters. The French Government made conciliatory advances toward the United States. Mr. Adams, who always knew his own mind, resolved to meet these in the same spirit. He determined to send another embassy to France.

This measure was like a sudden thunderbolt to the Federalists. Hamilton and many of his followers desired a lasting rupture with France.

From this time Mr. Adams and a large, influential section of his party were irreconcilably opposed to each other. The majority of his cabinet, even, sided openly or secretly with Hamilton.

The mission to France proved a success. Napoleon Bonaparte had now become First Consul of France, and was the real government.

He had no designs on America, and all differences were soon adjusted with the young ruler, who had suddenly come to the foreground in French politics.

But though events justified Mr. Adams's policy, the Federalist leaders were implacable. Their passions blinded them to their own interests. The President's eyes were at last opened to the hostility of certain members of his cabinet, and he summarily dismissed them.

The mission to France, wise, statesmanlike, and patriotic a measure as posterity now admits it to have been, probably cost Mr. Adams his second term of office.

The election found the Federal leaders full of bitterness and rancor, which divided and weakened their energies, while the forces of the new Republican party, under the masterly guidance of Jefferson, were united and alert.

But it was probably Hamilton's pamphlet which dealt Mr. Adams's public life its deathblow. This pamphlet was designed for circulation only among the Federalist leaders, but it fell into the hands of Aaron Burr, and was at once given to the world.

While this paper arraigned the administration, and tried to prove its lack of wisdom, it yet closed with perfunctorily recommending Mr. Adams's re-election to the Presidency.

All Hamilton's dispassionate friends had entreated him not to publish this document, but the cool, shrewd leader was inveterately obstinate at this time.

Jefferson's party could not have desired a better campaign document. Even Hamilton must have perceived his mistake when it was too late.

Thomas Jefferson was elected third President of the United States, and Aaron Burr Vice-President.

The nineteenth century was just two months and four days old when John Adams, a cruelly mortified, disappointed, and, as he believed, shamefully wronged man, left Washington for the last time in the early March morning. He would not remain to welcome his successor.

The long, honorable, and brilliant public life of John Adams came to a close on that March morning. He was sixty-five years old; he was to live beyond the first quarter of the century that had just opened.

The simple home life which, at the height of his dazzling career in Europe, he had constantly longed for, now awaited him; but he did not return to it with the applause and gratitude of the nation. The Federalist party, dismayed and enraged at the triumph of their opponents, laid their defeat at the ex-President's door. They insisted that the French mission was the real cause of their overthrow. Mr. Adams found himself for a while the most unpopular man in America.

The active mind, withdrawn from public interests, did not devour itself. Mr. Adams was still eager and alert, as in his youth, over the great events of the world. He had his old delight in books and writing; he dwelt, with graphic, picturesque talk, on the scenes in which he had borne so conspicuous a part.

His pecuniary circumstances enabled him to live in the simple independence which had been the aspiration of his youth. His domestic affections were strong, and he found in his family and in the companionship and sympathy of his wife, a solace for all public ingratitude.

As years passed, Mr. Adams's violent feeling toward his political enemies gradually softened. He was incapable of small malevolence; he never sought, by working in the dark, to injure his worst foe. It is said that the only man whom he never forgave was Alexander Hamilton.

His weaknesses, his faults of vanity, obstinacy, bluntness, self-conceit, were precisely the kind to show conspicuously against his real greatness. They were not pleasant while he lived and they made him many enemies.

But he was, from first to last, unconscious as a child of these defects. Indeed, they were of a nature which he would not be likely to perceive. He was, therefore, with all his generosity, unjust to his opponents; he never could see the other side of the shield. He was, in his own opinion, immutably right.

Such a temperament has usually moods of imprudence and rash confidence. Mr. Adams was no exception to the rule. He talked and wrote much; he revealed his opinions of persons and events where it would have been wise to keep silent. This rash habit of speaking and writing could not fail to bring him into serious trouble, though it must be admitted he always, when the pinch came, stood courageously by his words.

Both Mr. and Mrs. Adams had great satisfaction and pride in the career of their son, John Quincy Adams. The mother lived to see her eldest boy Secretary of State during Monroe's Administration.

In time the great breach between Adams and Jefferson was healed. It took years for the former to forget and forgive. The reconciliation was largely due to Mrs. Adam's influence and efforts. Thomas Jefferson was the last man in the world to hold a grudge against his old friend because of the part he had played, or failed to play, at the inaugural ceremonies. The ex-Presidents had many sympathies and a world of experiences and reminiscences in common. They maintained a frequent correspondence for the rest of their lives.

Mrs. Adams died in 1818, at Quincy, where she had remained since the close of her husband's public life.

Mr. Adams survived his wife almost eight years. He received some agreeable public attentions. He was appointed a Presidential elector and voted for James Monroe. He also lived to see his son President of the United States.

His mind was clear and active to within a few hours of his death which occurred at sunset, July 4, 1826.

THOMAS JEFFERSON

THOMAS JEFFERSON was born April 13, 1743 in the Shadwell homestead. This was named from his mother, "who first saw the light in a London parish of that name." The homestead stood on a farm of nineteen hundred acres, in Albemarle County, Virginia.

The boy's father was Peter Jefferson, and his mother was Jane Randolph. She had passed her youth on one of the tobacco plantations of the James River, where Peter Jefferson saw her first, when she was only seventeen. He wooed and won and married her, and carried her away from the old stately home mansion, to his great, partially cleared farm on the banks of the Rivanna.

Young Thomas had a good start. His father was a land surveyor, only a few years before George Washington undertook the same business. The owner of Shadwell farm was a Hercules in strength and stature. He singly performed feats which taxed the powers of three strong men. But he was also a man of much intelligence, shrewd sense, and force of character. County honors naturally gravitated to such a one. In due time, the Shadwell farmer became Justice of the peace, Colonel of Albermarle County, and Representative in the House of Burgesses.

Jane Randolph, who came from the old Virginia stock, could never have regretted the choice of her youth, although her early married life must have involved many privations and hardships.

Thomas was the first son, but he had two elder sisters. Other children followed, until a large brood of Jeffersons had gathered in the farm homestead.

Peter Jefferson had to leave that young family fatherless. The stalwart man died suddenly, August 17, 1757. His death occurred when Thomas was fourteen. There was nobody to control or advise him. The mother, with her young family about her, herself not yet forty years of age, appears to have placed unlimited confidence in her boy. From that time he became his own master.

It had been the father's dying injunction that his son should be well educated. Thomas made up his mind to study with the Rev.

James Maury, whose school was then regarded as the best in Virginia.

The parsonage was only fourteen miles from the farm. Thomas entered the school, where he remained two years. By this time he was ready for the college of William and Mary.

This was situated five days' ride from young Jefferson's home, in Williamsburg, the capital of Virginia. He set out for it, a lad hardly seventeen years old, in the early spring of 1760. "He had never at that time seen a town, or even a village of twenty houses."

Dr. Small, Professor of Mathematics and Philosophy, was a conspicuous figure in Jefferson's college life. The Scotsman and the student became companions and friends. The elder had a genius for teaching, and inspired the younger's soul with great enthusiasm for study. But the college life was not wholly one of books. With his ardent, generous nature, Thomas Jefferson was sure to be a favorite with his classmates. Even at this age he won the attention of men of the world, men of high character and great abilities. George Wyeth, the lawyer, and Francis Fauquier, the Lieutenant Governor of the province, admitted the young student to their intimate companionship. All his after life he spoke with solemn fervor of the immense debt which he owed to three men: his beloved tutor, Dr. Small, George Wyeth, and Peyton Randolph. They were the models which he chose for his youth.

Yet, with all his omnivorous study and the society of his seniors, the boy from the Shadwell farm was by no means a prig. He had his share in the pleasures and amusements of the ancient capital. He had a passion for music, and his violin was a source of never-ending delight to him. He danced minuets late into the night in the Apollo, that "great room of the old Raleigh tavern," which was soon afterward to be put to a very different service.

Jefferson lost his heart within those old historic walls. The first romance of his life came to him before he was nineteen years old. The charms of Belinda, or Rebecca Burwell proved powerful enough to win the thoughts of the devoted student from his books but she was married soon afterward, and Jefferson's young romance was shattered. He believed his heart would never rally from that blow.

In April 1764 he reached his majority. He celebrated that event after the old English fashion, by ordering an avenue of locusts and sycamores to be planted near his house, though he was himself absent at Williamsburg.

The young owner of Shadwell must have seemed to his neighbors to have in him the making of a splendid farmer. There was much more in Thomas Jefferson which neither he nor his friends suspected at this time. But he was certainly an agricultural genius. He began now that habit of experiments with soils and plants which he kept up throughout his long life. He had a variety of garden books, in which he made endless entries. No changes of the weather, no aspects of sky or earth within his horizon, escaped him. The amount of work, planning and study, which he managed to put into every day was simply enormous.

In the summer of 1765 Martha Jefferson, a beautiful girl of nineteen, was married to Dabney Carr, the most intimate and beloved of Jefferson's college class mates. Young Carr had one of those rare natures, whose charm and lovable quality lend a fresh grace to life. Like Jefferson, he was a law student. Even before they became brothers-in-law the two were constantly together. They had a favorite resort two miles from the homestead, on a lonely mountain, five hundred and eighty feet in height. This afterward became the historic Monticello. It was richly wooded to the summit. Far up the mountainside grew a vast oak, under whose shade the young men made a rustic seat, and here they sat amid the wide green freedom and stillness, and studied their textbooks, and had long intervals of talk.

It was these hours which were afterward to make that spot so famous in history. The two entered into a covenant that he who died first should be buried under the mighty oak. Jefferson kept his word. Long afterward, the place formed the burial plot of his family, and at last, full of years and honors, he was laid by the side of his friend, beneath the very sods where they had sat and studied, and where they had held the long, wise, aspiring talk of their youth. It was the memory, too, of those days which made Jefferson choose that mountain top for his home.

In 1767, near his twenty-fourth birthday, Thomas Jefferson was admitted to the bar.

Jefferson had his young dreams, like George Washington, of going abroad. But the Stamp Act kept the newly fledged lawyer at home, as matrimony and Mount Vernon had done in George Washington's case.

Before he became engrossed in public events, however, Jefferson had entered into successful practice. His thorough preparation, as well as the times, were in his favor. There was much financial embarrassment among the old extravagant Virginia planters at that period. Jefferson's clients grew so rapidly in numbers that in seven years he had doubled his estate.

It was not until the year before he was admitted to the bar that he ever went beyond his native province. At that time he visited Annapolis, Philadelphia, "where he underwent inoculation for smallpox," and even got as far as New York. Here, in the little pleasant Dutch town of twenty thousand inhabitants, he chanced to find as a fellow lodger a small-framed, keen, intelligent stranger from Marblehead. His name was Elbridge Gerry.

The Virginian and the New Englander took a strong liking to each other. They little suspected the role each was destined to play in the fortunes of the nation.

In the winter of 1768–69, when Lord Botetourt, the new governor, came over from England, the old House of Burgesses was dismissed, and in the election which followed Thomas Jefferson was a candidate for Albermarle County. He was elected and entered on a public life which was to continue for forty years.

The first Virginia legislature in which Thomas Jefferson served forms a memorable chapter in American history. The British Parliament had now entered on that tyrannical course toward the Colonies which ended in the Revolution. Lord Botetourt, amazed and alarmed at the temper and purpose which his freshly elected House of Burgesses manifested toward the Parliamentary measures, dissolved the House.

A meeting was held next day in the Apollo—that old room at the Raleigh tavern where Jefferson and Belinda had danced so many minuets.

But the members had sterner work to do now than watch the smiles of beauty, or keep step to the joyous music. At that meeting the famous Nonimportation Agreement was drawn up, and eighty-eight members of the House of Burgesses signed it.

Virginia endorsed the compact of her legislators in the most emphatic manner. "Every man who signed the agreement was re-elected; every one who refused lost his re-election."

A little later good tidings came across the sea. The colonists had their brief hour of rejoicing. The party in the British Parliament favorable to America was in power.

Lord Botetourt, a high-spirited and honorable gentleman, informed the House of Burgesses that Parliament intended to remove the taxes.

But Lord North became Prime Minister. After that George III and he had everything their own way.

Lord Botetourt, indignant and mortified, demanded his recall. He did not live to receive it. It was believed that he died of grief, because he was unable to kep his word to the Burgesses.

The year 1769 found Thomas Jefferson an immensely busy man. His practice at the bar had increased to a hundred and ninety-eight cases before the General Court. Bands of workmen were clearing the summit of Monticello for his future home. An orchard was planted on a slope, and the busy lawyer, farmer and member of the House of Burgesses found time between the sessions to supervise the construction of a brick wing, which was intended to form part of a mansion.

During the winter of the following year, the old Shadwell homestead was burned to the ground.

Just twenty-three months from that day Thomas Jefferson was married. He, too, like Washington, had chosen a beautiful young widow whose name was Martha. She was the daughter of John Wayles, one of Jefferson's associates at the Williamsburg bar. She must have been married in her young girlhood, for she was a widow at twenty-two.

His marriage with Martha Skelton took place January 1, 1772. In a few days, the newly wedded pair started for their home on the mountain top, "more than a hundred miles away, in a two-horse chaise."

All accounts represent Mrs. Jefferson as a woman of much grace and charm of manner. Masses of auburn hair framed her fair, expressive face. Her tall, slight figure indicated only too well her fragile constitution. She sang; she played the harpsichord; and her musical gifts must have been a great delight to her husband. He had a peculiar tenderness and loyalty of nature, and while the woman he had chosen was the central joy of his life, he, in turn, made her supremely happy.

The home on the mountain summit commanded a magnificent prospect. Its stillness and coolness must have made it a delightful residence during the heats of the Virginia summers. On one side the mountain sloped abruptly to the valleys. On another, a mile and a half away, flowed the Rivanna, among the farms and wheat fields, and beyond its banks was a heap of "blackened ruins," all that the flames had left of the Shadwell homestead. At one point the Blue Ridge walled the horizon, a hundred miles distant, while two hundred to the eastward was the Atlantic. The little village of Charlottesville was only "three miles off."

Meanwhile, the events which ushered in the Revolution were marching relentlessly forward. Jefferson was married in January. In June of that year the King's little armed schooner, the *Gaspee,* of eight guns, was boarded and burned to the water's edge, while she lay aground off Narragansett Point, seven miles below Providence. The patriotic Rhode Islanders had at last been driven to desperation. They had bearded the British Government after bearing for years its oppressive and intolerable restrictions on their commerce. Its orders had been carried out in the narrowest and hardest temper by insolent and overbearing officials. The fire which had long smouldered in the breasts of the hardy, resolute race which had settled along the New England seaboard was sure, sooner or later, to break out and sweep everything before it.

"The burning of the *Gaspee,*" with all the attendant circumstances, rang through the Colonies. That bold deed could not fail to fire the blood of men in whose veins ran the free old Anglo-Saxon strain. A new feeling of common sympathy and interest was aroused in the Provinces. It was the immediate cause of another famous meeting in the old Raleigh tavern. Thomas Jefferson and Dabney Carr, with several other young members of the House of Burgesses, were assembled here one evening in the early March of 1773. The question which absorbed them was the attitude which Virginia, the eldest and most powerful of the Colonies, should assume toward Rhode Island at this juncture. The young Burgesses felt unbounded admiration at the daring act of the brave little Province. They glowed with sympathy for her wrongs; they felt these as their own. But the great outcome of the meeting and another held on the day following was the circular letter, written and dispatched to the various Colonial Assemblies.

The Committees of Correspondence had been organized. These were followed a little later by the Continental Congress.

When they emerged from the Raleigh tavern the brothers-in-law little suspected the great historical importance of the work in which they had borne a share. But this was the last important act of one of the pair. Dabney Carr died suddenly of malignant typhoid fever. He had been married eight years. His small home, a few miles from Monticello, held a brood of six children.

His beautiful young wife lost her reason for a while at the shock of his sudden death. Jefferson took Martha, the sister, with her young family of children, home to Martha, the wife. He adopted them all—three sons and three daughters. He brought them up as tenderly, as generously, as carefully, as he did his own.

When, at last, they laid him in his old age and his greatness, by the side of Dabney Carr, he had kept faith with the friend of his youth.

Children of his own came to him. The eldest, who bore the beloved name of Martha, survived him, but the others, of whom there were five, seem to have inherited their mother's fragile constitution. Four died in infancy. Mary, the fourth child, reached young womanhood.

All the children were girls, except one son, who lived only a few days.

The year 1774 brings the reader out on the great highway of American history. The Revolution was on its way. People felt its coming in the air before they realized what it meant. While the whole land was shaken with its approach, Thomas Jefferson was in the thick of events. Yet the lawyer from Monticello never in these exciting times lost his coolness or his serenity.

When the new Governor, Lord Dunmore, dissolved the refractory House of Burgesses, there was another meeting at the Raleigh tavern. This time the Committee of Correspondence was instructed to propose the organization of a Continental Congress. Its members, composed of deputies from all the Colonies, were to meet annually.

Before that year had closed the name of Thomas Jefferson was enrolled on the Bill of Attainder which the British Government was preparing against leading American rebels.

The year 1774 was a busy one for Jefferson. He was enlarging his house for the occupation of his numerous family; he was busy with his agricultural and professional duties, and he was also preparing a draft of instructions for the Virginia members of the Congress which was to meet at Philadelphia in September.

It was characteristic of his calm, peace-loving temperament that, in these stormy times, his cherished idea was an address to the King. In this he felt the whole Congress must unite. The members should utter bravely in the royal ear their wrongs and grievances. Nothing could have been more offensive to the narrow-minded, arbitrary, obstinate King than the home truths of this plain, forcible, but respectful petition. He did not deign to take the slightest notice of it.

The Colonies had sent the flower of their manhood to the Congress assembled in Philadelphia, "in a plain brick building up a narrow alley." These sixty members represented the greatest statesmen, the most gifted orators, the commanding intellects of the Provinces.

Everybody knows that Jefferson's great work in the Continental Congress was the Declaration of Independence. This immortal document was not prepared until the summer of 1776. Even after the day of Concord and Lexington, there were many delegates who still clung fondly to the hope of a reconciliation with England. Perhaps Jefferson had been among the number until he learned in September 1774 of the fate which the dutiful petition, much of which was composed by himself, had met at the hands of the King.

The journey from Monticello to Philadelphia required more than a week's traveling. The road lay largely through the wilderness. Jefferson made his long trips back and forth as public or private duties summoned him. He was at home in March when his mother died. On the following June he was in Philadelphia, preparing the Declaration of Independence.

It was well that Massachusetts had sent her bold, resolute, patriotic delegate from Braintree to the Continental Congress. There were men among the members who, even after the evacuation of Boston by the British, flinched at the prospect of irrevocable separation from the mother country. A Declaration of Independence must mean that. It must involve, too, a long and unequal struggle, at best, with the most powerful enemy in the world. It is not strange that brave men's hearts failed them sometimes, when they contrasted the might of England with the weakness of America.

John Adams took upon himself the great task of carrying the Declaration through Congress. It required his immutable conviction, his absolute devotion to his country, and his supreme fearlessness, to spring into the breach. At this great crisis the Virginia and the Massachusetts barristers worked in perfect harmony. In a speech of masterly argument, of solemn, passionate fervor, that carried him and his hearers out of themselves, John Adams pleaded the cause of the Declaration before his colleagues.

No other man could have done this with such effectiveness. The speech and the hour were perhaps the greatest of the speaker's life. When he ceased, the end was achieved.

On July 4, 1776 the Declaration of Independence was signed by all the delegates. Henceforth there could be no drawing back. "The Declaration of Independence is probably," says a high authority, "the most famous state paper in the world. It is the charter of human freedom. It was greeted with shouts, bonfires and processions."

Jefferson was now in the full tide of public life. Honors and responsibilities were rapidly heaped upon him. In the autumn following the Declaration of Independence he was appointed by Congress to represent, with Dr. Franklin and Silas Deane, the United States at Paris. The offer was a dazzling one to a young man of thirty-three. Jefferson felt all its allurements. With his alert intelligence, his keen observation, his delight in congenial companionship, Paris, two decades before the French Revolution, would have been a most fascinating place for him. But Mrs. Jefferson's health made it impossible for her to accompany her husband. He would not leave her behind for all that Europe could offer him. He declined the mission.

He was again elected to the Assembly. He was placed on a variety of committees. The lawbooks of Virginia bristled with all sorts of medieval traditions, with iron rigors and cruel punishments. Jefferson was bent, heart and soul, on making a sweeping reform in the ancient, tyrannous legislation and he gave the best of two years to revising the laws of Virginia.

Meanwhile the war of the Revolution went its long way. The young nation passed through all the dark days which followed the evacuation of Boston. In due time came the surrender of Burgoyne, and the war was brought under the very eyes of Monticello, when four thousand English and German prisoners of war were marched and quartered close to Charlottesville by order of Congress.

It was in keeping with Jefferson's character to do all in his power to alleviate the tedium and discomfort of the war prisoners in the very shadow of his home. He extended many courtesies to his foes, and made many friends among them.

On June 1, 1779 Thomas Jefferson became Governor of Virginia. It was a position full of responsibility and difficulty at that time. The flower of Virginia was, of course, in camp with Washington. The weak and scattered militia could do little to protect a State whose unguarded coasts and numerous rivers offered such temptations to sudden incursions of the foe. Three weeks before Jefferson's inauguration a fleet of two thousand troops had landed, plundered, ravaged, burned and murdered, without encountering any obstacle. There was much apprehension, too, about the Indians. Worst of all, Virginia was impoverished. Her militia lacked everything necessary for defense. The former Governor, Patrick Henry, had hurried off all the home supplies to General Gates, in North Carolina. The latter was all that stood between Cornwallis and the firesides of Virginia.

When the great fleet of sixty vessels entered Hampton Roads and lay there, waiting to co-operate with Cornwallis in laying waste Virginia, Jefferson's hands were tied.

Happily the North Carolina militia held Cornwallis at bay, and, after a month's waiting, the fleet disappeared from Hampton Roads.

Certainly Jefferson had hard lines from the beginning. If he was not a born soldier he was a man full of energy, resource and determination. He faced the situation with coolness and courage. Yet it was one to appall the stoutest heart. There was no force but a half-armed, scantily-clothed body of militia to resist the march of Cornwallis into Virginia or the hostile fleets upon her coast. It was a time that tried men's souls, and the Governor had to bear the brunt of things.

There was no peace for the inhabitants. One invasion was followed by another. The air was full of alarm and terror.

Sunday, the last day of the year 1780, was perhaps the darkest day of all those dark days. On that morning a fleet of twenty-seven sail rode in Chesapeake Bay. Benedict Arnold was in command. Wherever he went, he would be likely to make short, stern work with the country he had betrayed. At that time Jefferson was alone. He hurried his family to a place of safety thirteen miles distant. Then he spurred his horse toward Richmond, the new capital, until the animal broke down. "The Governor of Virginia was compelled to borrow an unbroken colt." When at last he reached Richmond, he found the foe there before him.

Arnold remained at the capital twenty-three hours. One suspects that, brave as he was, he must, after his treason, always have felt uneasy when he was outside British lines. Jefferson's prompt action had roused the militia on every side, and breathing vengeance, they marched on Arnold's track.

But he got back safely to his fleet and fell down the James, having to content himself with the havoc he had made at the capital.

Four times in the spring of 1781 the Virginia Legislature fled on the alarm or approach of the British.

The following month Jefferson's hour of trial came. The redoubtable Tarleton, "with a body of cavalry two hundred and fifty strong," galloped near midnight into Louisa, a town twenty miles from Monticello. Before the next sunrise a rider spurred a horse white with foam up the mountain. He brought tidings of the approach of the foe.

The Legislature—what there was of it—was at Charlottesville. There was no doubt Tarleton was bent on capturing that and the Governor.

Jefferson confronted the peril coolly. The family had time to breakfast before they left Monticello to take refuge with a friend. Jefferson secured his most valued papers, mounted his horse, and rode off in the pleasant June morning.

There was no thunder of hoofs in the still air. He rode to a point where he could look down on Charlottesville. It lay peaceful in the morning sunshine. Jefferson had been hurried away from his precious papers by a militia officer who had rushed in breathless with the tidings that troops were ascending the mountain.

Jefferson now suspected this was a false alarm, and rashly concluded to return for his papers. As he rode back he discovered that his sword was missing. It had fallen from its scabbard. He turned to search for it, and once more glanced off at the little village of Charlottesville. It was swarming with cavalry! That lost sword had saved him from capture. Five minutes after he left his house Tarleton's men were inside it.

But before that year had closed the long travail of Virginia was over. A little more than five months after that morning flight from Monticello, Cornwallis had surrendered at Yorktown.

Jefferson returned to his beloved Monticello, at the close of the war, believing that his public life was over.

Following the birth of her sixth child, Mrs. Jefferson died on September 6, 1782 and shortly thereafter Thomas Jefferson was once more elected to Congress. He took his seat in November 1783.

But a greater honor and a larger sphere of action were awaiting him. In the following May Congress resolved to send another envoy to France. Thomas Jefferson was appointed to the new post. He was to occupy it for two years. His salary was to be nine thousand dollars a year.

But despite all that was novel, interesting and delightful in that new life of Paris, it had its drawbacks. Jefferson could not speak French, and at his age it is not easy to learn a new language. Then his salary was inadequate, as his position of foreign minister involved large expenses. The climate did not suit one accustomed to a clearer, warmer atmosphere.

But he saw all that was most brilliant, distinguished and charming in French society. The most illustrious people met under the American's roof. Despite his broken French, they liked him immensely. Every American was interesting at that time to Frenchmen, especially one who was cultured, a lover of science and a philosopher.

But much as Jefferson's tastes were gratified by the grace and elegance of French manners, his clear, penetrating glance was not deceived. That pierced beyond all the glory and beauty of art around him, beyond the splendor and luxury of life, to the heart of things. That saw clearly the unutterable misery, ignorance and oppression of the people. These aroused in him a feeling of intense pity, indignation, horror. His letters show the strength of his feelings. He believed that of the twenty millions in France, "nineteen millions are more wretched, more accursed in every circumstance of human existence, than the most conspicuously wretched individual of the whole United States."

Despite his own agreeable surroundings, Jefferson was under no illusions. His residence in France only strengthened, if possible, his loyalty to America.

He did his best for her interests during these five years. He worked with untiring industry to secure a more generous commercial treaty between the two nations. But old interests, traditions, abuses, all stood in his way. Outside of his official duties he labored unceasingly for his country. He wanted to introduce every valuable product and implement of the Old World to the New. With his passion for agriculture, he was always sending home "seed-grass, plants, roots, acorns"—anything novel in the vegetable world which he fancied might flourish in his native soil.

He was eager also to introduce American productions in Europe; and was untiring in obtaining specimens of the fauna and flora of his own country for propagation in France.

Jefferson had not been two years abroad when he went over to London to join Mr. Adams, who was having a hard time in "negotiating commercial treaties."

At this period the social atmosphere of England was anything but agreeable to Americans. George III naturally did not delight in their presence at his court. Jefferson's reception was hardly civil. He did not enjoy England or the English people. In the way of treaties he could accomplish nothing. Prejudice, commercial selfishness, and a bitter grudge against anything American, all combined to create the most rigorous monopolies. It was evident that English statesmen and English merchants meant to crush the manufactures and ruin the carrying trade of the young nation across the sea.

Now the Colonies had chosen to set up for themselves, they should have no chance of which England could deprive them. This was the temper which Adams and Jefferson had to encounter at court, in Parliament, and on the English Bourse of that day.

In about two months Jefferson was back in Paris. Here he was in congenial air. The most famous Frenchmen assembled at the board of the Monticello planter. Here they discussed great political problems, the signs of the times, the promise of the future.

For there was a new thrill and agitation in the air. People were talking about human rights, about individual freedom, about the dawn of a better and happier era, in a strain that had never been heard before. Long afterward Jefferson, in his quiet home at Monticello, must have recalled that illustrious company which, during these years, passed over his threshold, and remembered with a pang how many of these had perished by the guillotine.

His official position made the utmost caution necessary in giving expression to his feelings or convictions. But as time went on, his heart and soul must have been fired by the great events transpiring about him.

All that can be said here is that Jefferson witnessed the opening acts of the drama which was to convulse the world. He never got over the hope, joy and intoxication of those days. All the terrible ones that followed never shook his faith in the promise and the purpose with which the French Revolution had opened under his eyes.

Jefferson was present at the assembly of the notables in 1787. He witnessed the destruction of the Bastille in 1789.

Lafayette, and the leaders in all these great national events, were Jefferson's intimate friends. They came to him constantly for sympathy and counsel. But all his passion for freedom did not confuse his judgment. He felt that the French people were not ripe for the large freedom his own nation had secured. He constantly admonished his friends not to move too fast, to beware of extreme measures, to adapt their policy to the conditions and habits of a people unaccustomed to liberty.

It seemed a cruel fate that Jefferson should feel it necessary to leave France at this juncture. The engagement of his eldest daughter to her cousin, Thomas Mann Randolph, who had visited his relatives in Paris, was the cause of Jefferson's return to America.

Almost the first news that greeted Thomas Jefferson on his return home, was that George Washington, then newly elected President, had appointed him Secretary of State. It was a most unwelcome honor. Jefferson at once resolved to decline it, but Washington had set his heart on the matter. He himself was in an untried place; he wanted the strongest brains, the wisest statesmanship, the noblest talent of the country about him, in the new experiment of a Republican Government. At last, and with much secret reluctance, Jefferson accepted the position. A week after his daughter's marriage, which was celebrated at Monticello in the gay old Virginia fashion, he repaired to General Washington, who was at the seat of government in New York.

It was an immense change from the life in Paris. No doubt Jefferson found his high position anything but agreeable at the beginning. He had come from a social atmosphere full of the passionate hope and joy of the opening French Revolution. It was one which peculiarly suited his temperament, tastes and convictions. He seemed now to have entered another air, where he missed the old sympathetic comradeship.

Alexander Hamilton was Secretary of the Treasury. In that post he was to render the nation, at the dawn of its existence, incalculable services. The country, which had barely held together in the loose bond of her Confederacy, was on the eve of bankruptcy. "He restored the credit and developed the resources of the country. He inspired its moneyed men with faith in his large, original, financial measures." He had a brilliant, dominant, captivating personality. His position, and Jefferson's in the cabinet involved, of course, close political and social relations.

Every student of American history is familiar with the bitter feud between these great men. It must be read elsewhere. Each aimed to serve his country with disinterested patriotism. But the character and convictions of each were utterly opposed to the other. Alexander Hamilton was by instinct and training an aristocrat. He had a great liking for England; he sought, so far as possible, to mold the new Government, in its political and social forms, after the ancient model. Thomas Jefferson, despite his Randolph blood and traditions, was a born Democrat. He believed in the common people; he trusted them; he desired that, so far as possible, all political power should be left in their hands; he was suspicious of a strong Central Government. Any measure that bore the slightest tinge of aristocracy or monarchy at once aroused his alarm.

With characters and sentiments so radically different, the Secretary of State and the Secretary of the Treasury could not long maintain their first harmonious relations. In a little while the gulf had opened between them. It could not fail to grow wider and deeper.

Hamilton's career at this time forms one of the most brilliant chapters in American history. He was master of men and of measures. He largely created and controlled that great Federal party to which the nation owed its existence, and which included a majority of its men of culture, character and weight.

Meanwhile the French Revolution went on its terrible way. America had at first hailed her old ally with joy, as one ancient abuse fell after another. But at last tidings came across the sea that appalled the hearers.

Strange as it may appear now, there were in the United States, not so many years ago, two parties, whose sharp dividing line was formed by their French or English sympathies. It need not be said that Jefferson belonged to one party, Hamilton to the other.

The statesmen kept up a show of civilities long after they felt the strongest mutual antipathy. Each attributed the worst motives to the other. Jefferson honestly believed that Hamilton's "schemes" would work irreparable mischief to the country. He could not do justice to his colleague's splendid financial genius.

The latter, on his part, had no confidence in the impracticable theories of Washington's Secretary of State.

Jefferson, disgusted and exasperated, and finding his urbanity and philosophy taxed beyond endurance by the imperious Secretary of the Treasury, resolved to resign his place at the close of Washington's first term. But the President was strongly opposed to his leaving. He therefore consented to remain awhile. Jefferson was no doubt sufficiently unhappy at this period. An atmosphere of controversy was repugnant to him. He saw his great rival, his unscrupulous political enemy, as he regarded Hamilton, carrying, with his masterly tactics, measure after measure which he heartily disapproved: he longed passionately for the old farm life, the freedom and quiet of Monticello.

Meanwhile the Republic of France sent its first minister to the Republic of the United States. Genet came to America.

There is only space here for a glance at this important episode. The new envoy, fresh from the fiery atmosphere of French politics, had one supreme object in his mission. He fancied it would be easy to embroil America with England.

Young, rash, headstrong, he set about his work. He found many sympathizers, and succeeded in arousing the passions and prejudices of the people. The friends of France were his ardent supporters, and Genet gave Washington infinite anxiety and trouble.

Despite Jefferson's French predilections, he now rallied stanchly to the President's side, and thoroughly sustained his policy.

The storm at last blew over. Genet's proceedings were disavowed by his government.

The President's entreaties no longer availed to keep Jefferson in the cabinet. The first Secretary of State resigned his office January 1, 1794.

But the nation could not leave him alone to experiment with his crops, and delight his soul with architecture, and read his books, and talk in the pleasant evenings with his guests at Monticello. In 1796 Thomas Jefferson was elected Vice-President of the United States.

"It is the only office in the world about which I am unable to decide in my own mind whether I had rather have it or not have it," he wrote to James Madison. Indeed, the political atmosphere was such at this crisis, that there were plenty of reasons why a man of Jefferson's temperament should dread to enter it again. However, he accepted the appointment, and in due time went to the inauguration of John Adams at Philadelphia. "It is a curious and characteristic fact that he carried with him the bones of an enormous mastodon, to display to the amazed eyes of the savants at Philadelphia. He had just been made President of the Philosophical Society."

The next four years formed a stormy period for the country, for the President and the Vice-President. Here again French affairs were complicated with American politics; here again Jefferson was brought into deadly antagonism with his powerful enemy, Hamilton.

John Adams, the President, did his utmost for a time to relax the country's strained relations with France. But fate was against him. The embassy which he sent to the French Government proved worse than a failure. War appeared inevitable between the two countries, the old allies. Washington even, with all his affection for Lafayette, with all his memories of the time in which France, when his need was sorest, had come to his rescue, believed the danger so menacing, that he prepared, as a soldier must, to meet it. He left Mount Vernon to organize the new army of which he was to be commander in chief. Happily the temper and situation of France, the wisdom, courage and patriotism of the President, averted the danger. John Adams saved his country a war with France, and this noble deed cost him his second term of Presidency.

The nineteenth century opened on a stormy scene in America. The bitter quarrel between Adams and Hamilton had demoralized the great Federalist party to which the country owed its existence, its financial strength, its growing honor and power among the nations.

This was the era of the birth of the Republican party. It grew rapidly in numbers, strength and influence. The Federalists had been called the "party of the gentlemen," a distinction which, in a political campaign, would not be used to their advantage. The Republicans, on the other hand, proudly called themselves "the party of the people."

Thomas Jefferson was its organizer, its leader, its ideal. In 1801 it made him third President of the United States.

His entrance upon office formed an era of great changes in the

Administration. The inaugurals of our first two Presidents were full of stately ceremonials and elaborate etiquette, more or less suggestive of the pomps and pageantry of European courts. Everybody knows how Jefferson, true to his Democratic convictions, abolished all these. The third President of the United States rode into Washington on March 4, 1801, without guard or servant, dismounted, and hitched the horse's bridle to the fence with his own hands.

Yet in that old morning of the dawning century, America was going wild with joy over the inauguration of this tall, plainly dressed, unattended man. His hair was getting gray, and he was fifty-eight years old, when he went up in that quiet, simple fashion to take the highest place and the heaviest responsibility in the Nation.

From that time, so far as possible, all stately ceremonials and etiquette were swept away as by a magician's wand. There were no more splendid levees, no more stately and burdensome receptions. Everything was plain, quiet, simple, as Jefferson thought alone befitted the home and habits of the President of a Republic. His proudest ambition was to be a "plain American citizen."

It is always difficult, if not impossible, to keep the golden mean. When Jefferson resolved to put his fervid democracy into daily practice, he may sometimes have carried it to unreasonable lengths, as he did when he received the amazed and indignant British minister "in a shabby coat and with slippers down at the heels."

But Jefferson felt strongly that an example was needed, and if, on occasion, he went too far, he did not err on the wrong side.

It should never be forgotten, too, that he resolved never to appoint one of his own relatives to office. With his generous nature and his large family connection, this was a lofty and trying position to take; but he held to it unflinchingly. Here he must speak for himself: "The public will never be made to believe that an appointment of a relative is made on the ground of merit alone, uninfluenced by family views; nor can they ever see with approbation, offices, the disposal of which they intrust to their Presidents for public purposes, divided out as family property."

Washington and Adams had held the same views, although the former authoritatively interfered, when the rigid observance of this rule would have deprived the country of the immense services of John Quincy Adams during his father's administration.

Jefferson's first term of office was happy, peaceful and prosperous for his country. The purchase of Louisiana was the most remarkable public event of this period. The vast transfer of real estate, which gave to the American Government control of the mouths of the Mississippi, was achieved by Jefferson with masterly adroitness and statesmanship. The hour was in his favor. The French treasury was impoverished, and Napoleon Bonaparte, first Consul of France, resolved on breaking the Peace of Amiens, was sorely in need of money before he could again let loose the "dogs of war." He virtually admitted that the sale of the vast "Terra Incognita" of the West cost him a pang. But Louisiana lay far out of the track of his conquests, and he believed that England would speedily make a descent on the Gulf coast if he did not close with the offer of sixty millions for the French territory. James Monroe had appeared on the ground in the nick of time. He had the President's full confidence and the great sale was promptly concluded.

It seems incredible that a purchase of such unspeakable value to the American Republic should have met with outcry and denunciation at home, but it is none the less true that the party opposed to Jefferson fiercely decried the bargain with Napoleon.

Another of Jefferson's important measures at this period of his Administration was the bold course which he adopted toward the Algerine pirates. "It was the beginning of a series of acts which ended in sweeping the pirates from the Mediterranean."

The trial of Aaron Burr, the English outrages on American shipping in American waters, the miseries of the embargo, belong to Jefferson's second term. They made the Presidential pillow one of thorns. Mr. Jefferson was a lover of peace; he did his utmost to maintain it. The whole country, aflame over the long chapter of outrages on its shipping and seamen, thought forbearance had ceased to be a virtue. All Jefferson's old enemies would have enthusiastically supported him had he declared war with England.

"I have only to open my hand," he wrote, "and let havoc loose."

But he did not flinch. The embargo which he preferred to war proved, in its workings, a very inadequate measure. It certainly prostrated the commerce of the country for the time, and it did not accomplish what Jefferson had fondly hoped.

His first Presidential term had expired in the midst of honor and glory. The closing months of the second were clouded by public anxieties and private embarrassments. Jefferson longed for relief from the cares and responsibilities of the high post with the passionate longing of Washington a dozen years before.

Thomas Jefferson was perhaps the happiest man in all America when, March 4, 1809, he resigned the Administration to James Madison.

He returned to Monticello and lived there for seventeen years.

He made a profound impression upon the noblemen and illustrious foreigners who journeyed to Monticello to look upon him and hear his voice. Some of these carried back to Europe the declaration that the "Virginia gentleman was the most important man of his epoch."

Jefferson was during the last years of his life, as always, an ardent Democrat. His soul swelled with patriotic joy when he contrasted the freedom and prosperity of the New World with the oppression and misery of the Old.

"When we get piled upon one another as they do in Europe," he said, "we shall be corrupt as they are in Europe, and go to eating one another as they do there."

It irked Thomas Jefferson sorely that he was a slaveholder, though he appears to have been the mildest, most indulgent of masters. But he abhorred the system. Nobody ever uttered more solemn protests against slavery than the Virginian, who was born, brought up, and spent his life in its midst.

In October 1824 an event occurred which cannot be passed over in this sketch of Jefferson's life. This was the meeting between him and Lafayette. They had not seen each other for thirty-six years. Jefferson had passed his eightieth birthday. Lafayette was approaching his seventieth. That meeting forms one of America's great historic pictures.

After that visit less than two years more remained of Jefferson's life. A longer biography would have much to relate of these years. Despite the dignity, cheerfulness, serenity, that characterized them, they were clouded and harassed by financial difficulties.

The oak was bending to the storm at last. He who had always dealt in such large generosity with his fellow men, he who had so strong a hatred of debt, felt its burden on his age. He was forced to sell his precious library. There was danger that he would lose Monticello. When this became widely known, individuals rallied to his aid. New York, Philadelphia, Baltimore, sent him, through private channels, more than fifteen thousand dollars. He who had resolutely refused a loan from his native State, was greatly touched by this gift of individuals. "No cent," he characteristically said, "is wrung from the taxpayer. It is the pure and unsolicited offering of love."

As the summer of 1826 opened it became apparent to all that he was gradually failing.

He made, on his death bed, a remark full of the noblest magnanimity. "His calumniators, he had never thought, were assailing him, but a being non-existent, of their own imagining, to whom they had given the name of Thomas Jefferson."

At the last he had but one desire. This was to live until the 4th of July. But his exhaustion was so great that those who watched often feared his sleep would be the sleep of death before that day dawned.

But the strong life did not yield easily, and he still breathed when the day broke. He lingered on, slumbering much, occasionally speaking a few words, until a little past midday. When the sun set, on July 4th 1826, Thomas Jefferson had breathed his last.

JAMES MADISON

When the year 1770 dawned, it opened the most important decade in American history. In that year there was, in the old Princeton college, a young undergraduate from Virginia, who was a most zealous and tireless student. For the Virginia youth of nineteen allowed himself only three hours' sleep out of the twenty-four, the rest he devoted assiduously to study and recitations! The name of the Princeton undergraduate was James Madison; he had entered college at eighteen; he came of the old Virginia planter class, which, a little later, was to give the country so many of its early Presidents and statesmen. He was born in Montpelier, in Orange County, in the beautiful, picturesque country of the Blue Ridge.

The family tree struck its roots far back among the earliest years of the Province. The Madisons anchored on the Chesapeake shores fifteen years after the settlement of Jamestown.

James was the eldest son of his family, a fact which was of consequence in the eyes of the old Virginia law; he had four brothers and three sisters; he was a born student, caring, even in his childhood, little for play and the rough games that delight healthy, robust boys; he was naturally shy and thoughtful, and had a grave, mature air that must have seemed oddly in contrast with his years.

In those days, when schools were few and poor at best, he studied mostly under a private tutor in his own home. Even when a boy, he had acquired a good deal of Greek and Latin, of French and Spanish. There were probably few fellows as well equipped for the college curriculum as that youth of eighteen, who went up to Princeton from the foot of the Blue Ridge.

James Madison graduated in 1771. He remained awhile, however, to study with the president, Dr. Witherspoon. When the youth of twenty left Princeton, he carried to his home the groundwork of that wise and thorough scholarship which was to prove of such immense service to him in the great role he was to play before the world; but he carried also a weakened vitality; he had taxed it so heavily that it never afterward recovered itself, and it proved his discomfort and limitation all the rest of his life.

The wonder was that those twenty-one hours of study had not killed him long before he left Princeton; but he inherited the longevity of his stock.

At home he entered on the study of law, and taught his younger brothers and sisters. The small, pale, serious-faced youth was at this period much interested in theological studies. His fragile health exercised a depressing influence on his thoughts and moods. Before his life had really begun he had a strong feeling that it was approaching its end.

While James Madison was busying himself with law and theology, the storm of the Revolution was slowly gathering. All those great questions which preceded the War—questions of essential liberty, of the rights of freemen, and the relations of the Colonies to the mother country—must have aroused the eager interest of that luminous young mind and of that patriotic heart.

James Madison entered on his public career in 1776. The War of the Revolution was then a year old. Madison, though young and shy among his distinguished seniors, who were engaged in the work of forming a constitution for the State, made his mark—less in public debates than in private discussions and with his pen. Here his rich stores of learning and his calm and logical mind showed to best advantage. The young member slowly but surely acquired power and influence among his peers and with the people.

The following year he was a candidate for the General Assembly. He lost the election, but it was greatly to his honor. "He refused to treat the voters with whisky." It required much moral courage to do this. Drinking formed a necessary corollary of voting in the political habits of that age. But Madison had clear convictions on most subjects, and a conscience that would not permit him, when the test came, to flinch.

His position commanded great respect among people of weight in the province, and he was soon appointed a member of the Governor's council.

During his term of service Patrick Henry and Thomas Jefferson were Governors of Virginia. Both these men had a high regard for young Madison. Jefferson was eight years his senior. At this period that strong attachment was formed between the two which continued for the rest of their lives.

In 1780 Madison was elected to the Continental Congress. This was a high honor, and the man who received it was not yet thirty years old. He served through three stormy, eventful years. During this period, the War of the Revolution was brought to its triumphant close at Yorktown, and the Treaty of Peace was at last signed between England, France and America. Madison was in that old Continental Congress whose powers proved so inadequate to the needs of the Nation. It must have been a trying school for him, but it was an invaluable one. This was proved a little later when he, more than any other man, prepared the way to the Convention which framed the Constitution at Philadelphia.

In 1784 Madison left the National Legislature to enter that of his native State. A vast work lay before him. The old statutes were to be revised. A new spirit of progress and humanity was to be infused into the legislation. The old laws and usages which embodied much of medieval injustice and hardness were to be superseded by new and liberal ones. But Madison had to fight hard with prejudice and conservatism for every inch of the upward way. His great paper, the "Memorial and Remonstrance," which opposed taxing the people for the support of religion, finally carried the divorce of Church and State in Virginia.

Meanwhile the young Nation was going blind, helpless, struggling on its untried path. The inefficient Congress, the vast public debt bequeathed by the Revolution, the general disorder, insecurity and widespread impoverishment, were filling the country with foreboding and despair.

Madison's patriotic soul was deeply stirred by the condition of affairs. He saw the dangers into which the Republic was drifting. She would certainly go to pieces unless a stronger bond of union took the place of the slight Confederacy which barely held the States together.

The people who had gained their freedom after a struggle of seven years with the most powerful monarchy in the world, were jealous of their liberties. Behind any attempts to enlarge the national authority they beheld the dreaded specter of approaching monarchy. The soldiers of the Revolution, as they sat around their firesides or assembled in the ancient taverns to talk over their campaigns and discuss their grievances, grimly muttered "that they wanted no new king set up in America." It had taken seven years and Lexington and Concord, Bunker Hill and Yorktown "to get rid of George Third!"

The suggestion of a strong Central Government always aroused the suspicions and hostile fears of the veterans who had fought the battles of the Revolution. A power set above the States, controlling and defying them, at once assumed to their imaginations the hated features of monarchy.

The talk ran in the old taverns and around the firesides in this impassioned strain during the gloomy years which followed the close of the Revolutionary war. Meanwhile the country, which had bought its freedom with so great a price, and whose existence seemed the dawn of a better era for the world, was drawing nearer to that inevitable wreck which its enemies had exultantly predicted.

But one man—a small-framed, pale, thoughtful-faced Virginian—had the clear, forecasting vision of a statesman. He and a few others like him looked the worst in the face and did not despair. He believed that the remedy for all existing evils lay in an efficient national government. This alone would infuse new life into the paralyzed energies, revive the industries, and develop the resources of the Thirteen States. In a closer alliance lay their salvation. If they separated, formed small confederacies, or entered into foreign alliances, the work of the Revolution had been in vain. In a national government, invested with authority to act and to compel respect on its own soil and on that of every nation of the world, lay the sole chance for the future of the United States.

But it was one thing for James Madison to see this, and quite another to make the mass of his countrymen see it.

The greatest obstacle to the formation of a closer union was in the States themselves. Each of the "Thirteen" had her individual interests, her pet prejudices, her commercial ambitions and jealousies. Each, too, regarded her sisters with more or less distrust. In the face of all this, any attempt to secure a closer union by sacrifices for the general good must have appeared almost hopeless.

But James Madison had a calm, patient, hopeful temper, and underneath this glowed the zeal of the true patriot. He went at his Herculean task with great common sense and the utmost discretion. He had made a long step in advance when he carried a measure through the Virginia General Assembly which "invited the States to meet at Annapolis and discuss measures for the formation of a more efficient Federal Government."

This measure, instead of alarming the popular mind, appears to have been regarded with widespread indifference. It was certainly the day of small things for James Madison. Only five States thought his invitation of sufficient importance to send delegates to the Annapolis convention.

But before these delegates separated, another measure, also introduced by Mr. Madison, had urged the States to send their delegates to Philadelphia in May 1787 to draft a Constitution for the United States. This was throwing down the gauntlet. It was a frank admission that the old Confederate League was a failure.

The delegates met in Philadelphia, and George Washington presided, and what hard work and fierce controversies filled that old hot summer of 1787! When the Convention broke up in September the work was done; the Constitution had been formed, and James Madison was henceforth to be called its father. One war had been fought on the floor of the Convention, but the tug of a harder was yet to come. If the reluctant or hostile States could not be brought to accept the Constitution, all the summer's work would be lost.

Madison, Hamilton and Jay now did splendid service for their country, in that series of great papers which they contributed to the *Federalist,* and which with calm, unanswerable logic set the real issues at stake before the people.

A long, bitter contest, which cannot be dwelt on here, followed between the friends and foes of the Constitution. Many patriots regarded it as subverting the liberties of the people—as the first fatal step toward monarchy. But the States one after another fell into line and ratified. In due time, George Washington was, in accordance with the provisions of the Constitution, nominated first President of the United States.

The impressive ceremonies of that first inaugural took place in New York on April 30, 1789. The world had never witnessed a scene like that. A new hour had struck for humanity.

James Madison was elected a member of the first New York Congress. It met in the old City Hall of New York.

When Jefferson returned from his famous mission to France, and was about, with immense reluctance, to take the post of Secretary of State, Washington earnestly desired that Mr. Madison, for whom he had a strong liking, should accept the vacant mission. But Madison declined this, as he also did the post of Secretary of State.

Alexander Hamilton's time had come now. In a little while he was carrying everything before him. He was, with his splendid genius for finances, establishing the credit and creating the prosperity of the country. At the same time he was organizing the great Federal party, which was to control the nation to the close of the century.

Madison had worked harmoniously with his brilliant colleague during the critical period when the Constitution was formed and sent on its way. But now he drew back, disturbed and alarmed at Hamilton's sweeping measures, and at the large powers with which he was resolved to invest the new Government.

Madison was a democrat of the Jefferson type, though he was by temperament more conservative than his chief. He was much attached to France, and cherished grateful remembrances of her services to America in the Revolutionary War.

Hamilton, on the contrary, had strong English preferences and affiliations. He believed in conferring on the national Government as large powers, and on the States as limited, as was consistent with the Constitution. He was the leader and inspirer of the Federal Party. Madison came to be regarded as the head of the Republicans. This brought the former colleagues into political antagonism. An atmosphere of controversy was, however, extremely distasteful to Madison. "In all discussions he was the most courteous and conciliatory of political opponents."

He was forty-three when the love that was to make the content and happiness of his life came to him. He met Mrs. Dorothy Todd one day, when both were out walking in Philadelphia. The lovely face of the young widow of twenty-two at once attracted the lonely student. He soon sought an introduction. A little later, Mrs. Todd was writing to an old friend: "Thou must come to me. Aaron Burr says that 'the great little Madison' has asked to be brought to see me this evening."

In September, 1794, she left Philadelphia for Harewood, her sister's home in Virginia. Here, a little later, the marriage of James Madison and Dorothy Todd took place.

Dolly Madison, as she is known in history, came, like her husband, of sterling old English stock which had taken early root in the colony. She had been brought up in a home of great purity, simplicity and refinement. Her father and mother were members of the Society of Friends, and observed its rules rigorously. Dolly was a charming creature from her birth. The little, sweet-faced Quaker girl was a favorite with everybody. Her young life must have had its trials; for despite all the severe simplicity of her home, no fashionable belle's complexion was ever shielded with more care from every ray of sunshine. It must have tried even her sweet temper to be compelled to wear "a white linen mask, to have her sun bonnet sewed on every morning, and to have the little hands and arms thoroughly covered with long gloves before she started for school." But despite all these drawbacks, Dolly Payne had a happy childhood.

With the close of Washington's administration in 1797, Mr. Madison retired for a time from public life to the peace and delight of the home at Montpelier.

There had been talk of nominating him to succeed Washington in the Presidency. But Madison positively declined to enter the lists. He craved the peace and freedom of his own hearthstone.

But it was impossible for one who was so ardent a patriot, and who had so much of the statesman's quality, to lose his interest in public affairs. During the four years of Adams' stormy administration, Madison was keenly alive to all the great questions of the hour —questions very largely of foreign policy. Madison's deep, but calm, equable nature, must have been profoundly stirred by the passionate indignation against France which shook the country, and, at one time, brought it to the verge of war with its ancient ally.

As a Republican—more and more closely identified with that party as time went on—he must have shared Jefferson's sentiments and feelings at this critical period. Madison wrote, during these years, many papers, luminous, logical, and full of masterly reasoning.

It is not possible to dwell here on the strife and passions which filled America as the new century opened. The year 1801 saw the great triumph of the Republican Party. Thomas Jefferson was President of the United States; and very soon afterward James Madison was Secretary of State.

His office made it, of course, necessary to exchange Montpelier for Washington. In the big, dreary, unsightly capital, which, a few years later, was to excite such intense disgust in John Quincy Adams, Madison found his place, and his wife found hers. His relations with the new President were particularly harmonious and delightful. They shared each other's political views; they cherished toward each other the warmest friendship.

As the President had long been a widower, the duties of mistress of the new White House devolved largely upon Mrs. Madison. She filled that position with charm and ease.

Jefferson's first term of presidency was all prosperity, success, glory. The second term afforded so sharp a contrast that one might have fancied the gods had grown jealous. Foreign complications—the British Orders in Council—the Berlin and Milan Decrees of Napoleon, insulted the Government, crippled the commerce of the young nation, and goaded the people to the verge of war. Then, worse than all, was the atrocious impressment of American subjects on board American ships, into the British navy.

At the close of Jefferson's administration wide financial distress prevailed in the country, and the prosperous commerce of the previous years was almost destroyed.

All these things tended to embitter the contest for the election of his successor. "It was like a death-grapple between the two great parties, the Federal and the Republican."

The result proved a triumph for the latter. Aaron Burr's "great little Madison," the scholar of Princeton, the polished host of Montpelier, was elected President of the United States.

Jefferson went back to his farm and his library, happy to surrender the post around which the storms were beating so furiously, but rejoiced that the friend who shared his deepest political convictions would succeed him.

It was not in the nature of things that the scholarly, peace-loving President who went to the executive chair at that agitated time would have a peaceful administration.

England still continued to carry herself with all the old arrogance toward America. No statements of facts, no appeal to instincts of common right and justice, could move the haughty, insolent government. The time came when the outraged country could endure no more. On June 8, 1812 President Madison approved the act of Congress which declared war between the United States and Great Britain.

The history of that war cannot be told here. It can only be said that the feeble American navy, which had been the scorn and jest of England, won its first laurels in encounters with its powerful foe.

The American forces met on land with a series of disasters. The one, however, which overshadowed all the rest, was the taking and burning of Washington by a British army of five thousand men, who landed on the Patuxent, near the point where the river enters Chesapeake Bay. The enemy moved rapidly and without encountering vigorous resistance upon the unprotected national capital.

Everything lay at their mercy. The President, who was not a soldier, had hurried off "to meet the officers in a council of war." There was nobody to take command. Mrs. Madison, left at the White House, was in imminent danger of falling into the hands of the enemy. Her husband, too, could not return to her rescue, lest he should be captured. He sent messages, entreating her to fly in time, and "to save the cabinet papers, public and private." The mistress of the drawing room proved now what fine stuff lay under all her grace and gentleness. She secured the papers and the plate; she refused to leave the premises, though the enemy was close at hand, until a large portrait of General Washington "screwed to the wall" should be taken down.

In the hurry and confusion of the time, it was not possible to do this, so the frame was broken, and the precious canvas carried off.

During those trying hours, Mrs. Madison wrote some messages to her sister, which throb with the life and agitation of the time: "Here I am still within sound of the cannon! Mr. Madison comes not. May God protect us! Two messengers covered with dust come to bid me fly, but here I mean to wait for him."

At last, however, she was prevailed upon to enter her carriage and leave the White House, over which a little later the British soldiers were swarming, and which was burned that night.

At length, in a little tavern in an apple orchard, Mrs. Madison found shelter from the darkness and the furious storm which had begun to rage outside. Here at last her husband joined her; but at midnight, a breathless, panic-stricken courier arrived upon the scene, with tidings that the enemy had discovered the President's hiding place and was on his track. He yielded to the entreaties of his friends and went out in the storm which filled that August night with its fury, yet which was less to be dreaded than the foe close at hand: he found shelter in a miserable hovel in the woods, and listened through the roaring of the winds for the tramp of the British soldiers. James Madison lived to be a very old man, but he could never have forgotten that night in the lonely hovel with the storm lashing the low roof, where he waited, dreading the rush and the shouts that would be louder and fiercer than the tempest.

Day came at last, but it was long before Madison learned the welcome news that the British had retreated to their waiting ships. The President was saved, but the White House was a heap of blackened ruins.

There is no time here to linger on the events which closed the war in 1815. The Treaty of Ghent, the victory at New Orleans, which set the crowning glory on Andrew Jackson's military career, belonged to this period.

A little more than two years later James Madison's second presidential term expired, and he returned to the quiet, beautiful home at Montpelier. Here again, in his "dear library" as he called it, in the cultivation and adornment of his estate, and in the exercise of a large, gracious hospitality, the delicate, small-framed, scholarly ex-President lived a quiet life.

He had still some last service to render his native state. "In 1829 he was a member of the Virginia convention to reform the old Constitution. When he rose, after a long silence, to utter a few words, the members left their seats and crowded around the venerable figure, dressed in black, the thin gray hair powdered in the fashion of other days, to catch the low whispers of that voice."

A vein of humor brightened this grave, reserved nature, and made it gay and joyous as a boy's to those who knew it best.

"Madison had a strong relish for everything facetious and told a story admirably; his sunshine of temperament never deserted him. In the weary hours of pain, during his old age, his humor flashed up spontaneously as before. When some friends came to visit him, he sank back upon his couch with the smiling words: 'I always talk more easily when I lie!' "

Born and nurtured in the midst of slavery, he was, like Washington and Jefferson, opposed to it. As early as 1758, expressing in a letter to Mr. Randolph his wish not to enter upon the practice of law, he adds: "Another of my wishes is to depend as little as possible upon slave-labor."

Many of his contemporaries thought Madison lacking in warmth, enthusiasm, nerve. Perhaps this was true. Yet this lack may have been owing largely to that very enthusiasm for study which crippled his health in his youth and made him a semi-invalid all his days.

America will always owe a vast debt to James Madison for his services in critical periods of her history. His figure must always stand amid that group of immortal patriots with whom he was so long and closely associated.

He was at last much confined to his room and his bed; but the life in the delicate frame flickered on for many years and did not go out until James Madison was eighty-five. He tranquilly closed his eyes for the last time on June 28, 1836.

"Mistress Dolly Madison"—a fragrance seems to cling about the name—outlived her husband thirteen years. At the time of her death, July 12, 1849, she had reached her eighty-second year.

JAMES MONROE

At the battle of Trenton, fought amid the cold and snows of December 26, 1776, a young Virginia lieutenant carried himself with such gallantry that he won the praise of the commander in chief. "Perceiving that the enemy were endeavoring to erect a battery to rake the American lines, he advanced at the head of a small detachment, drove the artillery from the guns, and took possession of the pieces."

During the action a ball struck him in the shoulder. He received a captaincy for his bravery. His name was James Monroe.

The officer who received his wound and won his title at that time was a mere boy—less than eighteen. He was born in that old Westmoreland county, among whose river meadows George Washington sported away his childhood. The family emigrated to Virginia in 1652, and the race came of old Scotch cavalier stock. The father of James was a planter. His fine, fertile estate lay near the head of "Monroe's Creek, which empties into the Potomac." It was also very near George Washington's birthplace, although he had passed his twenty-sixth birthday a little before James Monroe was born.

Fortune smiled on the boy's beginnings. The tobacco plantations yielded large incomes in those days, and the childhood of James Monroe opened amid ease and comfort. What was better than that, too, he came of a vigorous, sturdy, freedom-loving breed. He breathed from his cradle an atmosphere in which liberty was held to be the noblest and dearest of man's possessions.

The planter's son had the best advantages which the old commonwealth afforded. He was sent to a "fine classical school, and at sixteen entered William and Mary College." Here he studied for two years, but it must have been study a good deal broken by the march of events. Lexington, Concord, Bunker Hill, must have been names that spoiled many a recitation. For the young undergraduate had inherited with his fire and pluck the liberty-loving instincts of his race. It was quite characteristic that after the Declaration of Independence he should throw up his books, leave college, "hasten to

General Washington's headquarters at New York, and enroll himself as a cadet in the army."

The trained British veterans were carrying everything before them. The Tories were triumphant and defiant. James Monroe took his place bravely in the ranks. He was with the army through all the sad reverses which make the darkest chapter in the history of the American Revolution. He shared the retreats from Haarlem Heights and from White Plains, and the miserable marchings through the Jerseys. At last he faced his enemies at Trenton, and in his first battle was wounded and made a captain.

In the later campaigns young Monroe served as aide on the staff of Lord Sterling, with the rank of Major. He was in the battles of Brandywine, Germantown, Monmouth. Washington, who had now conceived a high opinion of young Monroe's abilities, sent him to Virginia to raise a new regiment, of which he was to be colonel, but Virginia had poured her young men into the northern army until she had few left for her own defense. Monroe's temporary promotion served him an ill turn now, as he had "lost his place in the Continental line."

The young soldier then resolved to return to his books. He began the study of law with Jefferson, who was Governor of Virginia, who "had a large and admirable library," and who must have been the most delightful and stimulating of teachers.

Those were hard times for Virginia and her Governor. In the frequent British descents on her soil, the law studies were much broken into. Monroe was too ardent a patriot not to throw aside his books and hurry to the rescue when the invader was spoiling his native State. But the victory at Yorktown put an end to further British raids on the Atlantic seaboard.

Colonel James Monroe—he had received his commission, although he never organized his regiment—entered on his long public career at a very early age. He was only twenty-three when he became a member of the Virginia Assembly and also of the Executive Council. The following year he was chosen delegate to the Continental Congress. These were great honors for so young a man. He was fortunate enough to reach Annapolis, where the Congress was then sitting, in time to witness that great historic scene, when George Washington resigned his commission as commander in chief of the Army of the Revolution.

James Monroe went, heart and soul, into the service of this Congress. He was in its sessions at Annapolis, at Trenton, at New York; for his term extended through three years.

During this time he could not fail to be profoundly impressed by the inadequacy of the powers with which the old Congress had been invested by the States. He ardently desired that its authority should be strengthened and enlarged. The nation, after the close of the Revolution, had gone its blind, stumbling ways. The country was sinking deeper into impoverishment, disaster, and gloom. Business was prostrated, disorder was rampant, while each of the emancipated States regarded her sisters with more or less suspicion and jealousy.

The young delegate perceived with dismay the imminent danger of the Union's "crumbling to pieces." In the wide commercial distress, with the vast public debt weighing like an incubus upon the nation, and with all its energies crippled by its lost credit and its exhausted finances, the compact which had held the States together was rapidly growing weaker.

James Monroe bore an active part in events which led to the convention at Annapolis. But this represented only five States, and seemed absurdly unequal to the demands of the times when it broke up.

But it had recommended another convention to represent all the States and meet in Philadelphia during the summer of 1787.

The convention met. The Constitution of the United States was the result.

Before this New York and Massachusetts had had serious difficulties about a boundary line. James Monroe was one of the nine judges appointed to settle the dispute. This fact indicates the high opinion his contemporaries had formed of the young congressman's judgment and abilities.

It was in New York, while he was attending the session of Congress there, that he met and later married Miss Elizabeth Kortright, "daughter of Laurence Kortright, a former captain in the British army."

In 1787, the Constitution was framed and its acceptance by the States convulsed the country. Monroe, who had been much under the personal influence of Jefferson, and who entertained very ardent democratic ideas, was alarmed lest the Constitution should confer too large powers upon the central government. His fears led him, with many others, to believe that he detected a strong monarchical bias in the instrument. Madison, Hamilton and Jay were then straining every nerve to secure its adoption. Monroe, as ardent a patriot as any of the trio, held steadily to his convictions. Events were to amply prove his mistake, but history must record that he opposed the ratification of the Constitution by the States.

Soon after this had taken place, Monroe became a member of the United States Senate, where he remained for more than three years. Alexander Hamilton, Washington's Secretary of the Treasury, was at this time, in many respects, the most important figure in American politics. That fertile, imperious genius was laying the foundations of the new government; it was organizing the great Federal party; it was bracing the national credit; it was infusing new courage and energy into all the business interests of the country; it was inaugurating a new and large financial policy, with a splendid audacity and ability which dazzled the nation and carried everything along with it.

James Monroe took alarm at the power and success with which the brilliant and irresponsible Secretary was going on his way. Hamilton's audacious financial schemes bewildered the Virginian, who had no business genius. He doubted, too, the wisdom of Washington's public measures, in which the influence of his former aide was clearly apparent.

But all these interests were soon largely merged in another for James Monroe. His appointment as Minister Plenipotentiary to France took him and his friends by surprise. He had opposed the President's proclamation of neutrality between England and France; his sympathies were strongly on the side of our ancient ally. It was for this reason, and in order to restore the old friendly relations with that power, just now a good deal embittered toward America, that Washington sent the new embassy to France.

It is not possible to enter into the details of Monroe's mission in France. It is probable that his ardent, impetuous nature may have led him into some mistakes. He did not perhaps estimate the importance of maintaining harmonious relations with England, while his own government was dealing with all the great problems which it had to face at its birth. It should be remembered in his excuse, too, that it was not an easy matter to keep clear of offense with the stern, aggressive French Republic. Monroe fell more or less out of its favor, while he did not conciliate the authorities at home.

In 1796 he was recalled, and he returned to America in an aggrieved, resentful mood. He was received with great honor at a banquet by the Republican leaders in Philadelphia; but Washington evidently felt some displeasure when he wrote from Mount Vernon that "Colonel Monroe had passed through Alexandria, without honoring him with a call."

Monroe published a book in which he explained and defended his course in the foreign embassy with spirit and ability. The book at least created a profound sensation among the political leaders of that day.

Soon after his return Monroe was elected Governor of Virginia. He held that office for three years—the term allowed by the Constitution.

During the first years of that century, and while Thomas Jefferson was President of the United States, the sun of Napoleon Bonaparte was climbing to its splendid zenith. His name probably was on the lips of all civilized people oftener than that of any other man in the world. His career was watched in the United States with very different feelings. One party regarded it with unbounded admiration and enthusiasm; another feared and dreaded that triumphant, remorseless genius. The possession of Louisiana by the French, might, at any moment, jeopardize the cordial relations of the new governments. Jefferson had early perceived this. With all his partiality for France, he was too sincere a patriot to be blinded where the interests of his own country were at stake. He had long been resolved that if statesmanship and diplomacy could effect it, the United States should become the owner of the vast territory of Louisiana, which included the outlets of the Mississippi.

The necessities of Bonaparte were Jefferson's opportunity. The French Consul was straitened for money, as he was about to enter on that long and bitter struggle which succeeded the brief peace of Amiens.

Whatever dreams may sometimes have visited that teeming brain —that insatiate ambition—of establishing a vast transatlantic empire, Napoleon's present designs lay far out of the line of American conquests.

Spain had, a little while before, ceded Louisiana to France. Jefferson resolved to send Monroe to the legation at Paris to promote the great purpose he had so deeply at heart.

Monroe departed perfectly informed of the wishes of his Chief, and with large liberty of action in a case where there were no precedents to guide him.

The great sale was effected in less than a month's time. Louisiana cost the United States fifteen million dollars, when that sum meant vastly more than it does at this time. The French treasury was replenished, and Europe shook again with the tread of armies.

It has been said that "this was probably the largest transfer of real estate which was ever made since Adam was presented with the fee simple of Paradise."

Monroe's part in this great land sale, though it cannot be related here, was a very important one. His influence had much to do with bringing the matter to a successful issue. "He always regarded this as the most important of his public services."

Of course no one of the principals engaged in the famous sale anticipated its historic importance. Jefferson, writing about the coveted territory, a little while before, had described it as "a barren sand." Probably most Frenchmen regarded it in that light.

Monroe took leave of Bonaparte June 24, 1803. He was about to depart for England, to which he had been ordered by his Government.

Having arrived in England, Monroe found hard lines. The powerful government paid little heed to the remonstrances of the American Minister. It was useless to urge his country's grievances, to talk of the rights of neutrals, the outrages on American commerce, the impressment of American seamen.

Monroe's foreign mission had been a triple one. Besides France and England, it included Spain.

In Spain Monroe vainly attempted to reach any agreement with regard to the eastern boundaries of Louisiana. These had not been clearly defined at the time of the sale. The slow, stately, half-moribund court remembered its ancient glory in its present decay, and took alarm lest the young, energetic nation in the West should get some advantage in the Floridas.

Baffled in the Spanish mission, Monroe returned to England. Here he set to work with his usual vigor, aided by William Pinckney, who had joined him in the legation, to obtain a treaty which should in some faint way recognize the rights of American shipping and American merchants. But he had a haughty, obstinate and half-hostile government to deal with. It was only after long negotiations and immense concessions that he succeeded in obtaining a treaty. But it did not touch the vital point of the impressment of American seamen. It afforded no redress for the capture of American vessels and goods by English cruisers. The treaty was so unsatisfactory that Jefferson himself, with all his aversion to war, refused to ratify it.

Monroe's surprise and mortification when he learned this were extreme. His mission, which had proved such a brilliant success in France, was a humiliating failure in England. Yet the wearied, disappointed statesman had done his best to serve his country. It was not his fault, certainly, that England refused to give up the right of search, that Spain kept an iron grip on the Floridas.

At last Monroe returned to America. The chagrins and disappointments he had encountered in his foreign mission had not seriously shaken the faith which the Republican party reposed in him. It was now talking of nominating him for the next Presidency, but the choice, for various reasons, fell on Madison.

While he was in England, Monroe had become disgusted with public life; he desired to leave it and return to his estate and the practice of his profession. His salary did not meet the expenses, necessarily large, of his position. He had been compelled to make heavy demands on his private fortunes; he became alarmed at the state of his finances, and felt that he now owed all his services to his family.

But the time was still far distant when James Monroe should lay aside his armor. He was again elected Governor of Virginia in 1811, but was called from that post by the President, who appointed him Secretary of State. In the following year war was declared between England and America.

Vast cares and responsibilities now fell upon Monroe. He proved equal to all the demands made upon his energy and ability through those trying years in the nation's life. The President, who confided in him absolutely, at last induced his old friend to add to his other duties the enormous burdens of Secretary of War. During the confusion and disorder of that miserable time when Washington was entered and burned, Monroe showed that his old dash and bravery were not extinct. He was the master spirit of the hour. He made every effort for the defense of the capital; he did not hesitate to threaten with the bayonet those demoralized citizens who talked of capitulating to the enemy.

Placed at the head of the War Department, he infused new spirit and vigor into military affairs. "The treasury was exhausted; the government's credit was gone," when James Monroe pledged his private fortune to supply the country's pressing needs.

No reverses daunted that indomitable energy, that devoted patriotism. Monroe was bent on securing the victory of his country. He proposed to increase the army to a hundred thousand men. This unpopular measure would, if carried out, be certain to defeat his election for the next Presidency. James Monroe was certain of this, but he did not flinch.

When England sent her great fleet and ten thousand veterans, the flower of her victorious armies, to New Orleans, to secure the mouths of the Mississippi, James Monroe dispatched orders to the governors of the Southwest. The strong, trenchant sentences have the ring of that courage with which, years ago, the college youth had led his small column at Trenton against the advancing redcoats. "Hasten your militia to New Orleans. Do not wait for this government to arm them; put all the arms you can into their hands; let every man bring his rifle with him; we shall see you paid."

A little later the battle of New Orleans was won, and soon afterward America learned that the Treaty of Ghent had been signed.

There was no need of the hundred thousand men.

In 1817 James Monroe became President of the United States. The new administration, called "the era of good feeling," from its lack of all disturbing issues, proved in many respects the most peaceful which the country had known in its twenty-eight years of presidents.

Soon after his inauguration Mr. Monroe set out on an extensive trip through the country to inspect the various military posts. The journey must have been much like a triumphal progress of kings, although the object of all the enthusiasm, the processions, the welcomes and banquets, wore "a blue homespun overcoat, light-colored underclothes, and a military cocked hat, the undress uniform of the officers of the Revolutionary War."

The sight of the "old cocked hat" roused immense enthusiasm in all the Revolutionary veterans who beheld it. The President visited the Eastern cities. Boston gave him a grand reception. A cavalcade met him on the Neck; Dorchester Heights, the Common, the forts in the harbor, fired salutes. Monroe must have enjoyed all these demonstrations in his simple, quiet way, though he loved his country more than any honors she could bestow on him.

The long Presidential tour included the Northwest as far as Detroit, and occupied four months. The wearied and much feted President reached Washington about the first of October.

James Monroe's administration was far less eventful and dramatic than his foreign missions.

At the close of four years he was re-elected to the Presidency. His popularity is best attested by the fact that only a single vote was cast against him.

The affairs which during the double term principally engaged the attention of the President and his cabinet were the "defense of the Atlantic seaboard, the promotion of internal improvements, the Seminole War, the acquisition of Florida, the Missouri Compromise, and resistance to foreign interference with American affairs."

All these subjects are familiar ground to the students of American history. James Monroe earned his most enduring laurels in the declaration which was of such immense importance to Europe and America, and which will always live in history as the Monroe Doctrine.

James Monroe lived seven years after his retirement. But these years were not merely the restful ones of advancing age to that ardent, energetic nature. He was Regent of the University of Virginia; he was a local magistrate, and also a member of the Virginia Convention; he had a large correspondence at home and abroad and retained an active interest in public affairs.

At this time his fortunes had greatly dwindled. He had neglected them while he was engaged in public life, and the positions which he had occupied had involved expenses which his salary did not defray, and which compelled him to draw heavily on his private resources.

The thoughts of parting with Oak Hill, his home, was distressing to him, but he had to face it. "No private subscription came to honor or relieve him."

When Lafayette learned the condition of his old friend's affairs he came promptly to his aid, and in the most delicate and generous manner conceivable placed part of his Florida lands at Monroe's disposal.

But the offer was not accepted. The old man, whose health was much broken, could no longer endure the loneliness of Oak Hill. He went to New York to live with one of his daughters and died there July 4th, 1831.

JOHN QUINCY ADAMS

It was June 17, 1775 throughout the British Colonies of North America. In Massachusetts it was the day of Bunker Hill.

On that day a boy, with his mother, still a young woman, had climbed one of the hills in the parish of North Braintree, and the two stood with faces turned eager and intent in the direction of Boston, ten miles away.

This was by no means an unusual spectacle. On that summer morning the heights in the vicinity of the small, blockaded, seaport town, were occupied by anxious, breathless crowds, all gazing toward the dense clouds of smoke which hid the warships in the harbor.

Those crowds heard with blanched cheeks the heavy incessant cannonading of the British fleet. They heard the American volleys answer bravely back; they saw red flames dart and leap through the dense smoke. A little later, Charlestown, "with its five hundred houses and its one church steeple, that had shone a pyramid of fire," was a heap of blackened ruins.

To the gazers on the heights the scene before them was literally one of life and death interest. Husbands and sons, fathers and brothers, were in the thick of the fight. On the issue of the battle hung the fate of the Colonies, the future of America. When that June night fell upon smouldering Charlestown, the Battle of Bunker Hill had been fought, and Massachusetts had seen the darkest, most glorious day in her history.

John Quincy Adams was, at that time, close to his eighth birthday, for he was born July 11, 1767. He was the eldest son of John and Abigail Adams, of Braintree.

The boy bore the name of his maternal great-grandfather, John Quincy, who was dying at the time the child was baptized. "It was filial tenderness that gave the name," he wrote long afterward. And then he adds, in his characteristic way, "There have been through life perpetual admonitions to do nothing unworthy of it."

The early years of his life were passed between Boston and Braintree, as the family changed their home from one place to the other.

John Quincy Adams was a grave, thoughtful boy, caring less for play and games than he did for the talk of his elders. Ingrained truthfulness and honesty, as well as fearlessness and obstinacy, were salient qualities with him, almost from infancy.

At the time when he watched the Battle of Bunker Hill, he no doubt had very decided opinions on all the great questions at issue between England and the Colonies. But the time for discussion and argument had gone by. Two months before the British fleet cannonaded Charlestown Neck, the long drama of the Revolution had opened with the fight at Lexington and Concord.

The most momentous event in John Quincy Adams's boyhood occurred more than two years after the Battle of Bunker Hill, when his father, at the close of 1777, was appointed envoy to France, and decided that his eldest son, then in his eleventh year, should accompany him to Europe.

They had a long, stormy passage from Boston to Bordeaux, and the keen, observant boy was placed at a school in Paris, where he rapidly acquired the French language.

A year and a half later the two returned home, and during the long voyage young John gave English lessons to the ambassador and his secretary, whom the French Government was sending to America.

The return home was destined to be a brief one. In about three months the two sailed again in the same vessel, the father having received a second diplomatic appointment to Europe.

The next years afforded the boy rare opportunities for seeing the world and for meeting illustrious persons. He accompanied his father to Holland; he had brief periods of going to school at Paris, at Amsterdam, at Leyden. The chances for study, though he probably made the most of them, were short, for the boy's good fortune seemed to reach its zenith, when, just before he attained his fourteenth birthday, he found himself engaged in a diplomatic career. Francis Dana, envoy to Russia from the United States, actually appointed the youth his private secretary. The journey to that cold, semibarbarous country must, in that faraway day, have been full of novel experience and adventure to the New England lad. The mission was not particularly fruitful of results; but after diligently discharging all his duties for fourteen months, young Adams left St. Petersburg and returned alone, making his long journey through Sweden and Denmark, seeing much with those keen young eyes, before he resumed his studies at the Hague.

He soon after rejoined his father in Paris, where the latter was engaged with Franklin and Jefferson in negotiating a final treaty of peace between Great Britain and her quondam Colonies. Here the boy became at once an additional secretary, and had his share in drawing up that famous instrument which settled forever the question of the independence of the United States.

This reads already like the history of a long, varied and eventful life. It appears incredible that the whole is a rapid and very incomplete sketch of a boy who had recently passed his sixteenth birthday.

Mrs. Adams, with her two younger children, joined her husband, and the long separation ended in a happy, peaceful year at Paris.

In 1785 John Adams was appointed Minister to St. James's but young John had made up his mind to enter Harvard.

He returned home, studied assiduously for a short time, entered the junior class at Harvard College, and graduated with honor in 1787. He afterwards studied law in Newburyport, and was admitted to the bar just after he had passed his twenty-third birthday. Almost as a matter of course he established himself in Boston. Clients appeared rather slowly for the first year, but during the three following ones their numbers grew steadily.

But the rising young lawyer's time and thoughts were not wholly engrossed by his profession. An intense, patriotic interest in public affairs was his birthright. He published over different signatures various papers, which attracted much attention at home and abroad for the ability with which they treated critical public questions, especially the new relations of America with Europe.

The writer of such papers could not long remain undiscovered behind the slight mask of his signature. It is believed that they were the immediate cause of his nomination by President Washington as Minister to the Hague. He received his commission on his twenty-seventh birthday. The embassy offered him must have been a welcome change from the drudgery of the Boston law office. Some passages from young Adams's diary show plainly that he had been much chafed by the narrow horizon of his life. He felt the stir of large and noble ambitions. He could not be content in that "state of useless and disgraceful insignificancy" in which he found himself. "At the age of twenty-five, many of the characters who were born for the benefit of their fellow-creatures have rendered themselves conspicuous among their contemporaries. I still find myself as obscure, as unknown to the world, as the most indolent or the most stupid of human beings."

In these words we have the key to John Quincy Adams's character. He wrote them, moved by no merely personal and ignoble ambitions. He had many faults, angularities, limitations. Unhappily these were much on the surface, and often embittered his relations with others, and made his path, sufficiently thorny at best, unnecessarily hard and rugged. But nobody, familiar with his history, can doubt that his supreme aim from first to last was "to live for the benefit of his fellowmen."

"A perilous voyage, a leaky ship, a blundering captain, brought him to the Hague October 31, 1794."

The young diplomat had entered upon a scene which might well have confounded the wisest, most experienced statesman. The French Revolution was still in its death throes. All Europe was arming for the great struggle with France. Adams had scarcely presented his credentials, when the Stadtholder had to flee before the French conquerors. The ministers of foreign courts, for the most part, followed him. The American remained. But he was now forced to use all his adroitness, his cool judgment, his sound common sense, in order to escape compromising relations with the powerful French and Dutch party. They made flattering overtures to the young diplomat, whose secret sympathies must have been largely on their side. But he preserved his balance through all those exciting times. The government, however, to which he had been accredited had disappeared, and there was really nothing for him to do, a condition utterly distasteful to his habits and temperament. He was debating whether to return home, when advices from the President caused him to remain. Washington, who always weighed his words, ventured on a prophecy, "that Adams would soon be found at the head of the diplomatic corps, be the government administered by whomsoever the people may choose."

He remained at the Hague, narrowly observing the march of events, and characteristically making the most of his time, "studying, reading, learning foreign languages, the usages of diplomacy, the habits of distinguished society."

It is impossible in this sketch to dwell on the episode of young Adams's visit to England. He found himself in an awkward position.

He was not minister to the court which, for its own purposes, attempted to treat him as one. He had, at best, only some "rather vague instructions to discuss certain arrangements between the two governments." His shrewdness and good sense again carried him successfully through all difficulties, though it was not easy to avoid giving offense when declining the diplomatic and social honors which were forced upon him.

He became at this time engaged to Miss Louise Catherine Johnson, daughter of Joshua Johnson, American Consul at London.

After a brief absence he returned to England, where his marriage took place July 26, 1797.

He was appointed Minister to Portugal at the close of Washington's administration. Before he had set out for the post it was changed to that of Berlin. At this juncture a delicate question presented itself. John Adams had succeeded Washington in the Presidency. The sensitive honor of both father and son took alarm, lest the continuance of the latter in public office should now be open to the charge of nepotism. On the other hand, it seemed cruel that the son's career should be cut short in the midst of its promise by his father's success. The young man did not hesitate. He was ready to resign his office at once, and in a manly and spirited letter to his mother declared that he "could neither solicit nor expect anything from his father."

Washington now came to the aid of the perplexed President. He insisted that the son "ought not to be denied that promotion in the diplomatic service to which his abilities entitled him."

Accepting this view of the matter, Mr. Adams was appointed to Berlin, but he had some difficulty in gaining admission to the city. "The lieutenant on guard at the gates had never heard of the United States of America, and one of his private soldiers had to explain to him what they were!"

Mr. Adams's mission to Berlin promised to be hardly more fruitful than that at the Hague. The new nation across the seas was of little consequence in the eyes of the ancient governments, absorbed in French politics, with which their own existence seemed so closely bound up. It goes without saying that Mr. Adams did all that he could to serve his country, and succeeded at last in securing a treaty of amity and commerce between Prussia and the United States. His work was done now, and he applied for his recall home.

It came as one of the last acts of his father's administration.

On April 5, 1802 the Boston Federalists elected him to the State Senate. He promptly accepted the office, though it must have seemed to his contemporaries a vast descent for a man who had represented his country eight years at the courts of Europe. But they probably thought more of the contrast than he did himself. One of John Quincy Adams's finest qualities was his readiness to serve the people in any office which they bestowed upon him.

He did not remain long in the State Senate, yet the time was not too brief for him to display his independence of thought and action, and greatly irritate some of his supporters. However, he could not have alienated the majority of his party, for the next year they sent him as Senator to Washington.

In October he set out for the national capital—the rude little village which must have shocked the representatives of foreign courts, accustomed to the splendors of European cities. Mr. Adams may not have cared what they thought about it, but he was concerned to find that Washington "held no church of any denomination."

He probably was not prepared for the intense hostility which he at once encountered. In its atmosphere he must have gained a more vivid comprehension of all that his father had undergone. The triumphant Republicans, the disappointed and exasperated Federalists, who chose to hold the elder Adams responsible for the defeat of the party, alike vented their malice on the son. He was met on all sides with coldness, if not with insults. "Any motion that he made was sure to be lost. Any measure that he supported was certain to meet with virulent opposition."

A man with a less tough-fibered character, less sustained by a firm sense of rectitude, might have been overborne by this powerful hostility. Mr. Adams felt it acutely, but it was not in his nature to succumb. Time worked in his favor. At the end of four years the rancor of both parties had largely worn itself out. The Massachusetts Senator at last took the role among his colleagues in the Senate to which his abilities entitled him.

A Federalist of that period would doubtless have justified his opposition to Mr. Adams by the simple declaration that "his party could not trust him."

There was much apparent truth in this allegation. With his strong personality, his independence of thought, speech and action, it was impossible for John Quincy Adams ever to work on mere party lines. He was always sternly conscious that he owed his highest allegiance to his sense of duty. When, with such a man, it came to a question of right, party affiliations and interests were like flax in the flame.

Burning questions now came to the foreground in American affairs.

There was the purchase of Louisiana, which necessarily involved its future admission to the sisterhood of states. It encountered at the time the bitter, determined hostility of the Federalists. John Quincy Adams, wiser than his constituents, approved of the sale, won from Napoleon's necessities, and brought down on his head the vials of Federalist wrath.

One cannot have the faintest idea of the temper of that old time, without bearing constantly in mind the fact that in all questions of foreign policy, the Federalists ranged themselves stanchly on the side of England, while the Republicans were passionately devoted to France.

The echoes of the French Revolution had not died out of American air. All the prejudices and passions which it had inflamed, still colored the sympathies and shaped the opinions of parties. Mr. Adams had none of the strong English bias of his colleagues in the Senate. His long residence in Europe had afforded him opportunities for forming opinions and reaching conclusions which no other of his countrymen had enjoyed. A mere stripling, he had borne a share in negotiating the treaty of peace between the two countries. But it does not appear that he was, even then, blinded to the sentiment and policy of England toward her former Colonies. He believed the British government inveterately hostile to American interests. On this matter he and his party in the Senate were as wide apart as the poles. But that fact did not influence him. If ever a man had the courage of his convictions it was John Quincy Adams. No party traditions, no personal interests, no regard for constituents, could sway him an inch. It is not surprising that when the crisis came and Adams actually supported the President's nonimportation act, that the amazed, disgusted Federalists of Massachusetts cried out that their Senator had betrayed them.

A month after this the British government issued that famous proclamation which declared the European coast blockaded from Brest to the mouth of the Elbe. This was a tremendous blow aimed directly at American commerce. "At that time the word neutrals included little but Americans." Napoleon retaliated by his "Berlin Decree," which declared the British Islands blockaded. "No vessel," ran the edict of the mighty autocrat, "which had been in any English port could thereafter enter any port in his dominions." So America was placed between two fires. Early in the following year England forbade all commerce of neutrals between the ports of her enemies. The "British Orders in Council" followed one after another. They were aimed at the carrying trade of the United States. Napoleon was again prompt with retaliation. His next measure, called the "Milan Decree," virtually made him master of the shipping of America. But if the shipmasters obeyed these orders, no resource remained but to burn every vessel in American harbors to the water's edge.

No wrong, however, was so keenly felt by the young nation as the practice of British impressment. All other acts paled before this monstrous one. It seems incredible now that Americans could, at any time, have submitted to so great an outrage. It is to John Quincy Adams's eternal honor that, at this juncture, regardless of party allegiance and interests, he took a bold and independent stand. It seemed to his brave, resolute spirit that the Federalists were under a spell of alarm and dread when it came to taking any measures against English wrongs, even against this crowning one of impressment of American citizens. His soul recoiled at the idea of submission. He beheld his party embarrassed and timorous, where he felt the only hope of redress was in a vigorous resentment of England's conduct. He did not, even in his most passionate moments, desire that the country should rush, ill prepared, into a war with her powerful enemy; but he was ready for any measure, short of the last appeal, which should manifest America's indignation.

These feelings explain Mr. Adams's position. In the year following the nonimportation act, the administration brought forward a bill for establishing an embargo. This measure by no means met with Mr. Adams's full approval. It was not what he desired, but it was, at least, better than nothing. He voted for the embargo.

Then the Federalists turned on him. Their wrath was terrible. It is but fair to say that, blinded by passion, they believed that he had basely deserted their ranks. It was not wholly their fault that they could not reach his outlook, see things from his wider point of vision.

But chagrined and enraged, they could think of no language inflamed and rancorous enough to describe the conduct of their senator.

But the Federalists did not end with words. They made haste to shake off the "traitor" and "renegade," as they delighted to call him. They nominated his successor in the Senate under circumstances devised especially to insult him. "Mr. Adams was not the man to stay where he was not wanted. He sent in his resignation."

This was in 1808. On the 4th of March of the following year James Madison became President of the United States. Two days later he notified Mr. Adams of his intention to appoint him Minister Plenipotentiary to Russia. It was a new mission, but the Czar, friendly to America, had often expressed a desire that an envoy should be accredited to his court.

Mr. Adams's foes had their chance now. They voted against the mission. But Madison had set his heart on it. In June he again named Mr. Adams for the post, stating to the Senate that he had now additional reasons for sending an embassy to Russia. His wishes prevailed. This time the nomination was confirmed.

On August 5, 1809, as Mr. Adams's diary records, he left his house at the corner of Boylston and Nassau streets for his long journey from Boston to St. Petersburg. His wife, his youngest son and his secretary accompanied him.

Mr. Adams arrived on the scene of his new mission late in October. His reception by the Emperor Alexander was most gracious and cordial. In the splendid Russian court things went more smoothly for John Quincy Adams than they had ever done in the plain senate chamber at Washington. The new Minister did not find very much to do; but there was a great deal to see and to learn.

There was a gorgeous ceremonious life at that old court of the Romanoffs. Mr. Adams mingled with it, thoughtful, self-contained, observant. All the pomp and power never for a moment dazzled him. Simple and dignified, he must have been an admirable representative of his country at European courts.

Those four years and a half which Mr. Adams spent in Europe were breathless years for the world. The very air was full of the clash of armies. The name most frequently on all men's lips must have been that of Napoleon Bonaparte. In the Russian court they could hardly, one imagines, have talked about anybody else. When Mr. Adams went to Europe the great Corsican held its destinies in his hands. Before the American left, the wonderful drama of the invasion of Russia, the burning of Moscow, the retreat of the French armies, had all taken place.

The "last war" between England and America had meanwhile gone on its checkered way. The Americans had met with serious disasters on land, but had won some signal naval victories over their powerful foe. Both people were tired and disgusted with the war.

On August 7, 1814, eight commissioners met in Ghent to negotiate a treaty of peace between the two countries. Five of the party were Americans. One of these was John Quincy Adams.

The result was, after the long verbal battle, the Treaty of Ghent.

America was jubilant over its provisions. What England thought of them was perhaps expressed by the declaration of the Marquis of Wellesley in the House of Lords. He declared that, "in his opinion, the American commissioners had shown a most astonishing superiority over the British during the whole of the correspondence."

When Mr. Adams returned to London on May 26th, a commission was awaiting him. He was appointed Envoy Extraordinary and Minister Plenipotentiary to England. Washington's prophecy regarding young Adams was now fulfilled. He had reached "the highest rank in the American diplomatic service."

He remained in England more than two years. He does not seem, any more than his father before him, greatly to have enjoyed his elevation. There was comparatively little to occupy him. The Court of St. James was, throughout the Georgian era, a rather chilling atmosphere for an American Minister. This one's meagre salary, too, was the source of constant discomfort and annoyance.

When, on June 15, 1817, John Quincy Adams sailed from Cowes, he had closed his long and honorable diplomatic career. He was still in the prime of life, close to his half century. But when, that summer day, the English shores faded from his sight, he had looked on them for the last time. Henceforward his life work was to be in his native land. He returned now to a new post. He had been appointed Secretary of State in the cabinet of James Monroe.

The patriotic soul of John Quincy Adams was profoundly stirred by the aspect of the national capital. It must have been an ugly, dreary, most uncomfortable residence for the first three decades of its existence. What appearance it presented to the new Secretary of State, after his long familiarity with the splendid capitals of Europe, can best be told in his own words: "It is impossible," he writes, "for me to describe to you my feelings on entering this miserable desert, this scene of desolation and horror. My anticipations were almost infinitely short of the reality."

But the Secretary of State settled down to his work with his inveterate doggedness. So far as domestic affairs were concerned, Monroe's administration rolled its smooth course almost to the end, when it was shaken by personal rivalries. The party animosities which had marked the opening years of the century disappeared after the Treaty of Ghent. Neither Federalists nor Republicans had now any great domestic grievances or any widely divergent policies. With our foreign relations it was different. There was the great problem of South American independence and our own attitude toward the revolted Colonies in the face of exasperated Spain and disaffected Europe; there were the burning questions of Florida, of the Louisiana boundary, and of General Jackson's unparalleled proceedings on Spanish territory, all requiring in their settlement the most adroit handling, the most consummate statesmanship. These momentous affairs fell within Mr. Adams's department.

That was the day, too, of the Holy Alliance. There were strong grounds for fear lest the members of that formidable power should take it upon themselves to suppress the nascent South American Republics. The monarchical and religious prejudices of the Alliance would inevitably cause it to side strongly with Spain against her former Colonies.

All the great European powers were, at this juncture, undergoing the conservative reaction which had followed the French Revolution. Great historical events, among them the rising of Greece, appealed strongly to the sympathies of America, and were liable to produce demonstrations which might, in the sensitive condition of the times, embroil us with foreign powers. Mr. Adams had to guard rigidly against this possibility. He took the ground and strenuously maintained it, that "America should keep wholly out of European politics." Not even when it came to entering into a league with England for the suppression of the slave trade, would he yield an inch.

Several of the most prominent and popular American statesmen were eager to succeed Monroe in the Presidency. It had hitherto been the practice to award the high prize to the Secretary of State.

This fact, no doubt, explains much of the bitter opposition which

John Quincy Adams encountered during the Monroe administration. He bore it with invincible courage, but his feelings were deeply pained and outraged. While his conduct may have won the respect of his political rivals, it was not likely to conciliate them. But Mr. Adams was seldom careful to placate people. He had too inflexible a nature, too belligerent a temper to court popularity.

He asserted that he should do "absolutely nothing" to secure the Presidency. There was something morally sublime in this position. He held to it through tremendous temptations, for he was not, like Washington, indifferent to the office.

But despite intrigues and machinations, despite the wide popularity and military fame of his strongest rival, the proud, frigid New Englander was elected President of the United States.

At his inauguration, March 4, 1825, he wore a black suit, wholly of American manufacture. Washington had set that example.

When the ceremony was over, his rival, General Jackson, hastened to cordially greet the new President. One regrets to add that this forms the last courtesy on record between the two.

John Quincy Adams's administration opened with the close of the first quarter of the nineteenth century. The Republic, which had at its birth so many new problems to face, and which had been so vast an experiment on the part of the statesmen who organized the government, had by this time won her place and her name among the family of nations.

America was at peace with all the world.

But though the promise was outwardly so fair, the elements of discord were secretly at work, almost from the moment of Mr. Adams's installation. No stone was left unturned by his political opponents to secure the next Presidential election for that impetuous western soldier who had such a hold of the popular imagination. General Jackson's friends were shrewd, keen, alert. They were versed in political strategy. They knew how to handle the masses, to bend events to the accomplishment of their plans. The man at the head of the nation, his mind occupied with the large problems of the statesman and patriot, had little time or taste for entering into the lists with his political opponents.

The passion and virulence of the campaign of 1828 repeated in some of its aspects that of 1801. It closed with the election of Andrew Jackson to the Presidency.

The younger Adams bore his disappointment—it must have been a severe one—with more philosophy than the elder had done. He acted his part with dignity in his successor's inaugural, and returned to the ancestral home at Quincy. With his passion for work, his dread of long leisures and the slow rusting of mental faculties, he set about preparing a memoir of his father, and also projected a history of the United States. The man of sixty-two had at that time little prescience that the most glorious part of his life was yet to come.

In 1830 when Plymouth district first proposed sending Mr. Adams to Congress, it was feared lest an ex-President would regard the office as too great a contrast with his former one. This doubt was expressed to Mr. Adams. The high character and true patriotism of the man showed themselves in his reply: "No person could be degraded by serving the people in Congress. Nor, in my opinion, would an ex-President of the United States be degraded by serving as a selectman of his town, if thereto elected."

The people of New England, or a large section of them, always understood John Quincy Adams's real quality. The Plymouth district sent him by a large vote to Congress, and from that time until his death, he represented that region.

He took his seat in Congress in December 1831. He had been elected by the "National Republican," soon to be known as the "Whig Party."

He at once characteristically declared that "he would be bound by no partisan connection, but would in every case act independently."

His position in the Twenty-second Congress was unprecedented. Every member must have regarded the ex-President with peculiar interest; but he himself records that "he experienced no annoyance on account of his descent in official life."

In a little while the nullification storm swept through Congress. Mr. Adams took a most intrepid attitude at this crisis, and maintained it through all the excitement. When the atmosphere cleared at last, it found him much disgusted with the concessions which the government had made in the interests of peace.

Years before, Mr. Adams had proved himself one of Jackson's stanchest defenders. But the strongest antipathy, both political and personal, now existed between the statesman and the soldier.

But it was in his position regarding slavery that Mr. Adams was to prove himself a gladiator. This tremendous question, coming to the front when the annexation of Texas began to be talked of, aroused all the moral and intellectual forces of the New Englander.

He brought to support his arguments, his vast stores of knowledge, his pitiless invective, his scathing satire, and more than all these, his indomitable physical and moral courage.

Mr. Adams's health broke very slowly. He had begun a diary as a mere boy in 1779. He made entries more or less frequently until 1795. At this time he set vigorously about the record and wrote regularly during the rest of his life.

The diary, which forms a vivid portraiture of the man and his times, contains a significant entry as early as March 25, 1844. "Physical disability must soon put a stop to this diary."

He had then been at work on it half a century. He goes on to speak of his "rising at four, of his smarting eyes and shaking hands."

One crowning triumph still remained for him. "The infamous gag-rule which he had long fought in Congress was suppressed."

There were no signs of mental failure in the old man when paralysis struck him in Boston on November 19, 1846. But the warrior would not lay off his armor. Three months later he went to Washington. It is pleasant to write that when he appeared on the scene of his many battles, all the members rose together. Various kindly courtesies, which marked the feeling of the House, were shown him. Afterward he was punctually at his post, though he spoke only once.

The last words in his diary were written to his son, Charles Adams on January 1, 1848, and they have in them the ring of all the writer's battling, triumphant years:

"A stout heart, a clear conscience, and never despair."

Mr. Adams was in his seat in Congress February 21, 1848. "He rose on the floor, with a paper in his hand, to address the Speaker, when he suddenly fell forward insensible. Paralysis had seized him again. He was conveyed to the hall of the rotunda, and then to the Speaker's room."

When he regained consciousness he said calmly, "This is the end of earth." Then he added, "I am content."

His invalid wife and his family were summoned to his side. But the long day's work was done. The time had come for rest. On the evening of February 23rd he died quietly.

They buried him under the portal of the church at Quincy, beside his grand old father and his noble mother.

ANDREW JACKSON

In October 1788 there came a day which was full of excitement and joy in the wild, beautiful valley of the Cumberland. In Nashville, the small western settlement, at the back door of civilization, the air was full of hospitality, of welcoming sounds and happy greetings. For on that day, warm and peaceful in the soft autumn haze, there rode out from the long, rough wilderness trail a procession of emigrants, "nearly a hundred in number." No wonder the little hamlet, with its cabins and block houses, went wild for joy over this reinforcement to its scanty population. Nashville was only nine years old at that time.

The cavalcade had come with its guides, its women and its children, from Jonesboro', a hundred and eighty-three miles to the east. It brought stirring news to Nashville. The States, one after another, had accepted the new Constitution, and the government would now be organized. George Washington was certain to be America's first President.

In the emigrant train rode a professional party which must have attracted attention at once. It was composed of a clerk, a judge, and several young lawyers. One of these was the newly appointed solicitor, or public prosecutor, for the district. He is the subject of this brief biography.

Andrew Jackson was twenty-two years old on that October morning, when he rode into Nashville. He was born in Union County, close to the boundary lines between the Provinces of North and South Carolina, on March 15, 1767. All sad fortunes darkened about his birth. Before that happened, his father had sickened and died suddenly. The family were still strangers in the New World. They had been here only about two years. They were of Scotch lineage from North Ireland. No doubt poverty drove the little household across the seas from Carrickfergus to Charleston. These people were sturdy and honest. Radical Whigs, stanch Presbyterians, they came with relatives and neighbors to seek a larger foothold, to find a fairer chance on the new continent—the father, Andrew Jackson, and his wife, Elizabeth, and their two little boys. They did not lose any time at Charleston. With true Scotch grit they faced their fate at once, and set out for the Waxhaw settlement, a hundred and sixty miles to the northwest, where they would find many familiar faces and countrymen. Here, on Twelve Mile Creek, a branch of the Catawba, in the midst of the pine wilderness, a clearing was made, a log house built. But in the spring of 1767, the rude home was deserted, and the family never returned to it. Mrs. Jackson was a widow and the boys were fatherless.

It was hard lines for that brave mother. She must have greeted the birth of her last boy with fresh tears of her widowhood. He was born in the home of her brother-in-law, but Andrew was only three weeks old when his mother carried him to the home of Mr. Crawford, another brother-in-law, with whom she had come to America. He was a man of some property. The widow was sure to be of service in his large family, with his feeble wife. And these were the beginnings of Andrew Jackson.

After all, they were not the worst ones. A tender, devoted mother watched over his childhood. No doubt he gave her plenty of trouble and anxiety—rash, wild, headstrong, as he must have been—generous, affectionate, lovable, too. For there was to be in him all his life, two different natures, each so positive, powerful, insistent, that it seemed the whole of him when it got the mastery. This made Andrew Jackson an insoluble problem to many of his contemporaries. It has made him ever since a puzzle to the world. He could not have failed to show something of this double character even during the first decade of his life.

In that thinly settled region, he had small opportunities for study. Perhaps these were, however, about equal to George Washington's. Andrew went to an "old field school-house," and learned "to read, to write, to cast accounts." It is extremely doubtful whether any books or any tutors could have made a scholar of him. His genius was one of action.

At last the War of the Revolution broke into the Waxhaws. Hugh Jackson, the eldest of the two brothers, and a mere stripling, joined the militia, did his part in the Battle of Stono, and died of exhaustion afterward. So the war came to Andrew's heart before it was at his door.

On May 29, 1780 the terrible Tarleton, with his three hundred horsemen, burst upon the militia in the Waxhaw settlement. The details of the battle are too sickening to dwell on. The militia, frightfully mangled, were carried to the old "log meeting house," where the women and boys, Mrs. Jackson and her sons among the foremost, came to tend them. Here the boy of thirteen had war in its most appalling form brought under his keen, all-observant eyes. He never forgot those days; indeed, he had one of those tenacious natures which never forgot anything that touched his heart or roused his passions.

And now havoc overran that fair world of the Carolinas. Nowhere else did the Revolution take on so fierce, so brutal, so fiendish a form. Men seemed to lose their manhood amid the fierce passions and cruel deeds of the long strife on the wild southern border. And a tall, yellow-complexioned, lank-visaged boy, with fiery blue eyes, was in the midst of the dreadful scenes. The iron entered his soul, and at last he took his part in the work. On August 16, 1780 the defeat of General Gates struck dismay and terror to the heart of the South. In the early autumn all the inhabitants of the Waxhaws who were not in the field, were again in panic-stricken flight, for news had come of Cornwallis's advance with those British troops at whose name every man, woman and child in the Carolinas had learned to shudder.

Mrs. Jackson and her sons had to make their wild flight with the others. Amid scenes like these Andrew Jackson's boyhood was nurtured. He was now at that formative period of his life when impressions are most vivid and lasting. No doubt the experiences of this time gave a permanent trend to his character. One cannot wonder that his young, passionate soul was fired with a deadly hatred of British soldiers.

Before the war was over his chance came. Neither Andrew nor his brother enlisted in any corps, but "they joined some of the small parties in the neighborhood, who rode about the country breathing vengeance on the foe." The young Jacksons had all sorts of adventures, hardships and hairbreadth escapes. At last a day came which must have made all their previous sufferings seem light. After a night of peril and exposure in a thicket where they had hidden, hunger drove the brothers in the morning to the nearest house. This belonged to their cousin, lieutenant Crawford. They found his wife here with her young children. The boys had crept cautiously inside. Nobody dreamed of danger. But their hiding place had been discovered. In a little while a party of dragoons burst into the house.

It is difficult to realize the scene which followed. Yet it was not an unusual one in that year of grace in the Carolinas. The house was ravaged. The dragoons "dashed crockery, glass and furniture to pieces, emptied beds, tore clothing to rags," before the eyes of the scared, helpless mother and her children. She looked on with her infant in her arms. The young Jacksons looked on, too, powerless to aid. But the younger was laying up the memory of that hour in his soul, and years later, on another field, and in another war, he was to exact the bitter price.

The brothers were at last mounted on horses and rode away in the train of their captors. Each had been cruelly wounded by the leader of the dragoons. It may not have been wise to refuse, as they did, when he ordered them to clean his mud-splashed boots, but they were prisoners of war, and the rude command aroused all the resentment of their young, fiery, Celtic blood. Andrew's head and hand were deeply gashed by the sword of the infuriated officer. Then Robert's turn had come. The blow on his head prostrated and disabled him.

In this condition the two were mounted on stolen horses and carried to Camden, forty miles away. Not a particle of food, not a drop of water, relieved the sufferings of that long ride. It appears incredible that their captors, who were men and not fiends, would not allow the parched boys to scoop up a little water when they forded the streams.

In the inclosure at Camden, greater misery, if possible, befell. They had no beds; their only food was a scanty supply of bread; their wounds went undressed. Smallpox made its appearance among the two hundred and fifty prisoners of war. The cup of Andrew's misery was full, when he was separated from his brother, robbed of his jacket and his shoes.

At last a gleam of humanity steals across the black picture. An officer of the guard, probably touched by Andrew's youth and misery, condescended to talk with him. Then the boy, with that passionate speech and manner, which was to exert such an immense power over the hearts of men, poured out the story of his wrongs and those of his fellow sufferers. The officer was amazed and touched. He started an investigation into the fare of the prisoners. The villainy of the contractors was unearthed. These, and not the military authorities, were starving the prisoners. After the boy's talk the rations were improved. "The prisoners had meat and better bread."

At last there was joy in the prison pen, for General Greene had come to their rescue. He drew up his brave little army, twelve hundred strong, on an eminence, within a mile of Camden, and waited for his cannon, which he had outstripped in his rapid march.

For six days he waited on Hobkirk's Hill. For six days the prisoners waited, too, full of intense, suppressed excitement. Their fate hung upon that little army on Hobkirk's Hill.

At last the day of battle came. One only of the imprisoned Americans witnessed it. This was Andrew Jackson. He had secured an old razor blade, "with which he hacked out a knot from the fence that had been recently erected on the summit of the wall which surrounded the inclosure."

With his eyes at the knothole, the boy watched the scene. The American army, confident of its strength, and not dreaming of a surprise from the inferior British force, lay encamped on Hobkirk's Hill. Lord Rawdon had planned his attack skillfully. The boy, peering through the knothole, descried the danger. He could not send across the intervening mile a warning shout that the redcoats were close at hand. He saw the first rush upon the unguarded troops. Even then, unprepared as they were, the horsemen made a gallant rally. They dashed into the midst of their foes and almost carried the day. The breathless crowd behind the boy at the knothole, listened to his report of the battle. Their own fate hung upon it. Suddenly the joyous words of victory faltered and fell, as the American fire slackened and receded. A little later "Greene was in full retreat."

From that hour despair settled heavily upon the prisoners. The young Jacksons sickened with smallpox. Robert's wound, never dressed, had not healed. But in that darkest hour help suddenly appeared. Mrs. Jackson had come from her home at Waxhaw to the prison at Camden. The mother must have pleaded passionately for her boys' release to the Whig captain, who held numbers of British prisoners. Negotiations were opened. At last an exchange was effected. It was greatly to the advantage of the enemy. The British gave up seven Americans for thirteen of their own soldiers.

The mother could hardly recognize her sons. Wasted with

hunger, wounds and disease, they came out of the Camden prison pen. Robert could not stand. There was nothing to be done now but make the long, weary journey back to Waxhaw. "Mrs. Jackson rode one horse, and Robert, too ill to keep his seat, was held upon the other." Andrew, "bareheaded, barefooted, with no jacket," dragged himself over the wilderness road. The party had almost reached Waxhaw when a cold rain burst upon them. "The boys had reached that critical period in smallpox when a chill usually proves fatal." In two days Robert was dead, and Andrew was raving in delirium.

Andrew Jackson had not reached his fifteenth birthday when he found himself alone in the world.

No consuming desire for study at this time braced the will and spurred the ambition of the boy from the Waxhaws. Yet in the grip of poverty he was probably conscious of some vague, indefinable power and purpose.

Andrew tried the saddler's trade and worked at it for six months. He visited Charleston after the British evacuated the city. Here his young blood took fire. "He squandered his slender means, got into debt, gambled, lost, and at the darkest moment won a high wager, left the table, and from that moment never played again."

Young Jackson studied law for the next two years. But he was never a model student. The wild, rough games of the age and the frontier, the horse racing and the cockfighting, still attracted him.

But at last Andrew Jackson was licensed to practice. There was no chance for the young lawyer in the old settlements. He sought a new field on the frontier. He obtained the appointment of solicitor for a vast district that lay far beyond the western wilderness. This frontier, then Washington County, is now the State of Tennessee.

This is the way it came about that Andrew Jackson rode that October day of 1788 into Nashville.

Andrew Jackson became now, and continued for the rest of his life, "the busiest of men." During the next seven years he was in constant peril, as he rode from court to court through a wilderness infested with hostile tribes. He never knew where the ambushed savage lurked on his path; he must always have been listening for the sharp crack of the rifle. Yet his nerves were a stranger to fear.

In a little while people began to find out that the new solicitor was no ordinary character. Everybody must have had decided opinions about him. The shrewd, rough backwoodsmen could not have been long in perceiving that young Jackson was not to be trifled with. Resolute, tenacious, utterly fearless, friend and foe alike knew where to find him.

Three years after young Jackson's arrival at Nashville, he was married to Mrs. Rachel Robards after her divorce. She was the daughter of Colonel Donelson, the Virginia pioneer who, nine years before, had brought his family, including his pretty daughter, from the Virginia homestead to what was then the old French trading outpost on the Cumberland.

In June 1796 Tennessee, after serious opposition, was admitted to the Union, and Andrew Jackson was elected to represent her in Congress. He was twenty-nine years of age at that time. He mounted his best horse and set out upon a journey of eight hundred miles to Philadelphia, the first Representative of Tennessee in the Congress of the United States.

This was his "first visit to any center of civilization." The Representative of the new State was described by one who saw him at that time as "a tall, lank, uncouth-looking personage, with long locks of hair hanging over his face, and a queue down his back tied in an eel skin."

But, however he may have been dressed, the new member was not abashed by the presence of his accomplished colleagues. He voted against the address which Congress had prepared for General Washington at the close of his Presidential career. The young lawyer from the wilds of Tennessee would not be deterred from expressing his convictions by any great name or splendid services.

He made a few speeches in Congress, in which he brought forward certain claims of his State "growing out of Indian wars" on her territory. He made the long journey home to find his popularity enhanced, and in the following autumn Tennessee sent him to the Senate. He had no opportunity to make a record there. But he satisfied his constituents, who, when he again returned to them, elected him "Judge of the Supreme Court, with a salary of six hundred dollars a year." The Governor had little more.

He was not yet thirty-two years old—Member of Congress, Senator, Judge of the Supreme Court! Certainly honors had been heaped upon his young manhood.

Andrew Jackson's life, during the closing years of the eighteenth century and the opening of the nineteenth, abounds with many striking incidents. The fierce feud with Governor Sevier, the terrible duel with Charles Dickinson, in which the latter lost his life, belong to this period.

At that time probably nobody was surprised when he resolved to combine his judgeship with storekeeping. He bought goods in the Philadelphia market and transported them by boats and wagons down the rivers and through the wilderness.

For a while things went prosperously, but in 1797 the Bank of England stopped payment. The effect of this reached even to the store of the judge merchant in the Cumberland Valley. Jackson's property consisted largely of real estate, but he had endorsed heavily for one of his acquaintances who failed at this time. Jackson had to meet the notes, and this involved the sale of his plantation at Hunter's Hill, thirteen miles below Nashville. His honor was without a flaw. "He resigned his judgeship, paid off his debts, and removed to a place two miles distant which was called the Hermitage." It was to become a historic name, although at the time he went there to live, there was only a log house upon the land.

But the business anxieties and troubles of this time made an indelible impression upon Andrew Jackson. He conceived a violent prejudice against "banks, banking and paper money." He had faith only in "cash dealings and hard money," and circumstances were fated to make Andrew Jackson's opinion of immense consequence for good or evil to millions of his fellow creatures.

He now set up business "in a block-house at Clover Bottom, seven miles above Nashville." Here the former Congressman and Judge displayed much business shrewdness and energy. He won a reputation not only throughout Tennessee but in the far Eastern cities for his ability and probity.

On June 12, 1812 war was declared between the United States and England. The news reached Nashville, and Jackson, who in 1801 had been appointed major general of the Tennessee militia, promptly offered his services and those of twenty-five hundred volunteers of his division to the Government. His hour had struck now.

The offer was accepted.

Jackson showed his mettle at once. It was severely tried at the beginning of the campaign. The General and his small army burned to atone by Southern conquests for the disasters which the

Americans had encountered at the North. But he was hampered and defeated on all sides by the authorities at Washington.

His forces marched, full of ardor, to Natchez. Here he was thunderstruck at receiving an order to disband his troops. The lion was roused now; he had ample provocation. Jackson resolved on the spot that no human power should force him to disband the brave troops who had marched with him through the wilderness.

The men "were without pay, without means of transport, without provision for the sick."

The General took upon himself all the responsibilities of the march home. The experiences of that time had fruitful results. Jackson learned to take matters into his own hands and to act, when the pinch came, utterly regardless of orders from his superiors.

During the return the soldiers also learned to know their General. Many of them had been reluctant to enter the service under him. He had the reputation in Nashville of a fierce, hard, passionate man. The high-spirited volunteers dreaded the outbreaks of that terrible temper. They discovered now how generous, how thoughtful, how patient, their commander could be. He understood by instinct how to manage those fiery spirits, to rouse their enthusiasm, to win their love.

During this march Jackson earned the name of "Old Hickory." It clung to Andrew Jackson for the rest of his life. It was worth more to him than any victorious laurels.

Jackson's conduct was highly applauded at Nashville, and the Government was at last forced to approve it.

The tidings of the massacre at Fort Mims spread through the Northern country at the very moment when America was holding its breath over the news from Europe and the dark close of Napoleon's day.

White men, women and children had been tortured, butchered, scalped, on the last day but one of that old summer of 1813. The fort, "a strong stockade of two enclosures, at the junction of the Tombigbee and Alabama rivers," had been surprised by the Creeks. A terrible struggle ensued; but when that August day's work was done, "four hundred corpses lay in the wooden fort."

Andrew Jackson, at Nashville, learned the horrible story.

For a while all went well with the troops, as they marched through the pleasant autumn weather. But after a time the General's stout heart began to quail. "He did not fear the Creeks, but he feared starvation." There were all sorts of delays in forwarding provisions through the wild, half explored country. Jackson suffered agonies of anxiety. But he would not return. He faced the terrible specter of famine as he kept on with his scant supplies, until his troops reached the banks of the Coosa. Here a battle between the whites and the Creeks was fought. Two hundred Indians were killed. The women and children were brought to the General's camp. His soul had been vexed, his patience exhausted by frequent mutiny among the troops. It was not surprising. The unused soldiers were homesick and starving in the wild Indian country. At one time their rations consisted "of a few crackers taken from the sick stores." Through some mistake not one was left for the General and his staff. They were forced to repair to the slaughterhouse to appease their hunger with the refuse. Jackson turned the affair into a joke. Such a man has in him the stuff of a born commander.

But despite all his popularity and the force of his example, hunger and homesickness proved mightier. The men at last came to a fixed resolve to defy their General, turn their backs on him and start for home. Their misery made them desperate; their term of service had nearly expired. But the fate of the southern country hung in the balance.

General Jackson tried arguments, entreaties, promises. Stirring scenes took place between the irate commander and his mutinous troops. At one critical moment, when a brigade was on the point of departing, the exasperated General, resolved to conquer or die in the attempt, caught up a musket and rode before the columns. The tall, erect figure, the white, determined face, the blazing eyes, the wounded arm in a sling, formed a picture which those who saw it could never forget. The brigade stood still in mute, sullen rebellion. The General swore he would shoot down the first man who dared to move. Every soldier knew he would keep his word.

The mutiny was quelled; but the fire only smoldered.

Despite his severity, Jackson's pity for his men was constantly coming to the surface in some characteristic speech or deed.

On one occasion a starving soldier approached the General, begging for food.

"I will divide with you my own," he replied, and drawing a few acorns from his pocket, he presented them to the man, saying, "That is all I have."

The fight at Fort Strother ended in a swift victory for the whites. Afterward the troops marched fifty miles to the "Horseshoe Bend" of the Tallapoosa. Here the Creek warriors, assembled in force, believed their position impregnable. This battle was the most important one of the Indian campaign. It raged from ten in the morning until dark, and when it closed "the Indians had been conquered in North America." The long feud between the white and red man virtually came to an end when Andrew Jackson led his victorious troops from Fort Tohopeka.

A little later the victor returned home. Nashville received him with triumph. The whole South was wild with joy over its deliverance from the savages. It was full of gratitude toward Jackson. All his severities were forgotten.

During the summer of 1814 vague rumors of British troops in Florida, the Spanish province, and of a contemplated British descent on New Orleans, began to fill the air. They reached the ears of the victor, who was resting and recruiting his shattered health at the Hermitage. Alarm and dread took the place of the recent joy and security, and from all the Southwest, men's thoughts and hopes turned to the General who had just won such laurels in the Indian campaign.

In May 1814 Jackson's great services were rewarded "by his promotion to the rank of Major-General in the United States army, with a salary of over six thousand dollars. For those times he was a rich man."

The fate of the Spanish territory was really sealed when Andrew Jackson, whose deeds always followed fast upon his words, made up his mind that "Florida must be ours."

He did not, of course, venture to avow this opinion openly. We were at peace, at least nominally, with Spain. Even Jackson did not dare at first to assume the responsibility of marching a hostile army upon her territories. "But the residue of the Creek tribe had taken refuge within her borders, and a British force had landed on her coasts." There could be no doubt that the latter intended an attack on the weak defenses in the Southern States. Of course the savages would join the enemy. Jackson's patriotic soul burned at the thought. He longed to make a descent with his militia upon Pensacola, and sweep the British men-of-war from the bay. But bold as he was, he would not proceed to these extreme measures without orders from the government.

Meanwhile, as he fumed and waited reluctantly, the British gave him his chance. The defense of Mobile forms another stirring chapter in the history of this time. It can only claim a sentence or two here. The great drama of the autumn that was to be so famous in American annals, opens with the rapid march of two thousand Tennessee troops to Mobile. The enemy had decided to strike their first blow at that point. Jackson threw a small garrison into Fort Bowyer's walls which were falling to ruins. A British fleet from Pensacola appeared off the shore. Sailors and Indians were landed a few miles from the fort. The Tennessee troops had not made their forced marches of four hundred miles through the wilderness an hour too soon.

Hot work soon ensued between the fleet and the gallant little garrison. The fleet poured its broadsides into the old, tumble-down fort. The latter answered by its steady cannonade. The issue for a long time seemed doubtful. But at last, the *Hermes,* one of the four ships of war, "her cable cut, raked from bow to stern by the hail of shot," ran aground. This was the last of the *Hermes.* The captain removed his crew and set fire to the vessel.

The dark night, the sea, the fleet, and the coast line were splendidly illuminated by the burning ship. The rest of the vessels weighed anchor and disappeared. The land force of marines and Indians vanished in the night silently as specters.

In the morning the little garrison poured out from the miserable defenses. Their losses amounted to only four dead and four wounded. At Mobile, General Jackson had a day of agonizing suspense. The first tidings announced the defeat of the garrison. He was mustering his troops to repair to the scene of action and retrieve the day, when a courier dashed in with the glorious news.

So on Mobile Point the campaign had opened for Andrew Jackson with victory.

On November 3, 1814 General Jackson set out for the old Spanish town of Pensacola, with its fine harbor, on the Gulf of Mexico. He had three thousand troops. They carried no baggage. Three days later they halted within a mile and a half of the town. Jackson had acted without orders from his government. But he evidently did not entertain a doubt that it would sustain him.

In his first message to the Governor, he disavowed any hostile intent on Spanish subjects or Spanish property. His aim, he declared, was directed solely against the enemies of the United States. These, the British and their Indian allies, were sheltered in the forts. He therefore demanded their surrender, "but he also pledged his honor to restore the forts as soon as the danger was over."

This unparalleled challenge to a foreign power with which the United States was at peace, received at first no reply. Maurequez, the Spanish governor, was simply thunderstruck by its audacity. His sympathies, no doubt, were with the British and the savages. But the enemy, strong in numbers, and flushed with recent victory, was at his gates. He consulted with his officers. At last he brought himself to the point of replying, "Governor Maurequez could not accede to General Jackson's request."

The night was far advanced when the messenger returned with this answer.

"Turn out the troops." That was all General Jackson's comment.

Wild consternation filled the old Spanish town of Pensacola on the morning of November 7, 1814. The American forces had stormed the place; they had entered the town; they had already carried two batteries, when the distracted Governor, throwing to the winds all his stately old Spanish dignity, rushed into the streets bearing a white flag.

A little later the Governor and the General stood face to face. The town was at the mercy of the latter, and the Spaniard had to agree to the terms of the imperious American. He engaged that the forts should be surrendered.

All this time seven British men-of-war lay in the bay. But the Americans had entered the town by a route least exposed to a cannonade.

Though the town was Jackson's by the end of that brief autumn day, there was naturally some delay in surrendering the forts.

During the night a frightful explosion aroused the inhabitants of Pensacola. When the morning broke Fort Barrancas was a heap of ruins, and the British fleet had disappeared from the harbor.

Andrew Jackson had won his second victory!

There was no time to waste at Pensacola. The army returned to Mobile without the loss of a single man. But Jackson was bitterly disappointed at the escape of the fleet, which he feared might sail for Mobile. It never seems to have entered his mind that his unwarrantable proceedings on foreign territory could possibly be disavowed by his government or be questioned by a single American.

Andrew Jackson reached New Orleans early in December 1814. He had waited ten days in Mobile for the English fleet. Once assured that the town was safe, he had turned all his thoughts and energies to the defense of the great southern metropolis. He had been more than a week on the journey, riding seventeen miles a day over the wretched roads. Gaunt, yellow, shaken by long illness, as he rode with his staff, it must have seemed almost as though a dying man had come to the rescue of the city.

When Andrew Jackson entered the city in that autumn of 1814, he was a comparatively unknown man. Before the winter had closed he was the hero of the nation; he had proved himself one of the world's great military geniuses.

He found New Orleans indolent, supine, with little idea of the danger that was menacing her, and incapable of any effort to oppose it. Bitter local animosities divided her leaders. "Her inhabitants, composed of various peoples, had small confidence in each other."

With Jackson's appearance on the scene all was changed. The born leader had found his hour, had come to his place. Worn with his long travel and his chronic illness, he went straight at the work before him; he infused his own energy, promptness, decision, into the helpless,. bewildered city. There were no more halting counsels, no more dallying, halfhearted measures. The master was at hand to organize, discipline, inspire. It was all done like magic. Hope, courage, patriotism, succeeded the old indecision, perplexity and helpless panic.

Andrew Jackson believed—he somehow made the city of New Orleans believe—that, despite its immense disadvantages, its scant preparation, its small forces, it would sweep back the British fleet when the hour of trial came into the Gulf of Mexico.

Meanwhile the great fleet was coming, with its "fifty ships, its thousand guns, and nearly twenty thousand men."

Its officers were the flower of the British army. Victory was with them a foregone conclusion. They came fresh from the great battlefields of Europe, from the long wars of the Peninsula, from the glory of Waterloo! That vast armament felt so certain of victory! Its officers, its rank and file, and its sailors, regarded the foe with a supreme contempt. No doubt they felt it would be a mere play at war to end the contest between Great Britain and America by taking that low-lying, marsh-girdled, partly defended city of New Orleans.

And all that great armament had to reckon with was one man worn with pain almost to a skeleton, with stern, fierce eyes blazing out of his haggard, sallow face! The mere facts read like the wildest romance.

From the Island of Jamaica, over the tropical seas, through the soft autumn weather, the great fleet came!

At Lake Borgne a struggle took place with the few American gun boats which gallantly disputed the passage of the enemy. The engagement ended in an easy triumph for the British. A little later, the army had landed safely on American soil, and had taken up its march toward the city before New Orleans dreamed of its approach.

A little after noonday, December 23, 1814, General Jackson, at headquarters, learned the tremendous news. The enemy had come to a brief halt on a plantation nine miles below the city. The son of the owner had been captured. He managed to escape, mounted his horse, and spurred for New Orleans. The General listened calmly to the news. When he had learned the truth he turned quietly to his staff and said:

"Gentlemen, the British are below. We must fight them tonight."

And he did!

At four o'clock in the afternoon, just as the short winter day was growing into twilight, General Jackson watched from the gates of Fort St. George, the sloop of war *Carolina* weigh anchor and drop down the river. Then he took the road where the troops had passed to meet the enemy. He left the silent, lonely city behind him, with the scared women, the old people, and the helpless children.

There was a dim moon that night. The American army went silently to meet its foe. It had one immense advantage; it knew the "lay of the ground."

The British watch fires at last came in sight. They illuminated the landscape, so that the Americans could keep their own way and see the enemy perfectly. The *Carolina,* "anchored close in shore opposite the British camp, was to give the signal of attack. At half past seven the first gun was fired."

Then the ship's broadsides poured over the low, wet Delta where the British were encamped.

The confused, desultory fighting between the two armies on that winter night, lasted for about an hour and a half. All the time the *Carolina* poured broadsides into the darkness, not knowing whether her fire even reached the enemy.

The Southern night was chill and dark, and the Americans thought it prudent to retire from action and await the morning. But when the dawn broke and the fog slowly lifted, New Orleans, listening breathless for every sound of the distant battle, knew she was saved for that time. The *Carolina* had done deadly work in the British ranks. The advance had been checked.

By daylight, General Jackson, with his iron energy, set his army at the work of heaping up his famous intrenchments along the old Rodriguez Canal in the soft, wet soil of the Mississippi Delta. "The works were a mile long by sunset." Everybody had a share in the work. Hard hands and soft vied with each other in "digging the mud and planting the stakes." General Jackson seemed to be omnipresent. For three days and three nights the frail, gaunt body which held that imperious soul took no rest. The scant food he allowed himself was eaten mostly on horseback.

On that December 24, 1814, while the Louisianians were building their intrenchments, and a little way off the great British army, encamped on the low Delta, was watching the movements of the busy, swarming enemy, the Treaty was signed at Ghent at twelve o'clock which made peace between England and the United States.

But it would be weeks before the tidings could cross the stormy winter seas, and meanwhile brave men in both armies must keep at their work of spoiling and killing each other.

On Christmas morning there was wild rejoicing in the British camp. The great army, so used to victory, had been surprised and perplexed by the movements of the enemy. Its high confidence in easy victory had been a good deal shaken by the check it had received in its first engagement with the Americans.

But on Christmas morning, General Packenham had appeared to take command of the army. This was the secret of the rejoicings. He was the brother-in-law of the Duke of Wellington. This name, which was a synonym for glory and victory, and which thrilled every British soldier's heart, invested the brother-in-law with a borrowed halo. Yet General Packenham had had a brilliant military career. He had proved himself a brave officer and was distinguished for his humanity.

This brother-in-law of the great Duke, whose arrival inspired such fresh hope in the British army, looked over the situation and came to his first resolve. This was to blow up the schooner *Carolina,* which had made such havoc in the ranks during the late advance.

The work was done on the morning of December 27th. The little sloop was soon struck by the terrible cannonade that opened on her. She took fire; her crew were compelled to abandon her. There was a fearful explosion, a mighty cheer from the British ranks, a shiver of terror at the heart of New Orleans, and the *Carolina* had disappeared. But she was henceforth to have her place in every history of the battle of New Orleans.

The next day General Packenham "ordered a grand reconnoissance." The advance was made this time in the superb manner in which British veterans always moved to battle. Such a sight had never been witnessed on Louisiana soil. The American army, composed of untrained militia, gazed on the magnificent spectacle, half spellbound with admiring wonder. The morning, after days of chill and gloom, was lovely with the loveliness of the Southern winter. The burnished arms, the red and gray, the green and tartan uniforms, glittered in the sunlight.

But a man with gaunt, stern face and eyes that blazed like fire, was waiting for this splendid foe. Another engagement followed, short and sharp. The Americans had the advantage of position. They were perfect marksmen. Under their firing "the British ranks at last broke in panic, retreated, hid themselves. Their loss was nearly two-thirds more than that of the Americans."

Another advance took place on January 1, 1815 and took the Americans by surprise. The lifting of a heavy fog showed the enemy only three hundred yards distant. The firing, which at once began, made "confusion, disorder, broken ranks among the Americans."

General Jackson first learned the condition of affairs by the crashing of balls around his headquarters. The British had discovered these and were cannonading them. In a moment the General was on the ground, animating the soldiers by his words and presence.

"Let her off!"

With this order of Jackson's, spoken quietly, the firing from the American battery began. The engagement continued furiously for an hour and a half. When it ceased about noon and the smoke lifted, it showed the British batteries, which had seemed so formidable, and were in reality so slight, utterly demolished. The veterans had been scattered by the terrible firing. Every mound, every knoll, every slight hollow on the plain where the columns had stood in battle array, now sheltered brave but demoralized men. The shouts from the American lines shook the welkin.

But these several actions between the two armies were only the opening skirmishes of that great engagement which was to close the battle of New Orleans.

General Packenham at last made up his mind to carry the American lines by storm. It must have seemed to his army of brave veterans that the stars fought against them. But they labored under the disadvantage of being on strange ground. The American methods of warfare were not in accordance with the military tactics of European battlefields. The English soldiers had been devoured by impatience and chagrin at these weeks of long inaction, varied by miserable defeats. Their wrath was greater, because they held their enemy in contempt. It must have been a galling reflection to the veterans of the Peninsula and of Waterloo, that the untrained militia of the American Border held them at bay. The English army had confidently expected to keep Christmas in New Orleans, and it was still encamped on the black soil of the Delta.

General Packenham's plan was a simple one. It was to divide his army, recently reinforced by two regiments from England, "to send part across the Mississippi, to seize the enemy's guns and turn them on themselves. At the same time, he intended to make a general assault along the whole line of intrenchments."

It was a little after one o'clock on the morning of January 8th, 1815 when General Jackson called to his aids, who were sleeping on the floor at headquarters: "Gentlemen, we have slept enough. Rise! The enemy will be upon us in a few minutes."

About thirty hours before he had caught his first inkling of the British General's new plan. He was soon satisfied that the next engagement between the two armies would take place simultaneously on both sides of the Mississippi.

So, on that day of days in Andrew Jackson's life, he roused his staff at one o'clock. By four every man in the American lines was at his post. The daylight slowly penetrated the thick, gray fogs. After watching intently for about two hours, the Americans caught a faint red glow through the mist. It was the advancing redcoats. They came forward in solid columns, in superb array.

The Americans awaited, silent and grim. Those untrained frontier militia were the best marksmen in the world. When the signal came, the rifles poured out their sudden fire. Like sheets of deadly lightning it plowed and leveled the British columns. The swift, steady slaughter shook even the trained nerves of the veterans. When the ranks were once broken, it was impossible to re-form and advance under "that hail of musket-balls, powder and grape-shot." Now the fog had cleared, the vast scarlet masses afforded a perfect target to the Americans. The British, in their amazement and confusion, behaved as if they were under a fate, like the actors in some ancient drama. They stood helpless, while the sheets of fire mowed them down.

Throughout the battle the officers did their best to rally the troops and lead them into fresh action. But nothing human could stand that fire. In a little while the carnage among the officers was frightful. General Packenham was killed. Other generals were borne wounded or dying from the field.

The end came swiftly. Before eight o'clock on that January morning, headlong flight and total rout took place on the east bank of the Mississippi. It seems incredible, though it is none the less true, that the battle was fought in twenty-five minutes! Not that the firing ceased at the end of that time, for it was continued behind the low, scant American intrenchments for the next two hours. But the marksmen could only pour their fire into the thick smoke which hung over the battlefield. The extremities of the long lines had alone been engaged. "One half of the army had never fired a shot."

When the smoke lifted at last, there was no enemy in sight. The dead, the dying, the wounded, lay in full view. One is glad to learn that the Americans forgot all the joy of triumph in the pity and horror of the spectacle.

Seven hundred killed, fourteen hundred wounded, five hundred prisoners, were the result of that twenty-five minutes' work. The American loss was eight killed and thirteen wounded.

The British had made their attack, as General Jackson had foreseen, on both sides of the river. They won the day on the western bank. The road to New Orleans was open before them. But the adverse fate of the eighth of January pursued the victors. At the critical moment the artillery was wanting.

What was more, General Lambert, on whom, with the death of his superiors, the command had devolved, was not equal to the occasion. The loss of so many of his brother officers, with all the terrible events of the morning, had unnerved him. He had not the spirit to pursue his advantages, or even hold them. A little after midday the sound of a bugle outside the American intrenchments "brought the whole army to the edge of the parapet."

General Lambert had sent a white flag to the commander in chief. He agreed to abandon his strong positions on the opposite side of the river, and, after some delays, an armistice was concluded.

The "last war" between England and America was ended!

Of course New Orleans went wild with joy over her deliverance. She greeted the returning victor with ovations; she chanted Te Deums over him; she crowned him with laurels; she celebrated him with grand processions and gay illuminations. For a time the air was loud with laudation and gratitude. But as time passed on, low murmurs of discontent and anger began to be heard. The army had returned to the city two days after the victory, and the General continued to hold New Orleans in the iron grip of martial law. The citizens were held rigorously to military service. All exactions were submitted to without complaint, until tidings of the conclusion of peace filled the city with joyful excitement. The inhabitants now looked forward confidently to release from their ungrateful toils, but they had yet to count with their stern Commander. He would not relax an inch of his rigors until the tidings of peace were officially confirmed. Martial law was still maintained, and the citizens were held pitilessly to hard labor in the lines. The free American city had a taste of absolute rule. The discontent grew wide and deep. Only fear of Jackson prevented open rebellion. Anybody who dared to question that imperious will did it at his peril. Even the Judge of the United States Court was promptly arrested and imprisoned, because he had presumed to "grant a petition for a writ of habeas corpus." Other offenders met with scant mercy. No editor was permitted to criticise the General's highhanded measures.

At last the tidings of peace were confirmed. The Southern city breathed free again, and in her joy of victory, and her newly regained liberty, forgave, for the most part, her stern deliverer.

The Judge's chance came now. He returned to the city and fined Jackson a thousand dollars. The latter insisted on paying it, although some of his friends were eager to do this for him.

In April General Jackson returned to Nashville. The inhabitants gave their great citizen a reception which must have gratified him. He had won his laurels in two campaigns. Men said of him that he had conquered the red man and the British army. Honors and glories were heaped upon him. His name was spoken with enthusiasm in every part of the Union.

The summer of 1815 was spent in recruiting his almost wrecked health at the beloved Hermitage, and in the autumn General Jackson was sufficiently recovered to undertake a visit to Washington. His journey was like a triumphal progress. When he reached the capital, the hero of the battle of New Orleans was greeted with every possible distinction. He was the lion of festivities, the cynosure of drawing rooms. He carried himself through this trying ordeal with much dignity, and with that inborn grace which left nothing to criticise; but he was no doubt surprised and pleased, while his ambitions were stimulated by all this wide popularity.

Three years and three days after the battle of New Orleans, General Jackson was at the Hermitage when he received orders from the Government to put on his harness once more, and repair to the field. The old trouble with the Indians had broken out again. The Creeks had made a virtue of necessity and submitted to the white man; but they hankered after the old hunting grounds. In Florida the Seminoles, more or less encouraged by the Spaniards, had never consented to the surrender of their lands.

The long chapter of the Seminole War and all that came of it, can barely be touched on in this brief space. In the absence of the Governor, Jackson assumed every responsibility. His summons to the new campaign was like a bugle call to the yeomen of East Tennessee.

General Jackson left Nashville resolved, if necessary, to bring Florida to a stern reckoning. He had a long score of grievances laid up against the Spanish province. Under her flag, the hostile savages had found shelter. Beneath its protection, the English had formed their plans and sallied forth to make their attacks on the United States. In Jackson's eyes the neutral territory was simply the shelter of a dangerous enemy.

With these convictions, and with the temper they inspired, Andrew Jackson went to the Seminole war. The Indians in their long struggle with the white race had suffered cruel wrongs and oppressions. They retaliated with the vindictiveness of the savage. White men, women and children, who fell into their hands, underwent horrible tortures. Andrew Jackson firmly believed that these atrocities would never have been committed had the Spaniards and the English not been at hand to sow disaffection for their own purposes among the tribes.

On January 22, 1818 General Jackson left Nashville "at the head of his mounted riflemen and marched four hundred and fifty miles through the wilderness." This required forty-six days. The provisions, as usual, failed to arrive. It was simply a question of starvation or moving forward. It need not be said which horn of the dilemma General Jackson chose. At Fort Gadsden, where his hungry, impatient troops waited, the General learned that the flotilla of provisions which was expected from New Orleans had been delayed by the Governor of Pensacola. Then Andrew Jackson made up his mind to march into the neutral territory of his Catholic Majesty, the King of Spain, and seize Fort St. Mark's. That delayed flotilla, in his mind, furnished ample provocation.

The General, however, first dispatched a polite but sufficiently peremptory message to the Spanish Governor, who now allowed the ships to pass, and Fort Gadsden was provisioned. The General must have smiled grimly to himself. He had discovered the right way of dealing with the Spanish authorities.

Jackson had a large force, including two thousand friendly Creeks, with him. The day after the provision fleet appeared the army was en route for St. Mark's.

General Jackson had now crossed the Rubicon. After he had taken this tremendous step, there could, of course, be no half measures. Arrived at St. Mark's, he lost no time in informing the Spanish Governor that he had come to take possession of the fortress and garrison it with American troops while the war lasted! He condescended to justify the measure on the ground of self-defense. He affirmed that the savages were in St. Mark's and obtaining ammunition there. His action, he added, could not but be satisfactory to the King of Spain!

It took some time for the bewildered Governor to comprehend these demands and charges. He refused the first; he denied the second, with all the old Spanish punctilio and courtesy.

General Jackson wasted no words in parleying. He replied to the Governor's letter by taking possession of the fort. "The Spanish flag was lowered. The stars and stripes floated from the flag-staff. The American troops took up their quarters in the fortress."

General Jackson condescended to tell the amazed and helpless Governor "that his personal rights and private property should be respected; that he should be made comfortable as possible while compelled to remain at St. Mark's, and that as soon as transports could be furnished, they should convey the Governor, his family, and command to Pensacola!"

The victorious General was in no mood for mercy now. Two powerful Indian chiefs were taken prisoners at St. Mark's. They were hanged by his orders the day after he occupied the fort. The terrible atrocities which they had committed on white men and women were thus sternly avenged.

Another prisoner, of a different stamp, was taken. Alexander Arbuthnot was an old man, a Scotch trader, "an inmate of the Governor's family." When Jackson entered the fort, Arbuthnot's horse was at the gate. Its owner was on the point of leaving. But anybody within the fort was certain to incur the new commander's hostile suspicions. Arbuthnot's explanations did not satisfy Jackson. He was ordered into close confinement. In two days Jackson pushed on through the Florida swamps to the headquarters of the Seminole chief, in Suwannee town. When he arrived there, he found the Indians and Negroes had made their escape into the Florida wilderness where no white men could reach them. The prisoner Arbuthnot had written to his son, who was with the Seminoles, and forewarned of the danger, they had disappeared.

The Seminole War was over for the time. The General returned to St. Mark's, which he had left strongly garrisoned, in no gentle mood. He was naturally much exasperated at the escape of the enemy, for which Arbuthnot was responsible. With the army came another important prisoner of war, "Robert C. Ambrister, a nephew of the English Governor of the Island of New Providence, an ex-lieutenant of British marines."

The young officer had, with his attendant—a white man, and two black servants—stumbled one night into the American camp, upon the banks of the Suwannee. He was on his way to the Indians; his headquarters were Arbuthnot's vessel, a hundred miles distant.

Jackson learned these facts from Ambrister's attendant and instantly gave orders that the vessel should be seized.

The two British subjects were now put on trial at St. Mark's. "They were variously charged with inciting the Creeks to war, aiding and comforting the enemy, and supplying them with the means of war." Both were pronounced guilty. Arbuthnot was sentenced to be hanged; Ambrister to be shot.

The General approved the sentence. Both men were executed.

At Fort Gadsden, about to disband his militia, General Jackson, within a day's march of Pensacola, received from the Governor of West Florida, "a protest against his presence, and a threat of expulsion if he did not at once march out."

Certainly the Governor of his Catholic Majesty was only doing his duty toward the foreign invaders.

Jackson's reply was to order the troops to march at once for Pensacola. He entered the city. The Governor fled to Fort Barrancas and fortified himself there. Jackson approached and demanded the surrender of the fort. It was refused, and the batteries opened upon the invaders. But Spanish valor soon faltered before the American fire. Jackson was ready to enter Barrancas when the white flag appeared and the Governor surrendered.

Andrew Jackson's military career closed with this event.

Five days later he set out for Tennessee. Celebrations and banquets greeted his return home. The State sustained its great soldier. At a public dinner his course in Florida was entirely approved.

Europe was shocked at Jackson's behavior. It seemed a violation of all laws, divine and human. The old Spanish pride and honor were outraged by the American invasion of her territory and the indignities heaped on her Governor. England was aroused by the execution of British subjects. The popular feeling was so strong that Lord Castlereagh doubtless told the truth when he said, "he had only to lift his hand and there would have been war."

But at this critical time, Thomas Jefferson and John Quincy Adams sustained General Jackson with all their powerful influence. In December 1818 when Congress was forced to take up the matter of his crossing the boundaries, the irate soldier exclaimed: "There's a combination in Congress to ruin me!" He was, no doubt, fully possessed by this conviction, when he made the long journey to Washington in January 1819. His military course was now the subject of protracted discussion and criticism in Congress. His patriotism and ability received the warmest praise, but it seemed impossible, in the face of the evidence, to defend his course in the Florida matter. The slightest adverse criticism aroused the General's unbounded wrath. He believed that he had acted wisely in Florida. He felt that his sole object had been the interests of his country, and anyone who questioned this was certain to make a lifelong enemy of Andrew Jackson.

After all the discussion and excitement in Congress, no final action was taken against him. He became more popular than ever. He made brief visits to Philadelphia, and to New York, which he saw for the first time. He had one long ovation. Toasts, speeches, banquets awaited him. At New York he was presented with the freedom of the city in a gold box, and the military and the theaters celebrated his arrival.

When he returned home in March, Tennessee crowned all the honors and distinctions he had received, by meeting her illustrious citizen with an escort on the frontier, and a triumphal procession accompanied him to Nashville.

In 1821 Florida was ceded by Spain to the United States, and General Jackson was appointed Governor. In the new post he did not show to advantage. He was invested with great powers and he used them to the fullest extent. His treatment of ex-Governor Callava, the accomplished and stately Spaniard, whom he sent to pass the night in a calaboose, was an act which only the most absolute of rulers would have attempted.

General Jackson now grew wearied and disgusted with his office. In three months he resigned it and returned, a tired, weather-beaten man, to the Hermitage, in November, 1821.

The old log hut was now replaced by a handsome brick house with pillars and broad piazzas, and handsome stables in the rear. It stood in the midst of the fertile acres of his large estate. Here he intended to lay by his armor, and enjoy for the rest of his life the cultivation of his land and the peace of his home.

The most that Congress did now was to annul some of the least defensible of his late measures in Florida. The people were bent on supporting their soldier. The nation was keeping its greatest role for Andrew Jackson.

In 1824 the hero of New Orleans, or "Old Hickory," as his soldiers called him about their campfires, was proposed by the Tennessee legislature for the Presidency. Many people, no doubt, smiled derisively when they heard that name associated with such an office. Despite his great military successes, Andrew Jackson was still widely regarded by those who had not been brought into personal relations with him "as a rough, uncouth soldier, with a genius for fighting."

The four Virginians and the one New Englander who had occupied the nation's highest office, had been men of social distinction. They were accustomed to an atmosphere of culture and refinement. If such a word is admissible in a republic, they were aristocrats. It was instinctively felt by a large portion of the people that a President of the United States should fitly represent the social and intellectual life of the nation. The Tennessee candidate, it was said, had little respect for letters. "The Vicar of Wakefield was the only entire book he had ever been known to read in the course of his life."

Should the stately Washington, the sagacious Adams, the philosophic Jefferson, the scholarly Madison, the accomplished Monroe, be succeeded by the fierce, unlettered Tennessean, who made his own will the law of his life, who had stormed into foreign territory, who had, on slight provocation, executed American citizens and bearded kings by hanging and imprisoning their subjects?

This was the way in which a part of the people were talking about Andrew Jackson in that faraway summer of 1824. Even Jefferson, with all his Democratic sympathies, was dismayed at the prospect of this man's becoming President of the United States.

"He is the most unfit man I know of for such a place," he said, at Monticello, to Daniel Webster. "His passions are terrible," and he went on to relate how Jackson in his youth could never speak in the Senate, though he often attempted it, "owing to the rage which was sure to master him."

But in the winter of 1823–24 Andrew Jackson was, though very reluctantly on his part, once more in Washington, a member of the

Senate. He had accepted the election in order to please his friends, and was at the capital an object of supreme social and political interest.

Before the year had closed people had ceased to smile when Andrew Jackson's name was associated with the Presidency. The result of the election proved that he had barely failed of carrying it. His friends claimed that it rightfully belonged to him. And his friends were the great masses of the people. His popularity in every part of the Union was immense and unparalleled. His very name stirred hearts with a passion of love and devotion a good deal like that with which Napoleon Bonaparte's had once stirred the hearts of his soldiers.

John Quincy Adams was President of the United States. While he had been Secretary of War he had proved himself the stanch and powerful friend of Andrew Jackson. He had defended his measures in the Floridas, and vindicated his course—no easy thing to do—with outraged Spain.

But the great soldier and the great statesman met as friends for the last time when, after the ceremonies of the inauguration, Jackson, with great dignity and grace, congratulated his successful rival.

In a short time the two had become bitter and lifelong enemies.

Tennessee was defeated but not discouraged. The popular imagination was dazzled, the popular heart was stirred. The masses resolved that their idol should be President. No stone was left unturned to achieve his election. Through all the administration of John Quincy Adams, the opposite party, united, harmonious, tireless, was working for his rival.

The campaign opened with great excitement and bitterness. Jackson had many enemies. His life afforded salient points for severe and rancorous criticism, and his political opponents made the most of these.

But the result proved a great triumph for him, and the fiery, indomitable soldier took the place of the calm, frigid, but high-souled and scholarly statesman.

General Jackson carried to the White House the temper and habits of the soldier. It was inevitable that new principles and new methods should distinguish his administration.

The inaugural ceremonies were hardly over when there was widespread alarm among the government officials. These had, for the most part, retained their places through all the changes of administration. "There had always been a strong, instinctive feeling against removing any man in the public service solely for his political preferences."

Many of the officials at Washington had held their positions for years. "To dismiss them was to take away the sole means of existence for them and their families." But the new administration proceeded remorselessly. The blows fell swift and constant. That year of 1829 was a year of cruel anxiety and suffering at the capital. The removals were conducted in a prompt, pitiless fashion, which strongly savored of military tribunals.

"To the victor belong the spoils" was an epigram which had the ring of the camp, but it thoroughly expressed the spirit which governed the wide dismissal of those who were not partisans of the President. It is not easy to conceive of the immediate suffering which was caused by the creation of the "spoils system." Had the evil ended there it would have been a comparatively slight one.

A storm soon opened. It seems incredible that the social standing of the wife of one of the members of the new cabinet should have been the occasion of more excitement, "should have caused more angry discussion than some state measure of vast consequence." This was owing largely to the determined manner in which the President, whose chivalric sentiments and sympathies had been aroused, espoused the side of the lady and made her recognition a matter of political consequence.

The Bank of the United States, the issues with Clay and Calhoun, the dissolution of the cabinet, the removal of the Southern Indians to lands west of the Mississippi, all belong to the history of Andrew Jackson's first term of office. Dead issues, as they have long become, they were vital enough once to shake the country.

The political olympiad wore away, and the time came for another election. Jackson had entered into office with the expectation of leaving it in four years. But the country would not permit this. The next campaign was as bitter as Jackson's fiery partisans and bitter foes could make it. But the overwhelming majority with which he was returned to the White House, must have astonished both parties. It proved how strongly he was entrenched in the hearts of the masses.

Nullification, the removal of the deposits, the claims for the French spoliations, made the second term of Jackson's administration as agitated as the first. He showed himself in these varied crises, a true patriot. At times, too, he displayed the unerring instinct of born, if not trained, statesmanship. His measures, during the nullification epoch, earned the enthusiastic praise and gratitude of his most strenuous enemies.

The Jackson administration closed after eight years with honor and glory although it is true that the President had not left the White House before the business prostration began which was to make the year 1837 so black a one in American history.

He was an old man of seventy: the frail body which had held that invincible spirit so long was worn with years and pain when he returned at last to the Hermitage.

Like Washington and Jefferson, Andrew Jackson left the White House to become a planter for the rest of his days. The Hermitage was a splendid and productive estate. It was cultivated by a hundred and fifty slaves.

He remained to the last a singularly unlettered man. It has been said that "his ignorance was as a wall round about him, high and impenetrable; he did not even believe the world was round!" Harvard University, however, "conferred upon him her honorary distinction of LL.D."

The end came at last on June 8th, 1845. Thirty years and six months before that morning, the battle of New Orleans had been won. Andrew Jackson was seventy-eight years old now. He faced the last presence with the courage of the soldier and the faith of the Christian.

Looking back through the years at the life and character of this indomitable personality, the single figure at times seems to become two; one, hard, remorseless and stern, the other, gentle, kind and compassionate but both firmly united in the one man by a resolute spirit of defiance—to the world if need be—when, contrary to all else, he believed himself right.

MARTIN VAN BUREN

THE air was hardly clear from the smoke of the battles of the Revolutionary War, when Martin Van Buren was born, December 5, 1782, in the old town of Kinderhook on the Hudson, nineteen days before the treaty of peace between England and the United States had been signed at Paris.

Martin came of sturdy, old Dutch stock. His father was a farmer and kept a hostelry in the old river town. The elder Van Buren, shrewd and good natured, seems to have had a knack of making both farm and tavern prosper. Martin's mother is said to have been a woman of good sense and piety.

Martin was an active, keen, intelligent boy; he inherited, with the old Dutch fiber, the keenness and steady persistency of the breed; he must have had a smooth and cheery boyhood; he went to the best schools the Kinderhook of that day afforded; but there was another school, one which, in many respects, was to leave more permanent marks, under the old tavern roof. Here, after the ancient custom, neighbors and travelers met and discussed the signs of the times and the politics of the day. It is easy to imagine what names were oftenest on the lips of the habitués of the Kinderhook tavern and what political controversies those old walls witnessed. Inside them, the veterans of the Revolution must have lived their battles over again.

Martin, keen and alert, listened to the talk and made up his mind on all the matters under discussion. He must, following the paternal example, have been a very sturdy Jeffersonian in those days.

At fourteen, he had imbibed all the schooling which Kinderhook afforded and set about his law studies. He did not go to college, and was therefore forced to remain seven years in a law office before he could obtain admission to the bar. Six of these were passed at Kinderhook and the last one in New York, where he studied with William P. Van Ness, the friend of Aaron Burr, and his second in the famous duel with Alexander Hamilton.

The young law student was at this time brought much into the society of the brilliant Burr. That powerful, seductive personality must have had a strong influence upon the mind and character of the younger man. It was believed that Martin Van Buren showed throughout his life the influence of that year of fascinating and dangerous companionship.

In 1803 young Van Buren began the practice of law in his native town. This was a period of great political excitement throughout the country. The Federal Party, which had founded the Government, and which had so splendid a record during the first years of the nation's history, had, at the opening of the new century, been supplanted by the Democratic Party, whose leader and idol was Thomas Jefferson.

The young party was full of vigor, courage and aggressive force. The popular heart and instincts were on its side. Its sympathies had been wholly with that French Revolution whose echoes still lingered in American air.

The fair-haired boy had not listened in vain to the talk in the Kinderhook tavern. With his bright, precocious intelligence he had seized the meanings of the political issues at stake and formed his opinions, and adhered to them with true Dutch tenacity for the remainder of his life.

Martin was a born politician, although the environment of his boyhood and youth, no doubt, tended to develop and strengthen his native aptitudes in this direction.

But he did not, during his young manhood, neglect his professional interests for politics. He practiced law for six years at Kinderhook with an ability that insured his success in his profession. Then he removed to Hudson.

Just before he left Kinderhook, Mr. Van Buren married Miss Hannah Hoes. She was a native of the same town, and the two had been playmates and schoolfellows. Their married life of twelve years appears to have been one of great harmony, and when it was broken by her death, no other woman ever took her place in her husband's heart and life.

When he exchanged Kinderhook for Hudson, Mr. Van Buren entered upon a larger professional field. He spent seven years in this shire town of his county. Here he matched his powers with the most brilliant lawyers of the State, and won a wide legal reputation. At thirty he was elected to the State Senate. He had, by this time, become conspicuous in politics. He strongly supported Madison's administration, and heartily approved of the "last war" with England.

By this time Van Buren was in the thick of the political controversies of his day, and was displaying more and more of his remarkable qualities for party management and leadership. In 1816 he was again a member of the State Senate. During this year he removed to Albany, which afforded a wider arena for the exercise of his political talents.

From this time honors fell thick and fast to Van Buren.

In 1818 he brought about a fresh organization of the New York Democratic party, of which "he held absolute control for twenty years." He was attorney general of the State and also its governor. It has been acutely remarked of Van Buren that "he stood on the dividing line between the mere politician and the statesman, perfect in the arts of the one, possessing largely the comprehensive power of the other."

In 1821 New York sent Mr. Van Buren to the United States Senate. Three years later he was in the thick of that tumultuous campaign which ended with the election of John Quincy Adams to the presidency. Van Buren was, perhaps, his most formidable opponent. The New York Senator found his element in the heated atmosphere of politics. He was not an idealist; his genius concerned itself with the actual and possible. It had, many of his contemporaries believed, a keen eye to the main chance.

Jackson's election in 1829 was thought to be largely due to Van Buren's signal power of "directing and controlling political forces." The new President rewarded his services by appointing him Secretary of State.

In his new office, amid most critical social and political issues, the Secretary carried himself with consummate adroitness and tact. The favor of his Chief was of supreme importance, and nothing was allowed to stand in the way of that. To this period belongs the bitter personal feud with Calhoun, which had later such important consequences. But whether the issue was some great state measure, or a social affair so trivial that it was intrinsically ridiculous, Van Buren was careful to shape his conduct in a way certain to win the approval of the indomitable, fiery old hero of New Orleans. When the Cabinet was broken up Van Buren received from his partial

Chief the appointment of Minister to England. He arrived in London in the autumn of 1831. Here a mortification befell him which would have crushed a less elastic and self-poised nature. The Senate declined to ratify his nomination.

The English journals circulated the news, but Van Buren, with his Dutch pluck and aplomb, would not succumb. The evening on which his defeat was made public, the famous Prince Talleyrand, then French minister, gave a banquet. Mr. Van Buren was in the drawing room, as gracious, courteous, urbane, as though no thunderbolt had just descended on him. He returned to America to have his chagrin consoled by the increasing favoritism of Jackson, and to receive higher political honors than ever.

He was elected to the Vice-Presidency in 1832, and he who made it "the rule of his life never, if possible, to give fresh offense to an enemy, went, with smiles for all and reproofs for none, to take his place at the head of that Senate which had refused to confirm his nomination as ambassador."

In his new office he presided with such unvarying fairness and courtesy that he won the approval of both parties in the Senate.

The friendship of Andrew Jackson was to make the culminating good fortune of Martin Van Buren's life. The word of the great Tennesseean was all powerful with his party. As his own term was closing, he threw the weight of his vast influence into the scale of Van Buren's nomination for the presidency, and he carried his point.

On March 4, 1837 an immense crowd witnessed the inauguration of Martin Van Buren. It was a striking scene when he rode side by side with Andrew Jackson in a phaeton drawn by four grays to take his oath of office. Both the men were uncovered. The gaunt, iron face of "Old Hickory" must have formed an immense contrast to the shrewd, smiling, handsome countenance of his successor.

It was the new President's settled purpose to conduct his administration on the lines of his predecessor, but the circumstances of one term did not repeat themselves in the other. Before the close of 1837 that great financial panic which had, until then, no parallel in American history, shook the land. The widespread distress, the crashing of old and honorable business houses, the dismay and disaster of that gloomy year, were largely attributed to Jackson's highhanded measures with the banks. There was war, which shed no luster on American arms, with the Seminoles. To add to these domestic troubles, there were serious disputes with Great Britain about boundary lines, and an insurrection in Canada which involved the American Government and threatened another war with England.

The President must have found his high position full of trials and anxieties. However he might succeed in ameliorating the foreign difficulties, he could not relieve the financial tension at home. He and his party underwent a great eclipse in popularity. The Van Buren administration, which had opened so auspiciously under the smile of Jackson, drew to its close in the midst of a political campaign which filled the country with passionate strife. It ended with the defeat of the Democratic Party that had controlled the Government for four years, and in the election of William Henry Harrison to the Presidency.

Van Buren bore his defeat in his equable, smiling way. No political reverses could shake the calm nerves he had inherited from his robust Dutch ancestry. He had a fine estate at his native Kinderhook, and he retired to this to enjoy his leisure and wealth, and to dispense his hospitalitics in his generous and kindly fashion.

A month after he left Washington the nation was plunged in grief by the sudden death of the President. Mr. Van Buren went to New York and bore a conspicuous part in the funeral honors which were paid to General Harrison.

In 1844 a great effort was made to nominate Mr. Van Buren for a second Presidential term. But this time Jackson's influence and a strong proslavery sentiment carried the nomination for James K. Polk of Tennessee.

In 1848 the Free Soil Democrats nominated the old political chief once more for the Presidency. In accepting the nomination he "avowed his full assent to the antislavery principles of the party."

But it was not Van Buren's destiny to receive again the nation's highest gift. After this latest defeat he made an extensive tour in Europe. He returned to Lindenwald, his fine estate at Kinderhook, and here, amid the scenes of his boyhood and youth, the ex-President passed peacefully and gracefully into old age. "He had been in active political life from 1812 to 1848. No other man in the country had held so many great places."

In his political career all his bonhomie and courtesy had not prevented his having many bitter enemies. He was in character and temperament utterly unlike the seven Presidents who had preceded him. He had more moral pliancy; he was of a different strain; he had the shrewdness, the astuteness and the sagacity which go to make up the successful party manager, the born political leader.

Mr. Van Buren's serene old age passed into his eightieth birthday. He died July 24, 1862.

WILLIAM HENRY HARRISON

During the autumn of 1840 the whole country was aflame with political excitement. The Presidential campaign did not perhaps arouse intenser passions than the memorable one which followed the nomination of John Quincy Adams and Andrew Jackson. But the campaign of 1840 was conducted on entirely new lines. Its enormous mass meetings, its torchlight processions, its frequent parades and party emblems, all appealed to the popular fancy and stirred the popular heart. Never had such scenes taken place on American soil. The tumult, vehemence, passion, carried everything before them. "Log cabin and hard cider" formed the shibboleth of the young, vigorous, powerful party that was now moving heaven and earth to secure the election, which, for twelve previous years, had been carried with triumphant majorities by its opponents.

A curious distich had caught the popular ear. It was thundered from thousands of throats at great mass meetings, and sung and shouted by the little boys on the streets. It was an absurd little musical refrain which ran:

"Tippecanoe,
And Tyler too."

It was doomed by the trend of events to have anything but agreeable associations for the party who had made it their rallying cry.

Meanwhile Martin Van Buren at Kinderhook-on-the-Hudson, and William Henry Harrison at his farm at North Bend on the Ohio—the two candidates for the Presidency—awaited the turn of events, each in his characteristic fashion.

The latter had been nurtured amid the storms of the Revolution. He was born a little more than two years before the fight at Concord, his birthplace being at Berkeley, Virginia, and his birthday February 9, 1773.

He came of the sterling planter class which furnished so many of our early presidents. His father, a man in moderate circumstances, "was an intimate friend of George Washington's," a member of the Continental Congress, a candidate for the office of Speaker, though he yielded the place gracefully to John Hancock, and was three times elected Governor of Virginia—a brave, bluff, generous gentleman, who loved his country and served her with patriotic zeal; a man with a girth like Falstaff, and who enjoyed his joke better than anything else in the world.

His son, William Henry, was born a subject of George III a little while before the colony had made up its mind to shake off its allegiance to Great Britain. The boy was brought up amid noble examples and associations. He had every advantage which the father's comfortable means and position afforded. He went to the best schools of the time and place, and afterward entered Hampden-Sydney College, from which he graduated with honor.

Young Harrison had lost his father before he left college, and he went to Philadelphia to study medicine under Dr. Rush, and with Robert Morris for his guardian. Both these men were, like his father, signers of the Declaration of Independence.

Medicine did not, however, detain young Harrison long. His soul was fired by reports of the terrible Indian ravages on the frontier. At nineteen, in spite of the protests of his friends, he resolved to enter the army, and succeeded in obtaining a commission from President Washington.

With a frame so slight that it gave the impression of almost girlish delicacy, young Harrison set out for the frontier at the start of winter. General St. Clair had met a little before on the Wabash with the terrible Indian surprise against which Washington had, at their parting, so earnestly warned him. The hardships and perils of the service did not, however, shake the young Virginian's resolution. But he took his life in his hands, and made the journey to Pittsburgh on foot, and then descended the Ohio to Fort Washington, a remote outpost in 1793, but occupying almost the spot where the city of Cincinnati now stands.

In a short time he was promoted to a lieutenancy, and joined the army under General Wayne, or "Mad Anthony," as his popular title ran.

On August 20, 1792, as the whole army under General Wayne was marching down the Maumee river, they encountered an Indian ambush. One of the fierce, bloody battles of the frontier followed. It ended in victory for the whites. Lieutenant Harrison behaved with signal courage. He was in the hottest of the fight. He won the warmest praise from the General and a captaincy, and was placed in charge of Fort Washington. At this time he was only twenty years old.

When at last the British surrendered the military posts of the Northwest to the United States, Captain Harrison received and occupied them.

On November 22, 1795 he married Miss Anna Symmes, the daughter of Judge Symmes of North Bend, Ohio.

In 1797 Captain Harrison was appointed Secretary of the Northwest Territory. A little later he was its delegate in Congress.

In 1800 this vast area was divided into two parts. The western part, which included what now forms the States of Indiana, Illinois and Wisconsin, was then called "The Indiana Territory." Over this immense tract, as well as over that of Upper Louisiana, President Adams appointed William Henry Harrison as governor. "He was invested with almost dictatorial powers; he was ruler over almost as extensive a realm as any sovereign upon earth." He executed all the varied and trying duties of governor of that vast frontier with such ability and rigid integrity that Adams' successors, Jefferson and Madison, reappointed him.

In his position and with his great power and influence he had immense opportunities to aggrandize himself; but Governor Harrison's integrity was of the most flawless kind.

The Governor lived at Vincennes, on the Wabash. In all that wide frontier, where he held gentle yet firm dominion over the rough, fierce backwoodsmen, there were only two other white settlements.

The story of the Shawnee warrior, Tecumseh, and of his brother, the prophet, form a thrilling chapter in early Border history. Governor Harrison encountered in this subtle, powerful, determined pair, his most dangerous foes. Maddened by the steady advance of the settlers, and by the cession of large tracts of Indian hunting grounds, the two warriors resolved to rouse the tribes to a desperate and sanguinary war upon the widely scattered settlements. The brothers set about their work with all the Indian craft and cunning. They gained absolute control of the savages and inspired them with the fiercest enthusiasm, the most deadly vindictiveness. Governor Harrison had by this time thoroughly learned the Indian character and habits. In various ways he gained more or less knowledge of the designs of the brothers. Tecumseh visited Vincennes with a large party of his braves, in order to have a council with the Governor. He had always professed friendship for the palefaces and a sincere desire for peace; but during the council he threw off this mask. In fierce rage he told the Governor that he lied. Then a wild tumult ensued. The warriors brandished their war clubs. Nothing but the superhuman courage and the unshaken nerves of the Governor saved his life at this critical moment.

Meanwhile sickening work was going on among the scant settlements of the frontier. Revenge, patriotism, religious frenzy, were all kindled in the Indian breast. The war whoop rang suddenly where it had never been heard before. Men, women, children, were butchered and houses burned. The dreadful stories were brought to Vincennes and promptly sent to Washington. At last the Government was forced to heed the cry of anguish which rose from all the Western Border. President Madison issued reluctant orders for the Governor to move against the savages. He marched with about a thousand troops for Tippecanoe, the prophet's town on October 28, 1811.

In the valley of the Tippecanoe, just on the edge of a chill November dawn, in the midst of a drizzling rain, the terrible war whoop broke around the American camp fires. Before one of these, Governor Harrison sat in the midst of his aids. But he was too seasoned a soldier to be taken by surprise, though the fiendish yelling that rang through the woods might have made the strongest nerves shiver. The soldiers behaved admirably. They stood immovable until the day dawned and then charged with the bayonet. The savages broke and dispersed, though their prophet stood upon a mound and chanted a song of victory. But the savages now discovered that he had deluded them and his spell was broken forever.

Twenty-nine years later that battle of Tippecanoe was to become a great party rallying cry throughout the land.

Governor Harrison was forced soon afterward to encounter another foe. The "last war" with England opened, and the British descended from Canada upon the Northwest. They brought with them their savage allies, who "roamed burning, plundering, scalping over the frontier."

Those were dark days for America. General Hull surrendered

his forces at Detroit. President Madison promoted Governor Harrison to commander in chief of the Northwestern armies. "He was ordered to retake Detroit and protect the frontiers."

General Harrison succeeded, after almost incredible exertions, in raising from the scant population of the Northwest Border an army of rustic volunteers and militia, and marched them against the British veterans.

On September 10, 1814 Commodore Perry won his famous victory over the British fleet on Lake Erie. After the naval engagement General Harrison crossed the lake and dispatched a brigade to seize Detroit. He encountered the enemy on the banks of the Thames. He triumphed after a short, sharp action. Tecumseh, an ally of the British, met his death among his braves. The frontier was at peace once more.

Not long afterward, General Harrison resigned his commission.

In 1816 General Harrison was in Congress. He represented the District of Ohio. Before his election charges of corrupt dealings in connection with the commissariat had been made against him. He barely took his seat before he insisted that these charges should be thoroughly investigated. The result was his triumphant vindication. He was presented with a gold medal from Congress for his services.

He had no remarkable oratorical gifts. His most effective speeches were those which he made on his beloved Northwest. When he spoke of its interests, its increasing prosperity, the infinite promise of its future, the theme fired his soul and inspired his words, and at these times he would make a profound impression on the house.

In 1819 he went to the Ohio Senate. In 1824 he was one of the Presidential Electors and voted for Henry Clay. That year he went to the United States Senate. In 1828 General Harrison was appointed by President Adams Minister Plenipotentiary to the Republic of Colombia. In a letter to Bolivar, who was his friend, he eloquently entreated him not to accept the dictatorship.

"To be eminently great it is necessary to be eminently good," wrote this hero of the Northwest battlefields.

Andrew Jackson succeeded John Quincy Adams in the Presidency, and General Harrison was soon recalled from his South American mission. He returned to his farm at North Bend and settled down to agriculture. His income was very limited, although he might probably have been at that time the richest man in the United States.

But his honor was of that sensitive quality which would never allow him to reap any personal advantage from the many opportunities which, during his public life, had come in his way.

In 1836 General Harrison's friends nominated him for the Presidency. Van Buren, however, won the election. The terrible financial crash of 1837 followed, and in 1840 an unexampled political campaign shook the country. It was called "the log-cabin and hard cider campaign." The home of General Harrison at North Bend consisted, on its eastern side, of a log cabin, built by one of the early Ohio settlers, but it had long since been comfortably clapboarded. He lived with much simplicity, and hard cider held on his board the place which costly wines did on other tables of that day. Hence the significance of the party watchwords.

The North Bend farmer, the old hero of the frontier, the Whig candidate, carried the election.

The new President, now sixty-eight, was erect and vigorous. He had a long, thin face, with irregular features, and his eyes were pleasant and kindly.

But his hand had barely grasped the helm when it relaxed. He was attacked by pneumonia, and the iron strength which had borne all the hardships of the frontier succumbed. There were a few days of violent illness. Then the end came. He died on the fourth of April, 1841.

JOHN TYLER

On April 6, 1841 John Tyler became President of the United States. Two days before, William Henry Harrison had died in the executive mansion. The country, settling down into quiet after the most passionate of political storms, was suddenly stricken by a thunderbolt. Grief and dismay filled the heart of the nation. It was impossible to forecast the political future, or to estimate the extent of the calamity which had fallen upon the land.

It was the first time since the existence of the government that a President had died in office and the Vice-President had succeeded to his place. It must have seemed to the lately triumphant Whigs that everything in their political world was falling to pieces. They could have found little encouragement in recalling the political record of the Vice-President or the circumstances of his election. Everybody knew that he had been nominated to placate the Southern party, disappointed and resentful that its great leader, Henry Clay, had been defeated. The Vice-Presidency had not seemed at the time a costly sop to Cerberus. It included, of course, honor and high place, but there was a popular impression that the nation's second office carried with it little intrinsic authority. So John Tyler of Virginia was sent to the Vice-Presidency, and the South was more or less mollified.

John Tyler had been born in Charles City, Virginia, on March 29, 1790. He came of the old planter class, with its wealth and culture and high social distinction. All good fortunes smiled upon his birth and early years. His father had been a stanch patriot of the old Virginia type and was at one time Speaker of the Continental Congress.

The younger John proved himself a bright boy and developed a remarkable gift for scholarship in the happy old home, under the careful parental training. At twelve he entered William and Mary College, at seventeen he graduated with honor. It was a matter of course that he should follow in his father's footsteps and prepare himself for the bar. He studied in the elder's law office and enjoyed rare opportunities to equip himself for his profession. At nineteen he began to practice and had marked success.

Young Tyler had been brought up in the Jefferson and Madison political creed. It was a matter of course that he should become prominent in political life. For five successive years the almost unanimous vote of his county sent him to the State Legislature.

Young Tyler had won a high reputation as a lawyer before the last war with England was declared. His inherited patriotism now spurred him to take part in the contest. When the British ravaged the Chesapeake shores he set vigorous military movements on foot to resist them.

At twenty-six he went to Congress, where he showed himself a thoroughgoing advocate of the Jeffersonian policy. His long, thin features expressed intellectual force as well as resolution. His manners, with their social polish and grace, could not fail to be attractive, and he added to these the charm of his native wit and his kindly heart.

At twenty-three John Tyler made a marriage, which proved one of great harmony and happiness, with Miss Letitia Christian, a young lady of Cedar Grove, Virginia. The newly-married pair settled at Greenway, on a part of the Tyler estate.

Mr. Tyler left Congress to take his seat once more in the Virginia Legislature. In 1825 he was elected Governor of his native State, and young as he was, and powerful as were his competitors, he was re-elected to the office.

Afterward he went to the Senate. Despite his brilliant career he was not an orator, but he was a powerful and impressive debater. He distinguished himself in the Senate by his vigorous hostility to John Quincy Adams's administration.

But as time went on, the Virginia Senator became more and more opposed to Andrew Jackson's policy. The former, with his State-Rights sympathies, viewed with indignation what he regarded as the President's unjustifiable and autocratic measures. Mr. Tyler would not support the war on the United States Bank, which the relentless Jackson had resolved to carry to the bitter end. There were various social and personal matters mixed up with this period of the administration which cannot be gone into here. Mr. Tyler, who was at heart an ardent disciple of Calhoun, now found himself often voting in accord with Henry Clay when the latter opposed the highhanded

Executive. But the harmony between the State-Rights Virginian and the imperious and devoted Kentucky Unionist, though it was to have results of great national importance, did not reach below the surface of things. Mr. Tyler supported the censure of the President's measures in the Senate. Jackson was not the man to forget or forgive this. It must be sufficient to say that Mr. Tyler, on his re-election to the Senate, found it advisable to resign his seat.

After he had returned to his home he removed to Williamsburg, where his alma mater was situated and where his children could enjoy better opportunities for study. No doubt he reflected with pride upon his brilliant career in law and in politics, and had an agreeable consciousness that his native State had bestowed on him her highest honors.

Mr. Tyler still cherished and avowed all the principles of the political school in which he had been trained. He never broke from the old moorings of State Rights and Free Trade. But amid the wrangling and complicated political antagonisms and personal hostilities of the time, he was widely regarded as a Southern Whig, and it was the votes of Northern Whigs which, in the famous "log-cabin canvass," sent John Tyler, the Calhoun disciple, to the Vice-Presidency.

The day of trial had come for John Tyler. The Virginia Jefferson Democrat had been placed at a most critical period of America's history at the country's helm. New and over-shadowing issues were now steadily advancing into the political foreground. The annexation of Texas was beginning to arrest public attention; the air was growing hot with the great Antislavery contest; the exciting question of a National Bank Bill had soon to be met.

The new President showed plainly by his first measures his desire to promote harmony in his administration. He attempted to retain the Cabinet of his predecessor.

But the antagonisms between his principles and those of the party to which he owed his election were radical and admitted of no compromise. The separation which speedily occurred took place under circumstances which aroused the implacable hostility of his former supporters.

Mr. Tyler's position was not an enviable one. An honorable man could not fail to perceive that the Whig party had strong reasons for feeling that he had betrayed them. Yet he could not advocate their measures without doing violence to the deepest convictions of a lifetime.

The test came with the Bank Bill. It was twice prepared, and twice carried through Congress, and twice received the veto of the President.

The wrath of the Whigs was unbounded. The denounced the President in the fiercest language which disappointment and passion could suggest. The triumphant Democrats applauded him.

The administration proved a gloomy and unfortunate one.

Mr. Tyler made, it must be admitted, various efforts to conciliate those whom he had so deeply offended; but he did not succeed. He was a strong advocate of slavery, and here he came into direct contact with the feelings and moral convictions of a powerful and steadily increasing party at the North.

The President incurred much opprobrium among office seekers by his refusal to make removals on merely political grounds. Many of the men appointed in previous administrations "were his personal acquaintances, and had grown gray in the service." The President was a man of kindly heart and he said, justifying himself for not deposing the old public servants: "I cannot bear to have their wives and children come to me with accounts of their suffering when I can help it."

Personal griefs added their gloom to Mr. Tyler's stormy administration. His wife died at the White House on September 10, 1842.

The President must have experienced great relief when his term closed, and he could retire to Virginia and the rest and freedom of his home at Sherwood Forest. He brought a young and accomplished wife to preside there. On June 26, 1844 he had married in New York Miss Julia Gardner.

Under his own roof the ex-President could indulge his scholarly tastes and dispense his agreeable hospitalities, while he still took a profound interest in public affairs.

At last the Civil War broke. Mr. Tyler at first threw his influence on the side of the union element in Virginia. He went to Washington and presided at the Peace Congress in Willard's Hall, which was held just before the inaugural of Abraham Lincoln.

But it was too late to arrest the march of events. Mr. Tyler must have returned home a wiser and a sadder man. He had failed in his efforts to preserve the Union, and now he threw in his fortunes with those of his State, and the ex-President became a member of the Confederate Congress from his native State of Virginia. But John Tyler was an old man now, and the excitements and anxieties of that time must have worn heavily upon him. His health gradually broke and he died on January 18, 1862.

JAMES KNOX POLK

ONE can hardly read the name of James K. Polk without thinking of Andrew Jackson. The two came of that robust old Scotch-Irish breed which sent so many of its representatives to clear their farms and build their homes among the vast wildernesses of the Carolinas. They were a sturdy, resolute, freedom-loving race. They made their mark deep and strong on that new world where they settled.

The younger man's ancestors came first, for the two Polk brothers had settled on the eastern bank of the Catawba in the second quarter of the eighteenth century, while the Jacksons made their clearing on the Waxhaw creek, a branch of the Catawba, thirty years later.

James K. Polk was born in Mecklenburg County, North Carolina, on November 2, 1795.

James's father was a farmer, "a simple, unpretending man." The mother, Jane Knox, is said to have been a superior woman. When James was about eleven, the father removed with his young family to the West and settled in a rich valley on Duck River in East Tennessee. The Polks were in a log cabin in the primeval wilderness, and they had of course to encounter the hard fortunes and fight the brave battle of the pioneers. Before long the newcomers were joined by others, kindred and neighbors, from North Carolina. The farm clearings grew more frequent in the lonely wilderness along the Duck River banks. The elder Polk became a surveyor and a man of influence in the scant neighborhood. He made long surveying tours, on which he took his eldest son James, a bright, rather frail boy, who must have been excellent company, and who no doubt had fine times, helping to build the campfires and cook the game at nights in the Tennessee woods. James went to the common schools of that day and acquired the rudiments of an English education. He was fond of study and early set his heart on having a thorough mental training; but his father, in doubt whether his son's health would endure the strain of a long course of study, placed him in a store.

Life behind the counter was thoroughly distasteful to the boy, and after a few weeks the elder Polk relented, and the younger was thereafter permitted to follow his own bent. He found his true place at Murfreesborough Academy, where he studied industriously for the next two years and a half.

In 1815 he entered the sophomore class of the North Carolina University at Chapel Hill. Here he was a strenuous student, and graduated the best scholar of his class. He was twenty-three now, and his diligent study had shaken his health.

As soon as he recovered he went to Nashville, and began to study for the bar. The most famous man in Tennessee at this time was "Old Hickory," the hero of New Orleans. He was in the habit of visiting the law office of Felix Grundy, where young Polk was studying. The Hermitage was only a few miles from Nashville. The law student, like Andrew Jackson, had come from North Carolina and belonged to the same Scotch-Irish race. The younger man was brought thoroughly under the influence of that powerful, fascinating personality. It existed until it was broken by death, and profoundly affected the character and public career of James Polk.

He was duly admitted to the bar, and he returned to Columbia, in the "Duck River District," and began the legal practice for which he had so thoroughly equipped himself. Business, fortune, honors, fell to him rapidly.

James Polk had been brought up in the Jefferson school of politics and he followed the parental teachings. He grew into wide popularity as a political speaker and won the flattering title of the "Napoleon of the stump."

In 1823 Mr. Polk went to the Tennessee Legislature. It was a matter of course that he should enter with all the ardor and energy of young manhood into the campaign of 1824, which inflamed the whole country when Andrew Jackson and John Quincy Adams were candidates for the Presidency.

It is much to Mr. Polk's honor that he secured at this time the passage of a bill to prevent dueling.

In 1824 he was married to Miss Sarah Childress of Tennessee. It was a happy marriage. Mrs. Polk was a lady of fine character and of many personal charms. During her husband's Presidency she filled with simple, gracious dignity, the highest position which an American woman can occupy.

In 1825 Mr. Polk was elected to Congress. He was a member for fourteen years, a fact which affords a strong proof of his popularity with his constituents. He was an industrious member, "a frequent and popular speaker."

His convictions made him a Democrat of the most thoroughgoing type. He was, as a necessary consequence, opposed to all the measures of John Quincy Adams's administration.

When General Jackson succeeded to the Presidency Mr. Polk, who had now acquired much influence in Congress, stanchly defended the old soldier, although some of his measures rocked the country like an earthquake.

During five sessions Mr. Polk was Speaker of the House, where he must have witnessed many a stormy political scene. He was by nature amiable and courteous, but his strong proslavery sentiments no doubt lay at the bottom of much of his alarm lest the National Government should acquire too great control over the States. He was always a strenuous upholder of their rights and authority, and was always at watch lest the central power should overstep the lines within which, as he interpreted the Constitution, it was limited.

Jackson's famous administration closed with Van Buren's accession. Mr. Polk ardently supported the latter in his campaign; but in 1839 he resigned his seat in the House to become the candidate for Governor of Tennessee. He was elected and served for two years.

Then the Whigs had their day. After the famous campaign of 1840, another Virginian, General William Henry Harrison, took his seat in the executive chair. In the political overthrow of that time Mr. Polk was defeated in the Tennessee election for Governor.

Mr. Polk suffered another defeat when he had the same rival in 1843.

But his day of triumph was at hand. The great question of the annexation of Texas superseded every other in American politics. The country was aflame with excitement. Every one who desired the extension of proslavery territory was eager for the annexation of the immense southern area, which would afford material for several slave states.

Mr. Polk vigorously supported annexation. This fact, and the influence of Andrew Jackson, whose old age and whose growing physical prostration had not weakened his iron will, and who was still a power in American politics, secured the nomination of James K. Polk for the presidency. He was elected, and his inauguration took place on March 4, 1845.

Texas was annexed to the Union, and as a necessary corollary the war with Mexico followed. President Polk sustained it with all the authority and resources of his administration. Mexico was conquered at last, and the stars and stripes waved triumphantly over her capital.

Mr. Polk felt no doubt that he had achieved a splendid success when the treaty of peace was at last concluded between the two nations, and the United States, partly by war, partly by purchase, had acquired possession of the vast Southwestern areas of New Mexico and California.

Mr. Polk retired from office at the close of his first term. His abilities were not of a commanding order. But he had succeeded in the central aim of his administration. He immediately made a journey to the far South, and the honors and ovations which continually greeted him must have made all the way like a triumphal progress. He was still in the prime of his life, only fifty-four. The years must have seemed to stretch long and pleasant before him. His home, a beautiful mansion on Grundy's hill, in the midst of pleasant grounds at Nashville, awaited him. He had large wealth and ample leisure in which to cultivate his scholarly tastes and enjoy the domestic companionship so precious to him. But the end was close at hand. Cholera was in the air that summer. The ex-President, who had at times suffered from malaria, felt the touch of the pestilence as he passed up the river from New Orleans to Nashville; then he succumbed to the disease. It sapped his vitality, and when it was conquered at last it left him with no forces to rally and he died on June 18, 1849.

ZACHARY TAYLOR

THERE are several brilliant chapters in the story of this man's military career. Palo Alto, Resaca de la Palma, Monterey, are names that must be forever associated with his courage and valor, but the light of history shines clearest and strongest upon the figure of the old soldier on a single day and scene. The day is that of February 22, 1847. The scene is the battle of Buena Vista.

Yet it is no grand martial figure which one sees at the head of the scant American forces on that dismal day. It is a short, rather dumpy figure which stands on a height that commands a view of the plateau near the small hamlet of Buena Vista, where the desperate battle went on between Santa Anna's army of twenty thousand Mexicans and the American forces of five thousand. In this disparity of numbers lay, of course, the peril for the Americans. Santa Anna had come upon the little army when it was on the march, about fifty miles south of Monterey.

General Taylor's kind, honest, blunt-featured face was full of anxiety as he stood on the eminence, and overlooked the scene of that terrible fighting. The members of his staff, seeing the deadly peril to which their Chief was exposed, begged him to retire, but he refused to stir. The brave heart had not quailed when the Mexican host first came in sight, and poured in like the waves of the sea and almost surrounded the American forces. A dauntless soul was in the dumpy body of their commander. The Mexican General, confident and triumphant in the midst of his hosts, had, before the action began, sent a messenger, with a flag of truce and a stern summons to surrender, to the American outposts.

"General Taylor never surrenders," was all the reply sent back to Santa Anna's summons. The words were spoken by a man who never wasted any, and they had a sublime courage, uttered in the face of the twenty thousand Mexicans who had at that time nearly surrounded the Americans.

General Taylor was not the man to make light of the peril or underrate the strength of the foe. He had made the best possible disposition of his small forces. After the messenger had disappeared, the General rode along the ranks and said to his troops, "Soldiers, I intend to stand here, not only so long as a man remains, but so long as a *piece* of a man is left."

Soon after that speech the battle of Buena Vista began.

It lasted for ten hours. It should be remembered that General Taylor's forces, with the exception of about five hundred, were volunteers, and that many of them had never before been under fire. During that terrible day it often seemed as though Santa Anna's Mexicans would carry everything before them. They fought under the eyes of their fierce commander with the courage of desperation. They fought, too, for their soil and their firesides. They charged along the American lines with an impetuous fury which it seemed nothing could resist. But they encountered that old Anglo-Saxon valor that had plucked victory at vast odds on so many historic battlefields. The old pluck held its own now. When the dark closed about the ten hours' fight, seven hundred Americans, and about two thousand Mexicans, lay dead and wounded on the plateau of Buena Vista.

The night that followed was full of doubt and anxiety for General Taylor and his troops. Neither army had won a decided victory, and there was every prospect that the fight would be renewed in the morning. The tired troops, drenched and shivering, had no campfires through that long night. But when the morning broke Santa Anna had disappeared with his Mexicans.

With the battle of Buena Vista, General Taylor's military career in Mexico virtually closed. Laurels on other fields awaited him now.

Zachary Taylor was born on November 24, 1784 in Orange County, Virginia. His father, Colonel Richard Taylor, had been a stanch patriot and soldier of the Revolution. After the war closed he yielded to the attraction which at that period drew so many Virginians to the Western frontier. Zachary was an infant when his father and mother with their three children left the old home, and set out through the solitary wildernesses to make a new one in Kentucky.

They were one of the first settlers at a point only a few miles from the present city of Louisville.

Zachary's boyhood and youth were passed amid all the hardships and limitations of the frontier.

Zachary, bred on the Kentucky frontier, must have had his soul early fired by stories of the savages who were then ravaging the border settlements with torch and tomahawk. Tales of this kind would be sure to strengthen any drawings he might feel for a soldier's life. His father was a man of honor and influence in the growing Kentucky settlement. When the son was about twenty-four, the elder succeeded in obtaining a lieutenancy for him in the United States army. He went to New Orleans to join the troops, and soon afterward married Miss Margaret Smith, a young lady of one of the old Maryland families.

The "last war" with England brought to the surface the born soldier in Zachary Taylor. General Harrison on his famous march to the Tippecanoe, had built a fort on the Wabash, about fifty miles above his home at Vincennes. Captain Taylor—he had been promoted by this time—had been placed in command at Fort Harrison. The rude work consisted merely "of a row of log huts with a strong block house at each end."

In the early autumn of 1812 the shrewd, crafty Tecumseh, an ally of the English, led his braves in a night attack on Fort Harrison. The scene had all the unutterable horror of an Indian surprise. The savages with their blood-curdling war whoops burst from the forest upon the small garrison of fifty men—a large part of them invalids—and surrounded the fort. They fired one of the blockhouses, and its flames glared over the dancing, howling Indians. In the garrison women listened with sickening hearts to the unearthly sounds. The men, invalids and all, came to the defense with splendid courage, and at six o'clock in the morning the little garrison saw the savages, howling with baffled rage, disappear in the wilderness.

Captain Taylor was made a major general by brevet for his gallant defense of Fort Harrison.

The war closed between England and America without affording much active service to young Taylor. He was afterward ordered to the frontier. "At Fort Crawford, on the Fox River, which enters into Green Bay," the brave, resolute spirit passed years of his young manhood.

In 1832 a change came to this solitary life. Colonel Taylor—his promotions had not been rapid, but he at last gained this title—had an efficient part in the Black Hawk War. In this famous campaign against the redoubtable Indian chief there served under Taylor a tall, gaunt-framed young Illinois captain, whose name was Abraham Lincoln.

For twenty-four years Zachary Taylor's military service was the defense of the frontier. It must have seemed a thankless task, though it was one of immense cares and responsibilities. It demanded unceasing vigilance, prompt action in emergencies, and boundless courage.

In 1837 Taylor was ordered to march against the Seminoles who felt that they had been grievously wronged by the palefaces, and so took the revenge of the weak and the savage.

Taylor conducted the campaign with bravery and skill, won the title of brigadier general by brevet, served two years in Florida, then, wearied and disgusted, obtained at his own request a change to the Department of the Southwest, which embraced Louisiana, Mississippi, Alabama and Georgia. "He established his headquarters at Louisiana, and bought a plantation at Baton Rouge." To this quiet, pleasant retreat he removed his family. He had a home at last, in the real meaning of that word. In the Southwest Department General Taylor spent the next five years. His post was remote and did not bring him much honor, but he discharged all its responsibilities in his old, vigilant way.

In 1845 Texas was annexed to the Union. The inevitable consequence—trouble with Mexico—followed promptly.

General Taylor's part in the trouble was the soldier's, not the statesman's. It was his duty, as he interpreted it, simply to obey orders; so he crossed the Nueces, marched two hundred miles over what the Mexicans regarded as their territory, and established himself upon the eastern bank of the Rio Grande, opposite Matamoras.

Of course under such provocation war, sooner or later, was inevitable. A Mexican force crossed the Rio Grande. They attacked a squadron of United States dragoons ordered to watch them. The war had opened!

General Taylor's day had come at last. The victories of Palo Alto, of Resaca de la Palma, the taking of Monterey, brought the name, which had been buried so long on the western frontier, to the knowledge of the nation. It was on everybody's lips. Stories which struck the popular imagination were related of Zachary Taylor's heroism, of his homely simplicity of manners and tastes, and of his honest, straightforward, kindly nature. His troops called him "Old Rough and Ready." The homely, humorous phrase caught the popular fancy, as "Old Hickory" had long before.

The battle of Buena Vista closed the military career of General Taylor. After a time he returned home in a blaze of glory.

At this crisis there was very serious disagreement among the leaders of the Whig Party. They could not unite on a nomination for the Presidency, though they had a list of brilliant statesmen from which to select a candidate.

The idea suddenly struck some of the political leaders to seize this flood tide of popularity, and nominate the old frontier soldier. General Taylor, in his boundless astonishment, at first declined, and at last consented to accept, the nomination. The party managers now took possession of him, prepared his few communications to the public—he was not used to the platform nor given to the pen—conducted the campaign successfully, and Zachary Taylor was, in 1848, triumphantly elected President of the United States.

It was not an easy post for the brave, simple old soldier. Surrounded by all the splendors of the White House and burdened with novel cares and responsibilities, he, no doubt, often longed for the freedom and homeliness of his old camp life on the frontier.

But amid the many perplexing and harassing duties which were now forced on him, he showed a surprising grasp of affairs, and much of the statesman's intuition and large, patriotic temper.

But he was barely permitted to manifest his new aims—his unsuspected qualities. A sudden cold seized the old veteran, who had borne unharmed all the hardships and exposures of the military life of the frontier. The cold settled into an illness which after five days ended his life on July 9, 1850.

MILLARD FILLMORE

On July 9, 1850 Millard Fillmore became President of the United States. He went to his post, the successor of Zachary Taylor.

He was born in a log cabin at Summer Hill, Cayuga County, New York, January 7, 1800, the son of a poor farmer. He came of a brave, stanch ancestry which had planted themselves in the Massachusetts Colony. His mother was a native of the same State, and was a woman of character and intelligence.

The Fillmores emigrated to the western wildernesses of New York State and, like those before them, they had the hard lot, the straitened means of pioneers. Millard's home was of the humblest, and his opportunities were of the scantiest. A boy who came of an old New England race went, as a matter of course, to such common schools as his neighborhood afforded; but his lack of early advantages can be best illustrated by the fact that, in his early years, the household library consisted of but two volumes, and one of these was a Bible and the other a hymnbook.

The farm did not prove a great success, and the elder Fillmore resolved that his son should have a trial, at least, at some other business than that of cultivating the soil. Millard was sent at fourteen a hundred miles from home, to try his hand for a few months at "carding wool and dressing cloth." His employer proved hard and severe, and when the months had expired Millard "shouldered his knapsack," with its bread and dried venison, and set out on foot for home, a hundred miles off, through the primeval wilderness.

He appears to have worked for the next four years at the clothier's trade. It is significant that "the first book he purchased with his own money was a small English dictionary, which he studied while attending the carding machine." But his mind was awake and alert at this formative period. He had access to a small village library, and he made the most of it. He devoured "history and biography."

As time went on and he grew more eager for knowledge, a purpose also grew in his soul to make something of himself. At nineteen these kindling ambitions urged him to study for the law. He

the State, and who was "just entering on a brilliant political career."

It was Franklin Pierce's fate to be in the thick of politics from his youth. At the time he was preparing for the New Hampshire bar, John Quincy Adams and Andrew Jackson were the foremost figures in American politics. It is needless to say that the law student espoused the soldier's instead of the statesman's side, in the fierce campaign of 1828 for the Presidency.

Franklin Pierce was duly admitted to the bar and began the practice of law in his native town.

Hillsborough soon sent young Pierce, as it had sent his father, to the State Legislature, where he served four years; during the last two he was Speaker of the House.

In 1833 Franklin Pierce was elected to Congress. This was a great honor for so young a man. He was a faithful, strenuous worker in the House, though not prominent in debates. He supported all Jackson's measures and won the old hero's personal regard.

Franklin Pierce entered the Senate, its youngest member, as he was only thirty-three.

Jackson's pupil, the clever, adroit, political leader, Martin Van Buren, was just entering upon what proved to be his stormy Presidency.

The young senator's graceful, polished and fluent speeches won the interest of the chamber. A never-failing tact, a native courtesy of bearing and speech, and an unruffled temper, made Franklin Pierce popular in the Senate chamber, as they had in the old college halls of Bowdoin. He had many friends, even among his political opponents, and while he was the stanchest of Democrats, he had a felicitous way of ameliorating the heat and bitterness of political discussion.

In 1834 Mr. Pierce married Miss Jane Means Appleton, the daughter of a President of Bowdoin College.

In 1838 Mr. Pierce removed to the capital of his native State. Here he devoted himself to his profession and won a brilliant legal reputation.

When Mr. Polk became President he appointed Pierce attorney general of the United States, but the latter seems not to have had a greed for high offices. He declined the appointment, as he did the nomination for Governor of his native State.

But his profession had not extinguished his old military proclivities, and the war with Mexico opened a new career to the New Hampshire lawyer. He was appointed brigadier general, and sailed with the troops from Newport, Rhode Island, on May 27, 1847.

General Pierce returned to his home at Concord with the fresh laurels he had won on Mexican battlefields. He resumed his legal practice, but he was still deeply interested in politics. He gave all the weight of his character and all his public influence to the pro-slavery wing of his party. The South learned to know him, to regard him as belonging to itself. "He was the Northern man with Southern principles."

This feeling bore fruit at last. After ten days of balloting, the Democratic convention, at Baltimore, nominated the New Hampshire lawyer for the Presidency. It took the country by surprise, and Mr. Pierce's own words, best express his own astonishment when he learned of it.

The new administration proved a stormy one. This was in the nature of things. The question of slavery was becoming the central one in American politics. The shameful proceedings in Kansas concentrated the interests of the nation on that territory. The invasion of its polls, the election of its Legislature by armed mobs from other States, the appeal of its hunted and helpless inhabitants to the Government for succor and protection, fired the heart of the country. But all the President's sympathies were with the proslavery party. His words, his deeds, proved this only too well during his entire administration; and when it closed and he resigned the helm to James Buchanan, Franklin Pierce had "thoroughly alienated the North."

He returned to his home at Concord and then with Mrs. Pierce, spent a year and a half in leisurely travel through Europe.

After their return home Mrs. Pierce's health did not permanently rally, and she died in December 1863.

The Civil War was going its way of desolation and death by this time, but Franklin Pierce never did anything to alter the opinion of a world which had long regarded him as a "Northern man with a Southern heart."

He lived to see the Civil War close, and was near his sixty-fifth birthday when he died at Concord on October 8, 1869.

JAMES BUCHANAN

James Buchanan first saw the light of day while the French Revolution shook the civilized world, for he was born on April 23, 1791. Stony Batter was the homely name of his birthplace. "It lay in a mountain gorge in the midst of picturesque scenery at the foot of the eastern ridge of the Alleghenies." The boy's father came of Scotch-Irish breed. He had emigrated to America less than a decade before his son's birth. He cleared his farm and built his cabin on the frontier, and five years after his arrival in the country he married Miss Elizabeth Spear, an estimable young woman in the neighborhood.

James was fortunate enough, in the midst of his rustic surroundings, to have an intelligent father and a superior mother. It was fortunate for him, too, that when he reached his eighth year, the family removed to the village of Mercersburg, where James began his studies in English, Latin and Greek. So the boy, born in the shadow of the Alleghenies, was to have a fair chance to prove what stuff was in him. He was a bright scholar, and at fourteen was ready to enter Dickinson College, at Carlisle. Here he devoted himself to study, showed remarkable ability, and "graduated with the highest honors of his class."

At eighteen he began his legal studies at Lancaster, and at twenty-one was admitted to the bar. This was in 1812. It was a critical year in American history, and the young lawyer was deeply interested in political affairs.

James Buchanan was well equipped for his work when he set himself to the practice of his profession. The Lancaster lawyer soon acquired distinction at the bar. He secured a large and lucrative practice, and in a short time had won for himself an enviable reputation among the eminent lawyers of Pennsylvania.

In 1820 Mr. Buchanan was elected to Congress; he took his seat in the House and retained it for the next ten years.

In the campaign of 1824, when popular passions mounted high, the former Federalist used all his influence to secure Andrew Jackson's election to the Presidency. The hero of New Orleans never forgot his friends, and when, four years later, he succeeded John

Quincy Adams, James Buchanan was appointed Minister to Russia. He made his first entrance into court life in the summer of 1832.

He did good service for his country when he finally succeeded in negotiating a treaty of commerce with Russia.

With the fresh laurels he had won in the Russian mission, Mr. Buchanan returned to America to enter the national Senate. Here he unflinchingly supported all Jackson's measures.

In the Senate he was conspicuous for his advocacy of State Rights theories. His temperament was naturally conservative and inclined him to honor exalted place, power and high social rank. This fact, no doubt, strongly influenced his political sympathies. With all his skill as a lawyer, with all his experience and sagacity as a statesman, he had not a high and resolute spirit. Despite all the purity of his private life and his spotless integrity, he was lacking in will and moral energy. When he was brought in contact with powerful and determined natures, he did not confront them with a dauntless temper. In short, he was not a man for a great national emergency.

Mr. Buchanan sustained the unfortunate administration of John Tyler. When James K. Polk became President he made Buchanan, who threw his whole influence into the scale for the Mexican War, Secretary of State.

In all those great sectional questions which were now coming to the front in American politics, Mr. Buchanan invariably took the side of the South. He opposed the Wilmot Proviso and he approved of the fugitive slave law.

On the election of Franklin Pierce, Buchanan was appointed Minister to England. At the court of St. James he was a dignified and agreeable figure and made many friends.

But his attitude in the matter of Cuba, and his share in the conferences at Ostend, made an unpleasant impression both in Europe and America, and seriously threatened the relations of the United States with Spain.

Domestic affairs, however, soon wholly engaged the attention of the country. In 1856 the great political conflict took place which ended at last in the election of James Buchanan to the Presidency.

James Buchanan went to his new post under circumstances that would have tried the finest temper, the sternest stuff. The adroit politician, the polished diplomat, the bland, courteous gentleman, proved himself fatally unequal to the demands of the time and place. For the Civil War was now drawing near.

When the storm gathered there was a faint heart and a flaccid hand at the helm.

With all his Southern affiliations and sympathies, Mr. Buchanan certainly did not desire the destruction of the Union. Yet nonetheless, he, its President, looked on, dismayed, helpless, despairing, when the time came to act with promptness and energy. No word of high courage and dauntless resolve fell from his lips to ring through the North and stir its heart like the blast of a trumpet. During long months of doubt and waiting, he did not lift his hand to stay secession; indeed, his utterances for a while fatally encouraged it. The national forts were seized, the Union flag was insulted, the States went their own blind, mad way, unhindered by the man to whom had been intrusted the fortunes of the nation. He helped neither North nor South in the critical hour; he only lamented and watched and waited supinely. He was not the man for the place. This will always be the severest count which history will make against James Buchanan.

His Presidential career closed at last in calamity and gloom, and he no doubt found it an immense relief to leave the scene of his great triumphs and his greater failures, and return to the beautiful retreat which he had made for his old age at Wheatland, an estate about a mile from Lancaster.

He lived to witness the close of the Civil War, and died at Wheatland on June 1, 1868.

ABRAHAM LINCOLN

Abraham Lincoln was born in a rude log cabin on the Kentucky frontier on February 12, 1809 and came of rugged Virginia stock. The grandfather, whose name he bore, left the beautiful valley of the Shenandoah and pushed out on the western border before the War of the Revolution had closed. Thomas was the youngest of the three boys of the family; he stands a weak, helpless, bewildered figure between the two Abrahams—the sturdy old pioneer father, and the famous son. Perhaps the stern conditions of border life, which included battling with Indians and wild beasts, proved too hard for him. At least, he lacked the robust fiber which goes to the making of the born pioneer. He never had a chance to prove whether he was out of place. He was always "generous, good-natured, warm-hearted," because to be this was in the Lincoln blood. There were no schools in the wilderness, and he never went to one, never learned even to read or write—a fact more surprising now than it was in those distant times. He might have had a better chance, had not his father, while at work in the field, been shot down by a prowling savage. This happened two years after the migration from Virginia. The widow and her boys must have had a fight for existence in the log cabin on the lonely border. Thomas spent his youth as a hired laborer. At twenty-eight he built his own log cabin, and took to wife Nancy Hanks, a daughter of another Virginia emigrant. Here a daughter was born to them and later a son, whom they called Abraham, after his grandfather.

Inside the log cabin everything was so scant and bare that it seemed utterly comfortless; but the boy and girl must have had a homely, hearty, rugged childhood, with plenty of fun and rollicking thrown in, between the gentle, tender mother and the shiftless, easy-going father.

The son sprang up rapidly into slender, overgrown boyhood; he must have presented a singular appearance, with his odd, grave, strongly marked features, and his tall, bony limbs, when, at seven years old, he went to school for five months; he must have been a bright scholar, too, for he learned to read and write in that time.

This was opening a new world to a boy like Abraham Lincoln. It was to the father's credit that he "deplored his own lack of education, and was anxious his children should not suffer in that respect as he had done."

Perhaps the mother's influence had much to do with this feeling. She had enjoyed better advantages than her husband, and managed occasionally to get hold of a book and read stories to her delighted children.

When Abraham was eight years old, his father made up his mind to try his fortunes in Indiana. A pair of horses carried the few household goods, and the family of four left their log cabin, and the grave of a little boy who had been born after Abraham, and started on foot through the wilderness. It was a seven days' journey. It was not an unpleasant one, especially for the children, in the soft, western autumn weather, with plenty of game in the woods, and boughs to be gathered at nightfall for the long, delicious sleep under the stars. At last they crossed the Ohio, and, a few miles beyond, reached the site of their new home in southern Indiana.

Thomas Lincoln made shift to put up a hunter's cabin, or "pole shelter," in which his family shivered through their first Indiana winter. In the spring, with the help of his young son whose strength and size were far in advance of his years, he built a log cabin of the rudest description, and cleared and planted his land.

The wilderness was a solitary place for the new settlers. It must have been a happy day for "Abe" and his young sister Sally when old friends and neighbors of the Lincolns came to the new clearing and formed a settlement.

But the life in southern Indiana, whatever were its compensations, appears to have been hardly an improvement on the old one left behind in Kentucky. The face of the tall, gaunt, awkward boy, with all its lights of fun and humor, grew thoughtful and sad in that straitened, burdened life. After he had learned to read, he had an intense craving for books, but these were much like angels' visits in the Lincoln log cabin. What efforts that boy made, what miles he walked to get hold of a fresh volume, when he learned some settler owned the priceless treasure! Nobody could have had the heart to refuse his eager entreaties to borrow it. Whatever Abraham Lincoln read was stored away in some stronghold of his memory as a miser stores his gold. So, at one time and another, he feasted his soul on *Æsop's Fables,* on *The Pilgrim's Progress,* and *The Life of George Washington.*

The pioneer life is hardest on its women. Mrs. Lincoln broke down early under it. The woman of gentle, refined instincts seems to have been out of place in the rough border country. She sickened in the damp wilderness climate, and died about two years after the removal to Indiana.

Abraham was ten years old at that time. All his life he remembered the sad, patient, loving mother, with a great, reverent tenderness.

The home was doubly lonely and comfortless after she left it. The unthrifty father was helpless with his young boy and girl on his hands. Things appear to have gone from bad to worse for more than a year, and then Thomas Lincoln, awaking to a sense of the situation, did one of the wisest deeds of his life. Whatever were the man's failings, he seems to have had a fine instinct where women were concerned. He went back to the old Kentucky home, and when he returned he brought a wife with him. She was a widow—a Mrs. Sally Johnston—an old love who had formerly refused him. She brought with her her own son and two daughters, and a quantity of household effects, which utterly transformed the inside of that unfloored log cabin, the first sight of which filled her thrifty soul with dismay. What was much more, she brought her sensible, energetic, helpful nature, and her warm, generous woman's heart.

With the appearance of the new mistress on the scene there was an immense change for the better. The husband, whether he would or not, was forced to bestir himself and improve things. "A wood floor, a door that swung on hinges, and glass windows" were now added to the cabin. The wife's energy infused a new spirit into the household. The neglected appearance of her stepchildren had touched her heart. The boy and girl were now cared for and made comfortable in a way that was utterly new to them. Mrs. Lincoln soon made the surprising discovery that her young giant of a stepson could read and write. She encouraged his desire for study. When a school opened for a brief time in a log cabin a mile and a half away, Abraham attended with the rest of the young household; he made the most of his opportunities, but he never had more than a year's schooling.

The tide of emigration poured steadily and rapidly into Indiana, and "the woods ceased to be a wilderness" around Abraham Lincoln's home. A little way off, as the years went on, and the boy grew more lank, awkward, rugged with each, a store was opened, and a settlement grew about it which was called Gentryville. The name was chosen in honor of the storekeeper.

It was a great event in Abraham Lincoln's life when he earned his first dollar for himself. It happened curiously. He had shown his ingenuity and mechanical skill in building a boat stout and strong enough "to carry the farm produce down the Ohio to a market."

One morning, while he stood at the landing, "two strangers came down to the shore who wished to be taken out to the steamer in the river. Abraham was always ready to do a service, and he carried the men and their luggage out in his boat. He seems to have had no thought of reward, but as he was about to return each of the strangers tossed him a half dollar." His feelings at that moment must be related in his own words.

"I could scarcely believe my eyes. It was a most important incident in my life. I could scarcely believe that I, a poor boy, had earned a dollar in less than a day. The world seemed wider and fairer before me. I was more confident and hopeful from that time."

Amid the hard drudgeries on his father's farm, toiling on other men's land, reading, or rather mastering every volume on which he could lay his big, toil-hardened hands, Abraham Lincoln came up rapidly into his tall, muscular, vigorous youth. His outdoor life, his rugged training, had given him a constitution of oak and iron; his bodily strength, his physical feats, were the talk and wonder of the western settlement. In all games which required stamina, great power and tough muscle he was sure to come out winner. The bullies and roughs of the rude locality had learned to respect and fear him; he was eminently social, obliging, fond of games, of the frolic and fun which relieved and brightened the toilsome life of the settlers.

When he was nineteen, a fresh chance came to him. This was to go down the Ohio and Mississippi to New Orleans, in a flatboat "laden with a cargo of produce." The distance was a thousand miles. This must have proved a dazzling offer to the imagination of a youth whose longest trip had been the wilderness tramp from Kentucky to Indiana. The river voyage proved a financial success. It was full of novel sights, adventure, and interest to Abraham and his young companions. At New Orleans he was brought in contact with the dark side of slavery, with its degradation, its oppression, its barbarity. What he saw then made an ineffaceable impression on the youth of nineteen.

Before this time he had lost his sister Sally. She was married, a mere child, at fourteen, and died soon after.

The father grew restless again. In 1830 he sold out his squatter's claim, and removed two hundred miles to Illinois. The journey was made with ox teams, in the last weeks of winter, "over swollen streams and miry roads."

Before he left Indiana young Lincoln had reached his twenty-first birthday. It must have been one of joyful release from a yoke that had long chafed and galled him. The hopes and aspirations of his dawning manhood had been cruelly chilled and oppressed by the grinding toil and the hard circumstances of his home life. He was ready and eager for the battle with fate, when he would be no longer fretted and hampered on every side. He was now free to come and to go, to keep his own wages, and follow his own bent.

He helped to build the homestead on the "high bank of the north fork of the Sangamon River." Then he went out into the world.

Abraham Lincoln was now alone, homeless, penniless, in that young State of Illinois, which, a little later, was to crown him with honors.

The first year of freedom brought no better fortunes than the toils of a hired man in the farm settlements. Then there was another trip to New Orleans, made this time in a flatboat built largely with his own hands. The second trip proved, like the first, a financial success to his employers.

Abraham Lincoln, "hiring from job to job of uncertain work," was stranded at New Salem about midsummer of the year 1831. This was a small, new settlement, whose log and pine board houses were clustered on the Sangamon River, about twenty miles from its smart neighbor, Springfield. New Salem's chief source of prosperity was a mill owned by a Mr. Rutledge, the principal man of the settlement. The population comprised the lowest, coarsest and roughest elements of the border. The lank, awkward, solemn-faced youth had no employment, and was eagerly looking about for any work which would enable him to keep soul and body together.

Soon after he appeared at New Salem the rather surprising discovery was made that the newcomer could read and write. This was an accomplishment which gave one a certain distinction amid the rude, drifting population. On election day Lincoln was appointed clerk to record the votes at the polls. His service probably brought him more honor than emolument.

In that rough, drinking, fighting community, other qualities of the "farm-hand and flat-boatman" told in a little while. He proved honest, energetic, industrious when he had a chance to work. His courage, his "length of limb," his immense muscular strength won profound respect. He showed his prowess before a rough, vociferous mob in a wrestling match with the champion bully of the neighborhood.

After a time employment came to young Lincoln, which was certainly an improvement on all that had gone before. A Mr. Offert, storekeeper at New Salem, offered the young man, to whom he had taken a liking, the position of clerk and salesman. A little later the merchant rented the mill, and proved his satisfaction with his clerk's services by making him foreman.

At night one kindled shaving after another shone upon the page for which the reader could afford no candle. He heard some talk about grammar, and at once applied to the schoolmaster, a Mr. Graham, for enlightenment. Young Lincoln had a wonderful capacity for asking questions, and managed to gain some fresh information from every person with whom he talked. The schoolmaster happily knew of a grammar six miles away. Lincoln set off to find the owner, purchased the book, and in a short time thoroughly mastered its contents.

He also joined a debating club, and naturally subscribed for a paper. These were the days, too, when he "read and re-read Shakespere, and almost knew Burns by heart."

No doubt he was sometimes unhappy in this life-and-death grapple with his fate; he felt the goad of ambition, the restlessness of aspiring youth; but he had so hard a fight for every inch of the upward way that, had the grit been less firm, the purpose less earnest and noble, they might have failed.

The store and the mill did not prove a success. When the one was closed and the other had returned to its owners young Lincoln found himself adrift at New Salem. By this time he had many friends in the settlements. The rough associations, the rude life, were things that he took as a matter of course. If they left their mark on him all his life, it was in no degrading way; he learned to know the common people. In comprehension and sympathy he was a part of them, as he could never have been had his youth lain in less rugged ways.

In 1832 Black Hawk and his braves came across the Mississippi. The frontier was roused. There had not been such talk of war, such enlistments of volunteers, since Andrew Jackson led his Tennesseans against the Seminoles. Lincoln had, the previous year, been chosen captain at a militia muster.

With the rout of the savages the war closed, and Lincoln and his company returned to New Salem. In a little while he won fresh laurels in a new field; he made a speech before the debating club. Its force and homely eloquence took his rough audience by storm, and made a strong impression on Mr. James Rutledge, the president of the club, the owner of the New Salem mill. A few days afterward he advised Lincoln to become a candidate for election to the State Legislature.

The former "farm-hand and flat-boatman" must have been greatly taken by surprise. He modestly declined to run, urging his small acquaintance in the large Sangamon County; but Mr. Rutledge persisted, and the New Salem people sustained the mill owner. At last the young man yielded. He made stump speeches throughout the county. It was the year of Jackson's second election to the Presidency, and the frontier was shaken with the stormy campaign. Lincoln's first political speech is thoroughly characteristic:

"Gentlemen and Fellow Citizens: I presume you all know who I am. I am humble Abraham Lincoln. I have been solicited by many friends to become a candidate for this State Legislature. My politics are short and sweet, like the old woman's dance. I am in favor of a national bank. I am in favor of the internal improvement system, and of a high, protective tariff. These are my sentiments and political principles. If elected, I shall be thankful; if not, it will be all the same."

It is not surprising that Lincoln was defeated. But New Salem stood by him splendidly. She gave him two hundred and eighty votes; all she had but three.

The defeated candidate tried storekeeping—this time with a partner. The firm did not succeed. Lincoln found himself weighted with a burden of debts, while his partner proved worthless.

At this time he was appointed Postmaster of New Salem. The position did not involve large duties; the mail did not arrive every day. The tradition runs that the Post Office was Abraham Lincoln's hat!

A little later he was surprised by being offered a position as surveyor. He knew nothing of the art, but this was not an indispensable obstacle to one who had his habits of dogged, persistent study. The surveyor who wished to employ him as an assistant brought with him a manual of instruction in the art.

Young Lincoln took the book, buried himself in the country for six weeks, boarding with the schoolmaster who had first enlightened him regarding grammar. At the end of this time he had mastered the art of surveying.

Judicious friends, at this time, gave him wise and helpful counsels. One—a Mr. Stuart of Springfield—advised young Lincoln to study law. When he had made up his mind to prepare for the bar, he set about the work with his habit of iron determination. "He went to Springfield, borrowed a pile of books of Mr. Stuart, returned with them on his back to New Salem, and began his legal studies." He had now decided upon his future life work, and he put all his intellectual energies into his law reading. His study was the shade of an oak tree, but it turned out a better lawyer than many a luxurious library.

About this time he met Ann Rutledge, the daughter of young Lincoln's warm, personal friend.

He had now a fresh spur to his ambitions; he was eager to win honors that he might bring them to the beautiful maiden, whom he loved with all the strength of his deep, tender nature.

Again a candidate for the Legislature, he made another stumping tour through the county. The man had acquired a wider range, power, eloquence. His talk went straight to the reason and the hearts of his audiences. Very few amongst them suspected that a woman was his inspiration. At all events he was triumphantly elected to the State Legislature.

Miss Rutledge was betrothed to Abraham Lincoln. They were to be married, it was understood, after he had completed his legal studies.

When the Legislature assembled at Vandalia, then the capital of Illinois, Lincoln walked a hundred miles to join his colleagues. During the session he remained, for the most part, silent, listening, observant; but all his mental powers were deepening and expanding at this period. When the session closed he walked back to New Salem. He had meanwhile gained valuable knowledge and experience.

In 1835 Ann Rutledge's health began to decline, and she died in the last week of the summer.

There is something unutterably pathetic in that moan out of his loyal heart: "I can never be satisfied to have the snows, rains and storms beat upon her grave!"

In 1836 Sangamon County again sent Abraham Lincoln to the Legislature by a larger vote than any candidate received that year. He was, at this time, twenty-seven years old. He again trudged to Vandalia on foot. Here he met, for the first time, Stephen A. Douglas, then only twenty-three. The silent member of the previous session threw himself heart and soul into the business of this one. "He served upon the Committee of Finance: he at once took rank as an able debater and parliamentarian." Through his influence, and that of the other Sangamon County representatives, a bill was passed removing the Illinois capital to Springfield. Before the close of the session he boldly avowed his antislavery convictions. It required splendid moral courage for a young and modest man to do this before an assembly so hostile that only one member supported Lincoln. Those trips in the flatboats to New Orleans were bearing fruit.

"When the session closed he walked back to New Salem, his only baggage a bundle in his hand."

In 1839 Mr. Stuart proposed that young Lincoln should enter into a law partnership with him. It goes without saying that he accepted so flattering an offer. He removed to Springfield, now the capital, and began the practice of law.

From the time that he removed to Springfield the narrative of Abraham Lincoln's life is one of steadily growing success and prosperity. In a little while he had earned a wide reputation at the bar. His clear, forcible, logical presentation of a case had an immense influence on the minds of the jury; he employed no sophistries; he indulged in no plausible talk, which perplexed and confused the understandings of plain, honest men; "he had none of the graces of oratory; but he had an intuitive insight into the human heart, a clearness of statement which was itself an argument, with uncommon power and felicity of illustration, often, it is true, of a plain and homely kind."

"He would never advocate a cause which he did not believe to be a just one, and no amount of odium or unpopularity could dissuade him from undertaking a cause where he thought the right was with his client."

During this time young Lincoln was frequently a guest at the house of his intimate friend, Mr. Ninian Edwards. He met there Miss Mary Todd, a bright, vivacious young lady, the sister-in-law of his host. Like Lincoln, she was from Kentucky, although her home life and early advantages had been, in many respects, immensely superior to his own. But the young lady soon perceived, beneath all external drawbacks, the high abilities and sterling qualities of the young lawyer.

The romance of Abraham Lincoln's life was in the grave of Ann Rutledge; but the man's heart was lonely and empty. After a while he and Miss Todd were engaged. They were married, and Abraham Lincoln had what he never really had before—a home. This was in 1841.

The record of the next twenty years is one of constantly enlarging public life, of increasing responsibilities, of accumulating honors.

In 1847 the Sangamon district—always loyal to Lincoln—sent him to Congress. In all the vital questions which engaged its attention at that critical period the new member took a decided part, and defended his positions with great ability and earnestness. He left no doubt that he would follow his convictions wherever they might lead him.

They led him into an unflinching opposition to the extension of slavery; they led him also to delivering that series of immortal campaign speeches, in which he matched his strength against his powerful political rival, Stephen A. Douglas. Lincoln's speeches at this time made him famous throughout the country. The first one, delivered at Ottawa, was listened to by an audience of twelve thousand people. "Everywhere Mr. Lincoln proved his superiority, both in intellectual power and soundness of moral position."

But this position was an advanced one for those days, and the people of Illinois, though they were aroused and impressed, "were not quite ready to follow Lincoln." If Douglas had been worsted on the platform, he none the less went to the Senate.

No doubt Lincoln's disappointment was, for the moment, keen, though he said of his defeat in his quaint, homely fashion, "I felt like the boy who had stubbed his toe—too badly to laugh, and too big to cry."

By this time Lincoln had won a national reputation, and was recognized as one of the leaders of the new Republican Party. Invitations to speak crowded upon him; he went to Kansas, and afterward to New York and to New England; he captivated his audiences, whether they belonged to the Western frontier, or to the most polished and cultivated circles of old Eastern cities.

At Cooper Institute, where his audience was largely composed of the most distinguished citizens of New York, his speech aroused unbounded enthusiasm. His originality, his real greatness, and his odd personality, all served to make him an object of marked interest to the polished Eastern people among whom he was now thrown. This tall, gaunt, sinewy Western lawyer, with his shrewdness, his apt, homely illustrations that went straight to the mark, and his eloquence that held his hearers thrilled and spellbound, was something quite out of their line. Some of these were curious to learn, if possible, the secret of his power. To one of his new friends, who inquired about his early education, he replied in his frank, simple way: "Well, as to education, the newspapers are correct, I never went to school more than six months in my life; I can say this, that among my earliest recollections I remember how, when a mere child, I used to get irritated when people talked to me in a way I could not understand.

"I can remember going to my little bedroom, after hearing the neighbors talk of an evening with my father, and spending no small part of the night walking up and down, and trying to make out what was the exact meaning of some of their, to me, dark sayings.

"I could not sleep, although I often tried to, when I got on such a hunt after an idea, until I had caught it; and when I thought I had got it, I was not satisfied until I had repeated it over and over, until I had put it in language plain enough, as I thought, for any boy to understand. That was a kind of passion with me, and it has stuck by me, for I am never easy now, when I am handling a thought, until I have bounded its north and south, east and west."

The Republican Convention, which met in Chicago in June, 1860, was to prove the most momentous one which had assembled on this continent since that old one, which, seventy-three summers before, had framed in Philadelphia the Constitution of the United States. In its crowded, tumultuous assemblies one name was long and oftenest on men's lips for the Presidency. It was that of a great statesman and true patriot, William H. Seward. But when the Convention separated, it had, to the amazement of great sections of the country, nominated Abraham Lincoln.

During the summer and autumn which followed, the nation held its breath, awaiting the election on which such vast issues were to hang. In November it was known throughout the length and breadth of the land that Abraham Lincoln would be the next President of the United States.

During the winter which followed he remained at Springfield, watching the course of events, with his shrewd, intent, farseeing gaze. The South, gone mad with pride and rage, was resolved that the new President should have no "rights, power, or authority within her borders." By February 1, 1861 seven States had seceded from the Union.

Abraham Lincoln was barely fifty-three when he left Springfield, which he was never to see again, for Washington. He was really in his prime, but everybody thought of him as an old man. Those who liked him trusted him, spoke of him affectionately as "Old Abe." Possibly he was called that in his boyhood, in the rude home, and among his playmates. With those homely features and that solemn face, he must always have had an odd, unchildlike look.

Probably Abraham Lincoln was the saddest man—unless possibly it may have been George Washington—who ever went from his home to the Presidential post.

The history of the Civil War does not belong to this narrative. The part which Abraham Lincoln played during those four great historic years has been read by all men. We know with what tireless patience and courage he tried to conciliate his foes and avert the war. But when the storm broke at last, and there was no appeal between the North and the South but the God of Battles, we know, too, how grandly he met the issues and proved himself equal to the time, and how he freed the slaves and saved the Union.

Abraham Lincoln grew larger and wiser with the times, as all great souls do with occasion. There was necessarily much in the circumstances of his new position which afforded no precedents to guide him; and he was often obliged to fall back upon his own instincts, his rare common sense, his sound judgment. Much, of course, had to be tentative and experimental during the first years of his administration. He had to learn men, and the places they were born to fill, and this required time and trial.

His military training had been limited to a few weeks' service during his youth in the Black Hawk War. Yet the Constitution made him commander in chief of the great Northern armies, and he was held responsible for their organization, the conduct of their officers, and the success or failure in the field. The wonder is, not that he made some mistakes, but that they were so few.

The war went its long way of agony for North and South. In due time came that "Emancipation Proclamation," for which neither ruler nor people at the beginning had been ripe. During his first administration the nation and its President had grown slowly to trust each other; and when another election came around, the people's verdict again made Abraham Lincoln President of the United States.

By this time it had become evident to all who had the vision to pierce coming events that the cause of the Southern Confederacy—maintained at such great cost and with such high courage—was in its death throes. The second inaugural of the President had about it a calm atmosphere of assured coming victory. Sherman was making his historic march to the sea, and Grant was steadily approaching Richmond.

There came a day in April when the President learned that Richmond was evacuated. On that same day he made his entrance into the captured city. But the victor went with no signs of triumph. A tall man, with a sad, kindly, furrowed face, was seen moving on foot through the streets, leading his young son by the hand. Around him joyous crowds of colored people pressed, shouting and sobbing, and hailing him as their Liberator.

"The President took his hat off reverently and bowed; but he could not speak, for the tears were pouring down his cheeks."

When Abraham Lincoln left Richmond that day, his work was virtually done.

Less than two weeks afterward, April 14, 1865, the end came.

John Wilkes Booth, an actor, shot him as he sat in a box at Ford's Theater, and he died the next day. The war was over. His work was ended and Abraham Lincoln found the peace and rest he had never known in life.

ANDREW JOHNSON

On the morning of April 15, 1865 Andrew Johnson became President of the United States. The Vice-President of six weeks took his oath of office under circumstances which might well appall the stoutest heart. A man must have been more or less than human whose nature was not stirred to its depths by the conditions and events amid which the new Executive passed to the nation's chief place.

He had been elected Vice-President with scant knowledge of his real character outside that section of interior country where he had been born and played his part with signal honor and success. When the test came that tried men's souls, he had proved faithful to the Union; he had pleaded its cause with his ringing, fiery speeches, at the risk of his life; he had been hunted over the land; his helpless family had been forced to fly from their home. Yet Andrew Johnson's loyalty had proved of the highest strain. The fortune he had accumulated and the friendships of his life had all been sacrificed to his love for that old flag beneath which he had been born and reared.

But despite all this record of heroic endurance and loyalty, there lay a doubt and a dread at the heart of things—a feeling that this man, Andrew Johnson, who had just become President of the United States, was largely an "unknown quantity."

He owed nothing to fortune; his beginnings were the straitest and humblest; he was born in Raleigh, North Carolina on December 29, 1808. His parents were too poor to give him any advantages of schooling, at a time when these at their best were meager enough. When Andrew was five, his father was drowned, while heroically attempting to save a friend's life. The widow was left with her fatherless boy on her hands, and managed to keep soul and body of both together by her labor.

At ten, Andrew, unable to read or write, was apprenticed to a tailor; he worked at the trade until he was sixteen, by which time he had managed to learn his letters. At eighteen he removed with his mother to Greeneville, a small town in eastern Tennessee. Here he did, what proved to be the most fortunate thing in a life which held many of fortune's great prizes, he made a wise and happy marriage. With his active, vigorous personality, his strong, impulsive nature, there must have been something powerfully magnetic about Andrew Johnson. His wife is said to have been a very attractive girl, and her educational advantages had been superior to his own. With a woman's tact and devotion she set herself to teaching her young husband. She read to him while he worked, and during the evenings he was her intent and eager pupil. Under such an influence he soon acquired the rudiments of an education; he possessed much native ability and his memory had a lasting grip on anything which he learned. From the time of his marriage Andrew Johnson's progress was steadily upward.

At twenty the North Carolina boy was an alderman; at twenty-two he was mayor of Greeneville. About this time he was also appointed one of the trustees of Rhea Academy. He must have had unusual mental quality, as well as moral force, to attain these positions at that age. He had also a native oratorical gift, a power of pungent, fiery speech, which soon gathered about him eager and enthusiastic audiences in his neighborhood.

It was inevitable that a man of this kind should early become interested in politics. Young Johnson was in the State where Andrew Jackson was the central figure, and he followed his chief with all the devotion of his ardent, resolute, combative nature. The elder political leader had taken full possession of the younger's imagination. At twenty-seven he was elected to the Tennessee House of Representatives; afterward he went to the State Senate.

These, however, were but the lower rungs of that political ladder which he was destined to climb. In 1843 Tennessee sent him to Congress, and by succeeding elections he held the office for ten years. In 1853 he was Governor of Tennessee, and re-elected when his first term expired.

Andrew Johnson had the reputation among his neighbors and political colleagues of unflinching courage and unsullied integrity. This was greatly to his credit, but it must also be said that he was opinionated, obstinate and aggressive. Whatever he did he did with his whole heart and soul. When he was kindled into boundless enthusiasm for a cause or a measure, his fervid oratory, his strong, terse, pungent sentences, carried his audiences with him. In his best moments his forceful personality, his powerful declamation, and the courage and fire of the man, made an impression on cool heads and strong intellects. Of course, a Democrat of the Jackson type would, on all political issues, take the side of the people, and identify his interests with theirs.

Tennessee had not yet exhausted her role of honors for Andrew Johnson. In 1857 she sent him to the Senate. Here he worked faithfully until the prospect of secession set all the patriotism of his powerful nature aflame. On this issue the great popular leader separated from his party fearlessly, absolutely. No doubt he recalled Jackson's course in the Nullification era, and aimed at following in his predecessor's footsteps. It is certain that the Tennessee Senator left no stone unturned to save his State to the Union.

He made a grand figure as he stood almost alone amongst his political associates, and fought in the Senate against secession with a courage and zeal that would have delighted the soul of Andrew Jackson. Some of Johnson's speeches were like battle cries, and they goaded his opponents to frenzy.

But no menaces and no dangers could move him. In that mad time all terrible passions were let loose. Johnson was burned in effigy at Memphis. He returned to Tennessee to find a price set upon his head. His house was sacked; his wife, an invalid, and his child, were driven into the streets, and forced to wander houseless fugitives through the country. For a long time they remained in ignorance of his fate.

In February 1862 the capture of Forts Henry and Donelson restored a part of Tennessee to the Union. Johnson's turn came now. President Lincoln appointed him Military Governor of the State. He entered upon his office with a zeal which had been inflamed by his persecutions. "He sent the Mayor of Nashville and the City Council to the penitentiary for refusing to take the oath of allegiance." He threatened his enemies with prison and hanging. When the rebel armies again entered the State, and the timid began to falter, Governor Johnson's words went like an arrow to its mark: "I am no military man, but any one who talks of surrendering I will shoot."

The speeches and deeds of the loyal Tennessee Governor were widely related throughout the North and created profound admiration.

When the National Republican Convention met in Baltimore in

June 1864 and renominated Abraham Lincoln for the Presidency, Andrew Johnson was nominated for the Vice-Presidency.

A great mass meeting assembled at Nashville to ratify his nomination. The Governor addressed it with characteristic boldness. "In trying to save slavery," he said, "you killed it, and lost your own freedom."

Perhaps the greatest day in Andrew Johnson's life was October 24, 1864 when he made his famous address to a dense mass of colored people in Nashville. The hour, the scene and the circumstances, all combined to kindle his imagination, and to bring out the whole man at his best. The speech filled his vast audience with wild enthusiasm; but when Johnson reached his grand climax and declared himself the Moses who would lead the people from bondage into liberty and peace, the tumult that followed, the ecstasy of joy that broke out in sobs and shouts, and in a wild uproar of voices, baffled all description. As Andrew Johnson descended that day from the steps of the capitol, where, no doubt, every word of his burning speech had been uttered in perfect sincerity, he left the proudest scene of his life.

That speech electrified the North. A little later Andrew Johnson was elected Vice-President of the United States. Six weeks afterward he succeeded Abraham Lincoln.

There was alike throughout the North and the South, a belief that the new President would deal in a far sterner temper with the conquered people than his murdered predecessor would have done. Andrew Johnson came from a locality where all the passions of war had run rampant. They had filled all the fair land of East Tennessee with vindictive madness. The new President had been goaded by cruel wrongs to himself and to those dearest to him. It was feared alike by friends and foes that, now he was invested with the vast powers of the Presidency, he would use them in a highhanded and remorseless fashion. All Johnson's speeches at this critical period, as well as his own character, tended to emphasize the general impression that he would adopt a vindictive and resentful policy. He talked of "punishing treason and hanging traitors" in a way that ill accorded with that generous temper in which the North desired to close the long civil contest.

But in a little while, to the boundless amazement of the country, the new President's views and feelings underwent a total change.

The causes which brought this about have perhaps never been fully explained. His own character had much to do with the matter. Then he fell under powerfully persuasive and subtle Cabinet influences. It is a marvelous fact that in a few weeks the President's attitude toward the leaders of the rebellion and the conquered States, was precisely the opposite of his former one. He no longer denounced and threatened. All his speeches and acts indicated his inflexible purpose to forget the past and to exact no safeguards for the future.

It should always be remembered, in explanation of Andrew Johnson's course at this time, that he was by birth, instincts, training, a Southerner, though he had in the Civil War thoroughly identified himself with the North. But with the return of peace the old feelings reasserted themselves. The thought of becoming the friend and benefactor of the South must have gratified his vanity, as well as his more generous feelings. No doubt he had had in early life to endure many slights and indignities in a locality where the spirit of caste was strong and social exclusiveness had very much the force of law.

Andrew Johnson was not the kind of man to forget words or acts that had stung him; he could not fail to reflect that the tables were turned now. Those who had formerly felt themselves greatly his social superiors would be glad to sue humbly for his favor.

However natural this feeling was, it was not the magnanimous one of the true statesman. It was the President's misfortune that he could not in his high place divest himself of all merely personal considerations. His conceit, too, had been intensified by all the circumstances of his life. His inborn obstinacy, however it might have braced him in his early battle with fortune, could only be harmful where the interests of a great nation were at stake. In a little while Abraham Lincoln's successor had proved he was not the man for the time and the post.

The Reconstruction policy, the long and bitter quarrel with Congress, cannot be dwelt on here. As the controversy deepened, the President's anger was inflamed, his will was hardened, his tongue was loosened, he forgot the dignities of his position, and in his famous tour to Chicago, he denounced his opponents, inveighed against Congress, and lauded his own policy in a series of singularly unfortunate public speeches.

These coarse and denunciatory harangues, which had much of the rant and bravado of rustic stump oratory, disgusted and embittered the people. The party which had elected Johnson, the soldiers who had saved the Union, felt that he had betrayed them.

The President, exasperated by opposition, went on his mad, defiant course. He vetoed bill after bill which Congress had passed, until that body, insulted and outraged, resolved on his impeachment.

The trial of President Johnson took place before the Senate, and was conducted with a "solemnity, dignity and order befitting the occasion." The charges, however, on which he was tried did not make the real count against him in the thought of Congress or of the people. He was saved from deposition by a single vote.

There is no doubt that, to the last, he believed himself in the right. He probably anticipated that in the end the nation would vindicate his course by a re-election, but the nominations of 1868 convinced him of his mistake.

Andrew Johnson must have retired from the Presidency an embittered and disappointed man. In his own eyes he was still a hero; and in his prolonged battle with Congress, he always regarded himself as playing the part of a pure and enlightened patriotism.

The wife to whom his youth owed so much, was too broken in health to take on herself the duties of mistress of the White House, but her daughter, Mrs. Martha Patterson, took her mother's place. Its responsibilities were at this time particularly onerous. Mrs. Patterson entered the White House to find it in a greatly disordered condition, and she devoted all her energy and taste to supervising its restoration. Aided by an appropriation from the government, she succeeded in making a vast improvement in the interior.

The President's Southern friends had applauded his course, and it was a necessity of his ardent, active nature that he should resume his public life. After a period of rest he engaged once more with all his old fervor in the political conflicts of the time.

Six years after he retired from the Presidency, Tennessee once more sent Andrew Johnson to the Senate. A fortnight after he took his seat he made a speech which proved that time had not ameliorated the old temper, the old convictions and personal resentments.

In that session Andrew Johnson did his last public work. When Congress closed he returned to Tennessee, and in the following July 1875 he died suddenly while visiting his youngest daughter at Carter's Station.

ULYSSES SIMPSON GRANT

ONE evening, in the spring of 1861, there was great excitement at Hanover, a small town a few miles to the south of Galena, Illinois. The firing on Fort Sumter, the call for volunteers to defend the Union, had thoroughly aroused all the Northern land. A mass meeting had been appointed at the town hall, but the crowds that responded had proved too large for the building. At last they repaired to the Presbyterian church, an old brick structure with ample accommodations. On that spring night such meetings were being held over all the loyal country. The people of Hanover, fired by addresses ringing with courage and patriotism, were reluctant to separate. At last a comparative stranger in the crowded assembly was called upon for a speech; he rose with an embarrassed air; he was a man of rather heavy build, of average height, with square features and resolute jaw; he was conspicuous on this occasion for the old blue army coat—the only one in the audience—which he wore; he had been through the Mexican War, and later had been promoted to a captaincy, when with his regiment on the Pacific coast.

A silence fell upon the large audience, and all eyes were turned to the man standing there in his blue army coat. At last he said, in a quiet, familiar fashion, and with a good deal of effort:

"Boys, I can't make a speech. I never made a speech in my life. But when the time comes to go to the front, I am ready to go with you."

The man who said this in the old brick meetinghouse at Hanover was Ulysses S. Grant.

On the night when he made that brief speech in Hanover, Ulysses Grant was barely thirty-nine years old. There was nothing in his past or his present which made the outlook for his future a promising one. Indeed, most men in his case might have felt that the "run of luck" had been particularly against them.

There is no story of poverty and bitter hardships to record of his beginnings. They form, in this respect, a sharp contrast to those of Abraham Lincoln. Ulysses Grant was born on April 29, 1822 at

Point Pleasant, in Clermont County, Ohio. He came of old English stock; his ancestors had emigrated to Massachusetts during the earliest years of the colony. Nearly a century and a half later, one of the race was present at the battle of Bunker Hill; he afterward emigrated to Ohio. The old soldier was not thrifty, and his son, Jesse, had a hand-to-hand battle with fate in the new country beyond the Alleghenies. In time he had married, acquired a simple, comfortable home, and his circumstances were probably much better than those of many of his neighbors, when his son, Ulysses, was born.

In the autumn of the following year the family removed to Georgetown in the adjoining county. The boy's earliest memories clustered about this place, for the childhood and boyhood of Ulysses S. Grant were passed in this county seat, on what was then the Western frontier.

Ulysses' father combined leather manufacturing with farming. At seven or eight the boy drove the wagons loaded with wood from the forest to the house. "At eleven he was strong enough to hold a plow." After that time his history, until he was seventeen, is that of a contented, industrious, good-tempered home boy. The parents "never scolded or punished their children." If Ulysses, when the work was done, went his own way, it was one of simple, rational games and pastimes. He had a passion for horses, and was on the back of one as often and as long as possible; he went fishing and swimming in the creek in summer, and had jolly times skating and sleigh riding in the winter; a rather shy, silent, independent boy, not given to sowing wild oats, but putting his heart into his work or his play, and in either to be depended upon.

What was of vastly more importance, Ulysses had the best school advantages which the neighborhood afforded. These were slender enough at best. The father, an intelligent man, much given to reading, deplored his own scant schooling "which had been limited to six months," and was resolved that his young son should have a better chance; he sent him regularly to school, and this was better than not going at all, even with the very meager teaching he received.

He was seventeen when that event occurred which was to color and shape all his future life. The father had ambitions for his son, and when he learned "there was a vacancy from the district," applied for the appointment of Ulysses to West Point Academy. The appointment came in due time, much to the youth's surprise, not greatly at first to his pleasure; he dreaded the examinations, and, with his lack of egotism, feared that he should fail in them; but the father had set his heart on the matter, and his will was law; so Ulysses went to West Point. A part of the journey was made by river steamer, a part by canal boat. The boy saw everything with his quiet, observant eyes, among other things, and for the first time, a railroad. Still, amid all the novel scenes and experiences, the end of the journey was like a grim specter perpetually before him; and he would have been thankful if some "temporary injury" had disabled him, so that he could have escaped West Point.

He loitered a little at Philadelphia and New York; he arrived at West Point in the last of May 1839. Here, much to his surprise, he passed the examinations without difficulty.

His life as a cadet does not appear to have been particularly agreeable, as his record certainly was not a brilliant one. He had not the instincts and habits of the scholar, except for mathematics; for that he had a genius. He read much fiction at this time, and time hung heavily with him; he would have been glad, at least during the first year, if Congress had passed the bill under discussion for abolishing the Military Academy.

When General Scott came to review the cadets at West Point, young Grant was quite dazzled by the superb figure, the commanding air, the showy uniform; he regarded Scott as the man of men, and had a "momentary presentiment" that "he should one day occupy the General's place on a review." Beyond this he seems to have had no military ambitions and no intention of even remaining in the army.

At the end of two years he was home again for the summer furlough, but this time he went to Bethel, twelve miles from Georgetown, where the family were now living. His happiness was greatly enhanced by the possession of a young horse which had been purchased for his use during the furlough.

On his return to West Point time hung somewhat less heavily. The life there, with its unvarying routine, its rigid discipline, never suited young Grant; his health broke seriously before his graduation; he had a very stubborn cough, and there were fears that he had inherited certain consumptive tendencies of his family. But he rallied with the return home and with the long horseback rides.

Young Grant graduated about the middle of his class in 1843. Despite his first aversion to a military life, he had, before leaving

West Point, made up his mind to enter the army. He was "assigned to duty with the Fourth United States Infantry, at Jefferson Barracks, St. Louis. It was the largest military post in the country at that time."

So little wish or desire had the young lieutenant to remain in the army that, soon after he reached Jefferson Barracks, he applied for the post of assistant professor of mathematics at West Point. The reply was so encouraging that he was satisfied he should soon have obtained his appointment, had not the Mexican War broken out and changed all his plans.

At this time the annexation of Texas had become a matter of absorbing interest in the politics of the country. Young Grant had been, from the beginning, utterly opposed to a measure which shocked all his instincts of honor and justice.

He had obtained leave of absence for a short trip to Ohio, when his regiment was ordered to Louisiana. He was at home when he learned this.

Grant followed his regiment, the Fourth Infantry, to Louisiana, at Fort Jessup, between the Red River and the Sabine. Whatever ostensible reasons might be assigned for the presence of the United States troops on the scene, he knew perfectly well, as everybody else did, that they were intended as a menace against Mexico.

Little, however, as he imagined it, this Mexican campaign service was to prove invaluable to himself and to his country. In his subordinate place he was learning much of the business of war, and, in his shrewd, silent way, forming his own tenacious opinions. In that long campaign, and amid the good comradeship of army life, he was acquiring much knowledge of men, then greatly his superiors, whom he was afterward to meet as foes, on equal ground, and on vastly larger battlefields. He was faithful and untiring in the discharge of all his duties; but he exhibited no brilliant qualities. Nobody certainly credited him with a spark of genius, and he himself would be the last man to do that.

When the treaty was ratified and the victorious army left Mexico, Grant's regiment was ordered into camp at Mississippi in the summer of 1848. Here he obtained leave of absence for four months. He soon set out for White Haven where he was married to Miss Julia Dent, August 22, 1848.

In April of the following year he was ordered for garrison duty to

Detroit, Michigan. He remained here two years. In 1851 the Fourth Infantry was sent to California. It was a wonder that any of the regiment lived to get there, after the discomforts of the long, perilous trip, and the unutterable horrors of the Isthmus, which they reached in midsummer, and where they encountered cholera. Between the dying men and the defaulting contractor, Grant, who was regimental quartermaster, had his hands full. Early in December he reached San Francisco, with all the regiment that had survived the cholera. Here new scenes awaited him; he found himself in the midst of a strange, rough, picturesque life; in short, he was now in the midst of that gold-mining frenzy, which makes the early periods of California history more exciting and dramatic than the wildest dreams of the novelist. Lieutenant Grant had a chance to study the novel world about him in his shrewd, penetrating fashion, before he was ordered to Fort Vancouver on the Columbia River.

In 1853 he was promoted to a captaincy. His new command was stationed at Humboldt Bay, California, in the Redwood region; he remained here, however, only a short period.

By this time the charm of the Western life had exercised its fascination upon Grant; he had grown so attached to the country that he was resolved on making it his future home. But his domestic affections were very strong, and he could not be content to remain longer away from his wife and his two young sons.

The captain's pay was not sufficient to support the little family in California. He finally resigned his post and returned to the East. This was in the summer of 1854.

Captain Grant was now thirty-two: he had been in the army eleven years; he certainly had not a brilliant record and his promotion had been slow and slight.

The autumn of 1854 had no encouraging outlook. A man with Grant's military education and habits would not be likely to find farming a congenial pursuit, but this alone opened to him. Mrs. Grant owned a farm near her old home at White Haven, and here the family resolved to make their future home. But there was no house on the land: the owners had no money to buy stock. Grant faced his fate manfully and set about building a home for the wife and the boys; he worked hard at building the house, and performed the varied drudgery of farm work, just as he had done when he was a boy. Sometimes "he loaded a wagon with cord-wood and took it for sale to St. Louis." At last fever and ague came on and shook even his iron constitution. In a little while the farming proved a failure. The Grant farm was sold at auction.

A trial at real estate business with a relative in St. Louis followed. This did not prosper. Captain Grant did not have the moneymaking faculty.

In May 1860, he removed to Galena and took a clerkship in his father's leather store. His two younger brothers were there. It was the elder Grant's intention to establish his three sons in the business; but the second one died in the following year, of consumption.

This is a brief outline of the history of the man who stood in his old Mexican army coat in the brick Presbyterian meetinghouse at Hanover, and made his short, characteristic speech to the breathless crowd. Since he left the army, seven years before, his life had been a losing struggle with fate. He had not complained overmuch. Under the silence was a great deal of quiet, patient pluck. The best thing, thus far, that had ever come to him was the chance in the leather store and the prospect of the later partnership.

But the hour for the simple, quiet man to come to his place had struck at last. The North, waiting listless and incredulous while the South gathered its forces and trained its men for the coming struggle, was roused at last. The air was full of preparation for battle. The need of soldiers to defend the Union superseded everything else. There was an imperative call for capable and trained officers to command the enthusiastic, undisciplined volunteers, who had not the faintest idea what war really meant, and who now felt for the first time the passion of patriotism, the duty of living or dying for one's country.

Grant kept his word. The leather store at Galena knew him no more; he declined the captaincy of a company of volunteers, but he served them as drillmaster, and when the time came he marched with them to Springfield. On the point of returning home, he was accosted by the Illinois Governor, to whom he had never spoken, and was offered a position in the Adjutant General's office. This was accepted at once. From this time Grant had his hands full; he had charge of mustering the ten Illinois regiments into service.

A little later he had a new experience; he beheld for the first time a secession flag waving defiantly in the air. The scene occurred at

St. Louis, whither he had gone on his way to Belleville, the mustering place of the regiments of Southern Illinois. The sight of that symbol of rebellion kindled all Grant's patriotic wrath. A little later he saw it come down from the secession headquarters, and the old flag that he loved, in whose service he had spent his young manhood, and whose honor he was so splendidly to vindicate during the next four years, went up in place of the other.

About this time he made his application to General Thomas for command of a regiment. He merely stated his past services, and brought no influential names to back his application. Indeed, he felt some distrust as to his own ability to take charge of a regiment. But he might have spared himself all scruples. No notice was taken of his application.

This act must have been sufficiently mortifying. Grant, however, was to have his regiment. He had gone to visit his parents, now removed to Covington, Kentucky, and he had twice attempted to have an interview with General McClellan, whose headquarters were then in Cincinnati, but he had not succeeded. He aspired at this time to a position on the General's staff. On Grant's return to Springfield he learned that Governor Yates, impressed by the efficient service he had rendered in mustering in the regiments, had appointed him Colonel of the Twenty-first Illinois Volunteers. He joined them at their camp on the State fair grounds near Springfield. Ulysses Grant was now in the war.

He was with his regiment at Salt River in Missouri and a Confederate force was encamped at Florida, a small village, twenty-five miles away. Grant was ordered to move against the enemy.

It was a dismal march for the new Colonel and his unused troops. As they passed through the thinly settled country, the frightened people fled as they would before hordes of painted savages.

When at last they ascended the hill below which the enemy was supposed to be encamped, Grant, to use his own words, "would have given anything to be back in Illinois." The regiment reached the summit. There was no waving of flags, no flashing of arms, no sign of a soldier in all that wide summer stillness. The enemy had decamped in haste as soon as they learned Grant was on the march, and were now forty miles away. If he had dreaded to meet them, they were at least equally afraid of him. Grant was on the threshold of his new career. This experience was invaluable to the future General; he was never thereafter afraid to face the enemy in the field, though he admits that he often felt "anxious" on the eve of battle.

The new President was, in this terrible summer of 1861, desirous above all things to obtain officers of proved ability. Washburne, the new member from the Galena district, recommended Grant. He was accordingly promoted to the rank of brigadier general. This was an immense advance from that of drillmaster, a few weeks before, of the Galena volunteers.

Not long afterward he was assigned to the important command of the Southeastern District of Missouri, with its headquarters at Cairo, Illinois. It was here that Grant first showed his real mettle.

Kentucky was at this critical moment trembling in the balance, and Paducah on the Mississippi resolved to go the way of the Southern States.

On the day after Grant reached Cairo, he learned that the enemy was planning to seize and hold Paducah in the great State that, declaring herself neutral, was faltering in her allegiance to the Union.

It was early in the following morning when Grant and his two regiments debarked on the river shore at Paducah. During the night the little fleet had made the sail of forty miles, in steamers which lay at the Cairo levee. The Confederate flag was floating in the breeze of that autumn morning. The Confederate army, four thousand strong, lay scarcely a dozen miles away.

Grant's arrival was just in the nick of time. The inhabitants, amazed and alarmed, made no resistance. Grant assured them of his protection. The Confederate forces did not appear. The secession flag was lowered a second time and Paducah was saved to the Union. This was the beginning of that great military career which was to reach its triumphant close one April day, almost four years later, in the parlor of a private dwelling at Appomattox Station.

Between that morning of September 6, 1861 and that other afternoon of April 9, 1865, lie the names of Belmont, of Fort Donelson, of Shiloh, of Vicksburg, of Chattanooga, and later and last, of the Army of the Potomac. Each of these names means the story of a terrible battle—of a victory that was to amaze friends and foes, and a world which watched across the seas, intent, breathless, and largely hostile. In a little while Grant had learned the greatness and gallantry of the foe with whom he was contending.

The brigadier general of Cairo had meanwhile become the lieutenant general in the Army of the United States, and the Proclamation of Emancipation had freed every slave in the Union.

The series of splendid victories had not, of course, been easily won against so brave and determined a foe. Grant had had the usual fate of great commanders. At the beginning he had encountered distrust, jealousy, opposition. His reply was the all-sufficing one of some fresh victory on the battlefield.

The years which followed the close of the war, and the great questions which shook the country, the Reconstruction of the South, the relations of the President to Congress, belong to an ampler biography than this. The nation showed its faith in the Soldier with whom it had gone through the war by bestowing on him the highest place in its gift, the Presidency of the United States.

He was inaugurated with the most imposing display which the capital had ever witnessed. Naturally simple and unostentatious in his tastes, he yet enjoyed his fame and greatness, and all the visible signs of it.

His first administration went its smooth, prosperous way. When the four years expired, Grant was re-elected with great enthusiasm, and by an immense majority to a second Presidential term. This proved a period of great financial distress to the country. A terrible business panic prostrated the industries of the land, wrecked many fortunes, and filled the nation, which had gone on its prosperous ways, reckless and extravagant, with depression and disaster. The administration and the Republican Party were held more or less responsible for the financial reverses. Some of the President's most trusted advisers lost the confidence of the people. But they did not lose faith in their Soldier amid the general feeling of depression and insecurity with which his last term closed.

Soon afterward General Grant made a tour of the world. All his life he had been fond of travel, and had felt a strong curiosity to behold foreign lands. In the prime of his years, in perfect health, and with sufficient fortune at command, he resolved to indulge the longing of his youth and go around the planet.

The little party which accompanied him from Philadelphia, among whom were his wife and the youngest of his three sons, sailed on the steamer *Indiana* in 1872.

From the time that he landed on the English coast it was one long, triumphal progress for Ulysses Grant; his journey over the island, across the continent, around the world, reads in its simplest recital, almost like some Arabian Night's tale.

He who owed all his glory to the Civil War found no pleasure in military pomp and parade. He declined a review of the French army. The glitter of arms, the bravery of uniforms, the rhythmic march of columns, had no delight for him. "He never wanted to hear another drum beat."

Not long after his return he chose the city of New York for his home. She was proud of her illustrious citizen, and the Republic, if she may sometimes have forgotten to reward great historic services, was certainly generous to Grant.

After that April day when the North went wild with joy because the war was ended, Grant's position with the people much resembled that of the Duke of Wellington with the English nation after the battle of Waterloo.

Honors and wealth were heaped upon the victorious General. One subscription list raised him a quarter of a million dollars. Another provided him with a hundred thousand to purchase a home in New York for the remainder of his life.

He had a summer cottage at Long Branch. Its simplicity suited his quiet tastes. From its verandas he could watch the shipping of the world come and go, while grateful winds from the sea cooled the hot breath of the Northern summer.

In 1880 a determined effort was made by the Republican Party to nominate General Grant for a third term to the Presidency.

The effort met with prolonged and inflexible opposition; but so popular was the soldier, so insistent his support, that the contest became an extremely bitter one. It shook the Republican Party to its center, but at last the delegates to the famous convention at Chicago were induced to unite in nominating James A. Garfield for the Presidency.

Much that has been written about Grant's later years seems to cast a shadow over the fame and reputation of one of the greatest men in this country's history. The truth must be told, of course, but one mistake cannot blot out or even overshadow the fact that it was Grant's military genius which was the final, determining factor which saved the Union from separation.

In May 1884 the great blow fell. There was a period when the nation held its breath in dismay, learning that the weight of that great name had been lent to a delusion and a fraud.

But in a little while the truth came to light. The soldier, the ex-President, came out of the trial, which wrecked the firm in which he had been senior partner, with his honor and honesty undimmed; he had been the victim of too large a faith in others, and his own fortune had been engulfed with the ruined firm.

During the summer of 1884, while he was at Long Branch, General Grant began to feel mysterious pains in his throat. He at last reluctantly, and to gratify his alarmed wife, submitted to an examination. The recent suffering was explained as a "cancerous affection of the throat."

The disease made its approaches slowly but surely. All the heroism of Grant's nature, all its patience and quiet strength, came to the surface now. The man of the victorious battlefields turned, as his sun was setting, to his pen. With death staring him in the face, and with a sense of his broken fortunes harassing him by night and by day, he resolved to write the memoirs of his life.

To undertake such a task, and to carry it to its completion in a couple of large volumes, amid weakness, pain and growing disease, required a patient, sustained heroism, which, in some of its aspects, surpassed the greatest victory Grant had ever won on the battlefield.

In March 1885 a bill was passed in Congress once more creating Ulysses S. Grant a General of the Army. This gave him immense gratification. The old forces of his constitution rallied for a brief time. The contract for the publication of the memoirs was signed. Those Grant loved so devotedly were now amply provided for.

Early in June he went to a quiet cottage at Mount Gregor, near Saratoga and it was here that he died, on July 23, 1885.

RUTHERFORD BIRCHARD HAYES

"An officer fit for duty, who at this crisis would abandon his post to electioneer for a seat in Congress, ought to be scalped."

In August 1864 a brevet major general, who had won his title by gallant services in the West Virginia campaign, expressed himself in these words. They were the reply of the man who had been for the first time nominated to Congress by a district of his native State. He was in the field, and a friend urged him to return home awhile and campaign for the election. The man who made it was Rutherford B. Hayes. He was born in Delaware, Ohio on Oct. 4, 1822. His father had died in the previous July.

The Hayes family emigrated from Vermont in the early years of the nineteenth century, and had taken firm root in what was then the far West country before the elder died, or his son first saw the light of day.

The childhood and boyhood of Rutherford B. Hayes was a smooth, comfortable, prosperous one. In the quiet home there was no struggle with poverty for the widowed mother and her fatherless boy. Rutherford went first to the common schools in the neighborhood. Then he was sent to the academy at Newport, Ohio, and later he was at Middletown, Connecticut, where he prepared for Kenyon College in his native State.

Here the undergraduate showed his intellectual quality. He was not only a fine scholar, but he made his mark in the literary societies of his alma mater. He graduated in 1842 and won much praise for his valedictory oration.

He began his legal studies in Columbus, Ohio. Later he attended Harvard Law School for two years in order to equip himself thoroughly for the bar.

Young Hayes entered on the practice of his profession in his native State, at Fremont, called at that time Lower Sandusky, but his health now broke so seriously that he was compelled to give up all business and spend a winter in the South, where the milder climate restored him.

On his return to Ohio he established himself at Cincinnati, where the real abilities of the young lawyer, his high character, and his agreeable social gifts, won him many eminent friends.

In 1852 he married Miss Lucy Webb, the daughter of a physician in Chillicothe, Ohio.

A number of happy, prosperous years followed the marriage. Mr. Hayes had a successful law practice and occupied positions of honor and responsibility in the city government.

The firing on Fort Sumter was the signal for an immense change in his life. His antislavery convictions had been early formed and were very decided; he had joined the Republican Party on its organization. The strength of his opinions, the resolution and ardor of his character, were certain to bring him into the foreground of affairs at this time.

A great mass meeting gathered in Cincinnati. Mr. Hayes was in its midst and was appointed chairman to express the popular passion which at that time swept over the North, a great tidal wave, carrying everything before it. It was impossible that so ardent a patriot, so devoted a friend of the Union, as Mr. Hayes, should not come to his place and do his work in the hour when his country called upon her sons to save her.

In a short time the Cincinnati lawyer was appointed major of the Twenty-third Ohio Volunteer Infantry. In September 1861 General Rosecrans, under whom he was serving, appointed him judge advocate of the Department of Ohio, and in the month following he was promoted to the rank of lieutenant colonel.

At the famous battle of South Mountain, September 14, 1862, the new Colonel carried himself with great gallantry. A musket ball struck him in the left arm, but he refused to leave the field and at last had to be borne from it. His wound forced him to leave the army for awhile, but as soon as he recovered he was once more at the head of his troops.

It was at this time that the nomination to Congress occurred, with the characteristic refusal to obtain leave of absence and work for fresh laurels in the political field.

Despite his absence from the political arena, General Hayes won the election for Congress. In the following spring the war closed, and he took his seat in the House on December 4, 1865.

In his new field General Hayes did work which, though it might not be so brilliant as that which he had performed on the battlefield, was still of great service to his country. He did not display dazzling oratorical gifts, but he was a legislator of strong sense and solid judgment; his fearlessness, his high moral sympathies, his deep instincts for justice and right, won the respect and confidence of his colleagues. The measures which he promoted during that critical period of national legislation were always inspired by the large views and the magnanimous temper of the statesman.

In 1867 Hayes was elected Governor of the State. It is a sufficient commentary on his services in that responsible post, that he was twice re-elected to it.

In 1873 Governor Hayes resolved to return to private life and make his home in Fremont, Ohio, where he had settled in early manhood.

But the dreams of the quiet life and the fireside happiness with his wife and his children were not to be realized at that time.

The National Republican Convention which met at Cincinnati on June 14, 1876 had many brilliant and distinguished men among its candidates. At the last, however, Governor Hayes carried the nomination for the Presidency.

The contest which followed was strong and acrimonious to the last degree. Both parties claimed that it had elected its candidate. The country was shaken with the strife. Political passions flamed on every side. There were threats of civil war. Foreboding and dismay filled the nation.

The storm, however, quieted at last. Rutherford Hayes took his oath of office and was duly inaugurated President of the United States, and the country settled down tranquil and confident.

His administration was one which might have been largely anticipated from the character and convictions of the President. He had very decided opinions on civil service reform, and he made strong and courageous efforts to promote it. But so great and far-reaching a reform could not be accomplished in four years. The President encountered on this whole question bitter and persistent opposition from some of the leaders in his own party, though it is said that during this administration "there was far less meddling with party politics on the part of officers of the government than at any period since Andrew Jackson's time."

The new and lenient policy which the Executive adopted toward the Reconstructed States, ameliorated much bitter sectional feeling and proved in the end the highest wisdom.

It is certain that the administration, which began under so deep a cloud, closed amid wide tranquillity and prosperity throughout the country.

The ex-President returned to the home of his young manhood in Fremont. He was still in the prime of his years, and he was fully alive to all the great questions and interests of the day.

After his retirement Rutherford Hayes became the recipient of many honorary distinctions, and his time was much absorbed "in various philanthropical and useful enterprises." A greatly needed reform in the system of prison government received a large share of his attention.

The life of Rutherford B. Hayes does not afford to his biographer those dramatic incidents and contrasts which make the early lives of many of our Presidents so full of vivid interest and adventure. Born in a simple home, with moderate fortunes, reared amid refining and elevating influences, he had never known the struggle and grind of poverty; never had, in the hard upward climb, to break away from the power of early habits and of coarse associations.

The life of this man moved from his birth amid pleasant and prosperous ways, filled with busy activity which continued, even after his retirement from public life, in various philanthropic undertakings which he kept up until a few days before his death at Fremont, Ohio on January 17, 1893, at the age of seventy.

JAMES ABRAM GARFIELD

AMONG the opening days of September 1854 a young man, who would see his twenty-third birthday before that autumn closed, had achieved the great ambition of his youth. Whatever high honors, whatever large place, the future might have in store for him, it is doubtful whether any of its days could wear such a glow of hope and aspiration, could so abound with the satisfaction of noble purpose accomplished after long struggle, as those which closed the twenty-second summer of his life.

For James Abram Garfield was going to college. Infinitely important as this fact was to himself, it was at that time of little consequence to anybody else, with the exception of a small circle of his friends and neighbors, the majority of whom would probably have disapproved of his going at all.

The story of his youth, rounding now to its twenty-third birthday, is a story of pioneer life in northern Ohio. Its general features have a certain resemblance to Abraham Lincoln's early life; but the Ohio boy was born more than twenty years after the Kentucky one, so the beginnings of the younger were not so scant and hard as those of the elder. Still, James Garfield's youth is the story of a fatherless boy's long, brave battle with hard fortune, under the humble roof of a widowed mother left desolate by her husband's sudden death, and with almost no means of support for herself and her young children, in a clearing on the edge of the wilderness, in Orange, Cuyahoga County, Ohio.

The boy came of stanch ancestry on both sides. The Garfields were among the earliest Puritan settlers of the Massachusetts Colony, and James's mother, Eliza Ballou, came of the old French Huguenot breed, which left France with the revocation of the Edict of Nantes, and whose blood enriched the Protestant communities of two continents.

In the newly raised log cabin of the Ohio clearing the child who came of these two sterling races was born on November 19, 1831. James was the youngest of the children, a brother and two sisters having preceded him. He was about a year and a half old at the time of his father's death.

The boy was happily too young to comprehend the loss which had come to him just on the threshold of life. It meant struggle, privation, hardship, the wolf close to the door through all his boyhood and youth.

James was the youngest, the pet of the household; he was a bright, sturdy, resolute boy, much bent on having his own way—a fact which gave the doting mother a good deal of anxiety. He appears to have been always larger than his years warranted. There was certainly a touch of precocity in his learning to read by the time he was three. Brave, resolute, truthful, he must early have exhibited qualities which gave promise of a rare and earnest character. The mother, at her work,—she must have had scant leisure with her young household and her small farm—read poems, and told Bible stories to her children, all of which James greatly enjoyed.

He borrowed, like Abraham Lincoln, all the books, far and near, and devoured them. During the winters he attended the district school. When he was about eleven, the Orange boys formed a lyceum, and James eagerly joined the debating clubs, and these, no doubt, roused and stimulated his mind in various directions.

All this time he was doing a farm boy's work. He was about fifteen when the great ambition of the Garfield household was gratified, and they exchanged their log cabin for a wood house of four rooms. The orchard of a hundred trees, which the father had planted, stood, by this time, green and ample, about the small home. He had watched with immense interest the building of the new house, and he now made up his mind to become a carpenter. He followed the business for about two years, with intervals of farm work.

At this period he had frequent moods of discouragement, such as often come with adolescence. It must have been a peculiarly trying time to him; he was restless and pursued by vague longings and ambitions; he did not know himself, nor to what goal his aptitudes pointed. Everything was confused and tentative in his thoughts and his work; he must have had many gloomy hours. Nobody understood him well enough to advise or help him. His restlessness and his young imagination, which had been fed by tales of the sea, aroused strong desires for a sailor's life. While he was in this mood, he went to work for a while in his uncle's woodland near Newburg. He saw

Lake Erie, and the sight of the blue water suggested a trip on the lake boats as the beginning of a seafaring career.

When the wood chopping was done he attempted to find a place as "deck-hand or common sailor" on some ship, but his first application was so discouraging that he did not repeat it. A position, humbler if possible than the one he had sought, now opened to him. His uncle owned a canalboat which carried cargoes of coal from the mines to Cleveland. The nephew "engaged to drive the horses which drew the boat along the Ohio canal."

He had now reached the nadir of his career. The new work was outdoors, and in this respect suited his restless mind and body; but the labor brought with it associations which his careful mother would have disapproved.

He followed the canal work for about six months, and then he became ill. One day, weak and dizzied, he fell into the canal. That fall was a fortunate one for James Garfield, though he barely escaped drowning; he was now too ill to continue at his post, and with much difficulty he managed to reach home. A long and dangerous illness followed, but his fine constitution brought him safely through at last.

In the long leisures of convalescence new and serious thoughts awoke in his soul. They ripened at last into an invincible resolution to make something of himself, to set about getting an education.

As soon as he recovered he set about his studies; he had to do this by himself, as the household finances did not admit of his attending school. But he held to his purpose unflinchingly. It was certain during this time that, when he was not at work, he was at his studies.

James Garfield had made a long climb upward when, in 1849, he entered the academy at Chester; he remained there, more or less, for two years.

At eighteen the boy who had worked on the farm and tried carpentering and driving on the towpath, was teaching school in his native town.

Later he went to Hiram College, which had been recently founded by the Church of the Disciples. Mrs. Garfield had joined this simple and devout community, and her youngest son, whose religious convictions were always deep and vital, had become a member of the same body. At Hiram College young Garfield passed three years.

It was in 1854 that the uncle whose wood he had chopped, and whose canalboat horses he had driven, loaned his promising young nephew five hundred dollars to complete his studies at Williams College.

The student who had made such struggles and sacrifices to get to college, would not be likely, once there, to waste his opportunities. It is enough to say that young Garfield went at his work with the delight and thoroughness of the born scholar—that his range of reading was as broad as his time and classwork allowed. But he was not solely a student. With his abounding vitality, with his genial, cordial nature, he could not fail to enjoy the social life of the college.

At twenty-four James Garfield graduated and returned to Ohio. He was now fairly equipped and eager for the race. In a short time he was offered and accepted a professorship in Hiram College. A year later he was its President.

In 1858 he married Miss Lucretia Rudolph of Hiram. They had been students in the old days at Chester.

With his religious training and convictions he had at one time almost determined to study for the ministry, but soon after his marriage he resolved to prepare himself for the law, and with characteristic energy set about his legal studies; he pursued these under great drawbacks, for the duties of President of Hiram College were varied and exacting. It was fortunate that his early rugged life had given him such robust health, or it would not have borne the double strain of those years. While he was studying law, the instincts of the statesman became interested in the political questions which now began to come to the foreground. On the subject of slavery James Garfield, like Abraham Lincoln, took his stand early and kept it unflinchingly. He was, from first to last, its resolute, outspoken, consistent foe.

In 1859 he was, to his own great surprise, elected to the State Senate of Ohio. This was no small honor to a young man who had left his alma mater only five years before. He now entered upon public life, but he had no controlling ambition to remain in it. He had the instincts and tastes of the born scholar, and he did not even resign his position at Hiram.

But two years later the hour struck which stirred his whole soul with a passion of patriotism. He felt, as every loyal man in the North did, that he had a country to live or to die for. With his habit of putting his heart and soul into everything he did, he now set about assisting the Governor "in organizing the Ohio volunteers and in raising supplies for the army."

The whole business was novel and full of harassing perplexities to all who undertook it. Garfield rendered inestimable service at this trying time. He did everything in the spirit of a true patriot. While many were intent on reward and office, he did not solicit either; but in a little while both came to him.

A regiment of enthusiastic volunteers, composed largely of his college pupils, was organized at Hiram. The students were eager that their President should be appointed Colonel of the regiment. He felt himself unequal to the grand responsibilities which the command involved; but it was at last forced upon him, and Colonel Garfield marched with his regiment, the Forty-second Ohio.

Colonel Garfield won his first military laurels in the Big Sandy campaign. The rebels had swarmed into Kentucky, resolved to carry the reluctant border State into secession. Marshall, with his five thousand troops, was in the Big Sandy valley when Garfield went with his raw young soldiers to meet him.

After much marching and skirmishing the battle took place at Prestonburg. It must have been a trying moment to the new colonel, who had never himself been in an engagement, when he led his greatly inferior numbers to their first encounter with the enemy. It closed at last in a victory for the Unionists. Marshall's troops, as fresh as Garfield's, "were put to rout, and during the night beat a hasty retreat into Southwestern Virginia." The Big Sandy victory was doubly important because it was won against an enemy superior in numbers, and at a time when the Union armies had met with serious reverses.

The figure of the young colonel, as he tossed his coat into a tree and shouted back to his cavalry, whom he had first ordered to charge, "Give 'em 'Hail Columbia,' boys," forms the most striking and heroic picture of this campaign.

The remainder of Garfield's brief military career is in keeping with its brilliant opening chapter. He was promoted to the rank of brigadier general by the President, whose anxious and long vexed soul was rejoiced by tidings of victory from the West. The remainder of the year was full of varied military service for Garfield. But during that time he was in no battles. He was busy at the work of "reconstructing railroad bridges and re-establishing lines of railway communication for the army, beside serving on important court-martials."

Later, he was at the outposts with his brigade during the long siege of Corinth; but the hardships he underwent brought back his old foe, malaria, and he was forced to return to his home at Hiram, where he lay prostrated by illness.

As soon as his recovery permitted he repaired once more to the field. He now joined the army of the Cumberland, as General Rosecrans's chief of staff. It was at that time a position full of trials and heavy responsibilities. Garfield went through the battle of Chickamauga. It proved a lost one for his cause. Yet out of its very defeat he plucked fresh laurels for his own wearing. His perilous ride back to the scene of action after the reverse and flight on that terrible day, lifts him into the light of poetry and heroism. That ride, just at the critical moment, saved General Thomas's army, and as the night darkened over the field the enemy's columns retreated before the Union batteries.

That day's work was General Garfield's last on the field of battle. He earned there the title of major general. But his country needed other service from him now. He had been elected to Congress by his native State.

General Garfield was only thirty-two years old, and had been for two years and four months in the army, when he, in accordance with President Lincoln's strong desire, took his seat in the House of Representatives.

General Garfield had now entered the lists in which he was to do the longest and most important work of his life, for he was in Congress seventeen years.

Abraham Lincoln was shrewd at reading the characters and aptitudes of men. His estimate of young Garfield was amply justified by the latter's course in the national legislature.

The Ohio member rendered his country splendid service during a period that was full of new and untried issues for the government. During more than a decade and a half, he served his country with all the forces of his intellect, and with all the devotion of his heart. As a debater he soon took front rank among his colleagues. As one critical measure after another came up for discussion in those trying years of the nation's history, Garfield treated it in his masterly, exhaustive manner, and with all the force of his strong, aspiring instincts and convictions; he made many brilliant and effective speeches; he had a wonderfully happy way of pouring, by a few terse, rapid sentences, or a simple, pointed anecdote, a flood of light upon some confused or doubtful matter.

The man's nature, like his physique, was molded in large, generous lines. He had a glowing, abounding vitality. His temperament was invincibly hopeful and optimistic; he had unbounding faith in men and women.

General Garfield probably thought he had attained the summit of his political ambitions when Ohio elected him to the United States Senate; but there was a greater honor in reserve for him. In 1880 the Republican Convention at Chicago, after its famous week of tumultuous passions and fierce controversies, which held the whole country in suspense, nominated James A. Garfield for the Presidency.

The nomination was entirely unsought by him. He was a delegate to the convention, and had worked heart and soul for the nomination of his friend, John Sherman of Ohio, and he was probably as much astonished at the result as any of his colleagues in the convention.

The campaign which followed went the way of all campaigns. It was full of tumult and excitement, of noisy stump speaking and of cruel detraction, but the end came at last, and the long political storm subsided, when James Abram Garfield was, in November 1880, elected to the Presidency.

He who had chopped the farmwood and steered the canalboat, went from his quiet home at Mentor, Ohio, to take his place at the nation's helm. He was in the prime of his years, so young, indeed, that many a man who has won lasting fame, has, at Garfield's age, had all his lifework before him.

The inauguration took place amid the usual vast crowds, and with much heartfelt enthusiasm, which the character and history of the President inspired.

But, despite his brave, hopeful temperament, the new President did not underrate the difficulties and vast responsibilities before him. He frankly stated that, had he consulted his own likings, he would have better enjoyed being a "free-lance" in Congress.

The new occupant of the White House usually finds his first weeks there the most wearisome and harassing of his administration. Crowds of hungry office seekers consume his time and tax his strength, until he must ask his vexed soul whether this honor and high place are worth their price.

Garfield's experience, during the spring and early summer, was no exception to the rule. There is something pathetic in the exclamation wrung one day from his disgust and weariness: "I have been dealing all these years with ideas, and here I am dealing only with persons."

The morning of July 2, 1881 dawned upon a peaceful and prosperous nation. It found the President ready to lay aside his armor and take a short midsummer rest. That Saturday morning must have seemed, in a large sense, the crown and completion of his life. No other morning amid all his days of achievement and success could have held for him all that this one did. With his sensitive imagination he must have felt what the hour symbolized for him, as, standing on the White House piazza, he looked on its wide bloom and dazzling loveliness. He was on the eve of leaving for a few days the scene of his great triumphs and of his harassing labors and anxieties.

The President was on the point of joining his wife, who had been sent to the quiet and cool air of Long Branch. He was to spend the national holiday at Williams College, amid old, delightful memories and associations.

Beyond the visit to Williams spread the prospect of a restful trip with his convalescent wife on the coast, and among the mountains of northern New England. All this must have been in the heart and thoughts of the man who drove from the White House to the railroad station in the bright air of that July morning.

But, while walking through the station with James G. Blaine, a bullet from the gun of Charles J. Guiteau, a disappointed office seeker, struck him down.

Before noon the nation was stunned with tidings of the tragedy, and its shadow darkened all the land that was getting ready for its holiday.

The bullet did its work surely, but not swiftly, as in Abraham Lincoln's case. Long months of anguish followed for the sufferer. The wound, in the end, proved fatal and James Garfield died on September 19, 1881.

CHESTER ALAN ARTHUR

In September 1881 amid the mourning of the nation, Chester Alan Arthur became President of the United States. The land was darkened with the shadow of the tragedy which had placed him at the nation's helm, and any joyful inaugural ceremonies would have been singularly out of place.

Mr. Arthur took his oath of office under circumstances which could not fail to be trying to a man of sensitive feelings; he was well aware that the nation had accepted him perfunctorily as its Chief Magistrate, that he was regarded with doubt and coldness by the majority of his own party; he must have had a keen consciousness that his presence at the White House could not fail to be a bitter reminder of one so greatly loved and mourned, who had left it vacant.

It should always be borne in mind that our twenty-first President was acutely conscious of the deep cloud under which he entered upon his office. It was inevitable that he should be the object of more adverse criticism than usually falls to the lot of an incoming President.

The precedents in this case were not encouraging. The three Vice-Presidents who had succeeded to the executive chair on the death of the people's first choice, had made on the whole a disappointing record in Presidential history. This fact was sure to be recalled to the disadvantage of the present one.

The character, the personal and political aims of the man who had succeeded James Garfield, became suddenly a matter of immense anxiety to the nation. It was evident that the time which was thoroughly to test his quality had now come.

Chester Alan Arthur became President just before he reached his fifty-first birthday; he was born in Fairfield, Franklin County, Vermont on October 27, 1830. He was the son of a Baptist clergyman, who, in his early youth, emigrated from Ireland, and who was a man of strong feelings, decided theological convictions, and ardent devotion to his studies; he had various country pastorates, and with his large family and slender clerical income, must have found it a struggle to make both ends meet. Chester was the eldest son, and rigid economies were, of course, the habit of the household. But the clergyman was bent on giving his son an education which would equip him for the battle of life. Chester's boyhood had the great advantage of his father's library and his father's training.

He came up a bright, impulsive, active boy, and early showed his strong, domestic attachments and his frolicsome temper. When it came in his way to earn a little money, he did farm work, or any other odd job to which a strong, vigorous boy could set his hand; he must have inherited the parental aptitudes for study, for at fourteen he entered Union College; his social disposition and his youth interfered a good deal with his love of study; he was foremost in sports and adventures, especially if they had a spice of danger; he enjoyed to the full all the class games and fun, and liked torchlight processions, and to take his part in parades.

He graduated with an average record, and at once set about teaching school, which he tried for two years in his native state. Then, having saved a few hundred dollars, he went to New York, where he promptly set about preparing himself for admission to the bar. At this time he had large dreams of establishing himself in the West and winning fame and fortune in his profession; he at last made a trip there with a young friend and brother lawyer, Henry S. Gardner; but once on the ground, there appeared no prospect of immediate and striking success. The two, probably a little sadder and wiser, but by no means disheartened, returned to New York. They established a partnership and fortune smiled on them. The young firm entered on an extensive and lucrative practice. For the next ten years young Arthur devoted himself to his profession, and he reaped large rewards of distinction and fortune. The first partnership lasted for four years; then Arthur practiced alone for five, and afterward formed a brief second partnership. He became early interested in antislavery measures; his generous young soul was fired with indignation at the recital of William Lloyd Garrison's persecutions in Boston. Chester Arthur was thrown much among abolitionist influences, and became a strong defender of the colored people; his arguments in the famous Lemon slave case won him much honor, and he succeeded in securing the right of the colored race to ride in the New York streetcars.

No doubt his antislavery sympathies gave a complexion to his political career.

In 1855 young Arthur became judge advocate of a brigade of

New York militia; he was afterward appointed chief engineer on Governor Morgan's staff, and two years later he was inspector general of the State. These were high honors for a young man who had not yet reached his thirtieth birthday.

When the war broke out, and the great problem of supplies for the New York troops had to be solved, Arthur was appointed brigadier general; he served in this department for six months. When Governor Morgan was followed by Governor Seymour, Arthur's management won the highest praise from the officer who took his place.

In 1871 General Arthur, who had returned to his lucrative law practice, was appointed by President Grant, Collector of the Port of New York—he occupied this high office for four years and was nominated and re-appointed the same day. The matter was not referred to a committee. This was a marked courtesy. It had hitherto been shown only to Senators.

Presient Hayes at last resolved to remove Arthur from his post, but offered him a foreign appointment. The Collector declined to resign. No charge could be brought against him, except "his active participation in politics": he was known to be in strong sympathy with the Grant or "third term wing of the Republican party."

But the closest investigations failed to show a flaw in the Collector's integrity, and the President asserted his entire belief in General Arthur's official honesty.

General Arthur was a delegate at large to the Republican National Convention which met in Chicago in 1880. He ardently supported General Grant's nomination; but when, after the long, fierce controversy, the choice was declared for Garfield, Arthur was, by acclamation, nominated for the Vice-Presidency.

It is impossible to enter here on the strife over the New York appointments which followed the election of Garfield and Arthur, and which shook the Republican party to its center.

As the prospect of the President's recovery grew fainter, men's thoughts turned to Chester A. Arthur. It was well known to which side his political traditions and friendships had inclined him.

But during those trying months while the President lay fluctuating between life and death, Chester Arthur carried himself with a dignity and propriety which afforded no grounds for criticism.

From that time the partisan was lost in the President. His inaugural surprised the people by its temperate, reassuring tone, and he soon proved his determination to administer his high office in the interests of no faction. By his course he estranged some of his political friends, but "he had the noble consciousness that he had largely succeeded in healing the dissensions of his party."

Such an administration could not, of course, be a brilliant, aggressive one. But this latter would have been the worst possible for the nation. The country needed a period of calm, of assured quiet, to recover from the long strain and excitement through which it had passed.

To President Arthur's great honor it must be said that, during his three and a half years of administration, he gave his country what she most needed. Had he displayed a different temper; had he allowed his personal ambitions, his private partialities or resentments to dominate him; had he been bent on establishing his own policy and pursuing a strong, independent course, he might have plunged the nation, in its sensitive and excited mood, into political discussions and contests out of which vast evil would have flowed.

But the crisis brought out the nobler qualities of the man and the patriot; he himself never forgot that he was not the first choice of the nation, though he in the end earned its respect and its admiration. For the first time a Vice-President, called to the higher office, closed his administration amid the favor and confidence of the party which had elected him.

President Arthur's person was tall and well proportioned; he had a handsome, intelligent face and a distinguished presence. In character he was affable and genial; his affections were strong, and he was much beloved by his friends.

All his official intercourse was marked by unvarying courtesy, and he was the dignified and gracious master of the White House.

When Chester Arthur was about twenty-two he had married the daughter of Commodore Herndon, whose bravery was attested by the gold medal which Congress awarded his widow.

When President Arthur retired from the Presidency, and returned to New York, he was still in the prime of his life, and there was every reason to suppose that many years lay before him. But in the following year he had a severe attack of illness, and though he rallied for awhile, his recovery proved only transient.

His death was a surprise to his friends and to the country he had served so well. He died in New York City on November 18, 1886.

GROVER CLEVELAND

In the autumn of 1855 a young man entered a Buffalo law firm as clerk and copyist. He received the very small salary of four dollars a week for his services; his name was Grover Cleveland.

The young law student, who was now making a brave struggle for admission to the bar, had been born in Caldwell, New Jersey, March 18, 1837. His father was a Presbyterian clergyman whose English ancestry had settled in New England in its early colonial history. The mother was the daughter of a Baltimore merchant who came of Irish stock. Grover was named after the clergyman who had preceded his father at Caldwell.

When the boy was four the pastorate was changed for another at Fayetteville. Here he went to the academy and laid the foundations for his education. Afterward the family removed to Clinton, Oneida County, New York, where he resumed his studies at another academy.

With his resolute, sturdy nature, the Presbyterian parson's son was certain to set himself early and square at the battle of life, and it was almost a matter of course, that the household means of a country minister would be very limited. Grover, with his sensible, practical temperament, must have looked the facts early and courageously in the face, and resolved on having a hard battle with fate. At seventeen he was in New York City as clerk and assistant teacher in an institution for the blind. His elder brother, like the father, a Presbyterian clergyman, was teaching at the same place, and had, no doubt, secured a position for the younger.

He did not occupy it long. In 1855 he resolved to go to the West and make his place there; he went as far as Buffalo where his destiny was to keep him; he assisted an uncle in some literary work, and then entered a law office and set about studying Blackstone.

In 1859 Grover Cleveland was admitted to the bar; he remained for three years with the firm with which he had begun his legal studies. Afterward he became a member of several other law firms in the city.

By this time the father had died, and the widow and her family were left in those straitened circumstances which are so often the fate of clergymen's families.

Fortunately for this one there was a brother with a strong brain and a generous hand to come to its aid.

In the autumn of 1881 Grover Cleveland was nominated and elected mayor of Buffalo.

After his election he became known as the "Veto Mayor." It was certainly to his honor that he "used his prerogative fearlessly in checking useless and extravagant expenditures." The appropriations for the celebration of the Fourth of July were curtailed that the money might be more wisely expended on Decoration Day.

In the Democratic Convention at Syracuse the Buffalo mayor was nominated for the governorship of New York, and duly elected.

In this position he promptly showed his dislike of official parade and ceremony. He avowed, in his clear, terse style, his purpose "to serve the people faithfully and well."

He afforded an unprecedented spectacle in Albany when he went on foot through its streets to the capitol, accompanied only by a friend, to take his oath of office. As far as possible, he dispensed with official forms and ceremonials. "The Governor of the State lived simply, keeping no carriage, and walking daily from his house to the scene of his duties."

The "Veto Mayor" proved an honest governor. His opponents might disapprove of many of his political measures, but nobody questioned his integrity.

In 1884 the Democratic National Convention at Chicago nominated Grover Cleveland for twenty-second President of the United States. The campaign which followed was one of great rancor and bitterness. The Republican Party, which had carried the country through the grief and glory of the most momentous quarter of a century in its history, was shaken by dissensions and antipathies, partly political and partly personal. It was also weakened by the separation and opposition of some of its most prominent and trusted leaders. In November Grover Cleveland was elected President of the United States.

His administration was marked by those forcible and independent qualities which distinguished him as mayor of Buffalo and governor of New York. It is characteristic of such a man that he should exercise his veto power more frequently than most of his predecessors.

Mr. Cleveland was a man of large, rather massive build, with a strong, resolute, intelligent face, and with a quiet, simple directness of speech and manner.

His sister, Miss Rose Elizabeth Cleveland, a lady of literary tastes, whose writings give evidence of mental grasp and earnest thought, became, after her brother's inaugural, the mistress of the White House.

On June 2, 1886 the President was married to Miss Frances Folsom. The young lady was the daughter of his intimate friend and former law partner.

In June 1888 the Democratic National Convention assembled at St. Louis and re-nominated President Cleveland to a second term of office.

The main issue between the two political parties was the ever recurring one of the tariff. The quiet and good temper with which the campaign was conducted formed an agreeable contrast to the excitement and acrimony of the preceding one.

The President was defeated, receiving 168 electoral votes to General Benjamin Harrison's 233. He was again nominated, however, in 1892 and in November of that year again elected. The chief issue in the election was the McKinley Tariff, and on this issue the Democrats not only won the Presidency, but the Senate and House of Representatives as well.

* * *

The first act of Mr. Cleveland, on his second election to the Presidency, was to withdraw from the Senate the proposed treaty with the Hawaiian government, made by his predecessor, General Harrison.

The Fourth of March 1893, when Mr. Cleveland again took the oath of office, found the country plunged into a deep business depression. The Democrats attributed the cause to the financial legislation of the Congress of 1890, and the Republicans to the "free trade" opinions of their opponents. The President called a special session of Congress and advised relief along financial lines. At the first session of the newly elected Democratic Congress, a bill, remodelling the McKinley Tariff Bill and doing away with its reciprocity features, was, after a long and heated discussion, passed by both Houses of Congress. The President was displeased with the bill as a whole, but allowed it to become a law without his signature.

In 1893 the differences between our government and that of Great Britain concerning the Alaskan seal fisheries were settled by arbitration. In December of the same year Utah was raised to statehood—making it the forty-fifth State.

Two years later, in 1895, the administration found itself face to face with Great Britain on a question which threatened a rupture of the friendly relation which had existed between the two countries since the war of 1812. For a long time the governments of Great Britain and Venezuela had been engaged in a diplomatic controversy regarding the true boundary line between the latter country and British Guiana—a territory belonging to the former. Venezuela desired that the question should be settled by arbitration. This Great Britain refused to do. A war between the two countries seemed imminent. But as the result of such a war would undoubtedly be the adding of a vast expanse of Venezuelan territory to England's present possessions, thereby violating in the opinion of the administration the Monroe doctrine, the United States found itself side by side with Venezuela in insisting that the dispute should be settled by a court of arbitration. After many months of correspondence, England yielded to the desire of the two countries, and peace through arbitration had won another victory.

The second administration of Mr. Cleveland was a troublesome one. The financial depression continued, the inadequacy of the new tariff to furnish sufficient revenue to carry on the government, a strike of great proportions at Chicago, which forced the administration to send troops to that city to protect the mails, and the growing desire of the West for the free coinage of silver, brought such enmity against the administration on the part of its former adherents in the South and West, that the Democratic party found itself in the summer of 1896 threatened with disruption.

The Republican Convention for the nomination of a successor to President Cleveland met at St. Louis, June 16, 1896. The Democratic Convention met at Chicago the July following. The Republican Convention, after adopting resolutions in favor of a protective tariff and the "single gold standard," nominated William McKinley of Ohio for President. The Democratic Convention was a house divided against itself. A very large number of the delegates from the east and middle west refrained from voting. These delegates were bitterly opposed to three of the planks of the platform that had been adopted.

These were the planks advocating (1) the free coinage of silver; (2) the curtailing of the authority of the general government in cases of riot and disorder, and (3) the limiting of the tenure of office of the judges of the Courts. These delegates did not bolt the Convention; but later, in September a Democratic Convention, composed of delegates in sympathy with them, met at Indianapolis and placed in nomination General John McCauley Palmer of Illinois. The Chicago Convention had previously nominated William J. Bryan of Nebraska.

After an unusually spirited campaign, the Republicans elected their candidates. Major McKinley receiving 272 electoral votes to his opponent's 175.

Grover Cleveland left the White House a politically solitary figure but he commanded the respect and admiration of all. He became a trustee of Princeton University and was a dominant figure in the business life of his day. He died at the age of seventy-one at his home at Princeton, N. J. on June 24, 1908.

BENJAMIN HARRISON

Benjamin Harrison was born at North Bend, in the old Harrison homestead, on August 20, 1833. North Bend was the estate, or, as his sturdy old grandfather would have called it, the "farm" of the Harrisons, which lay on the Ohio River, not far from Cincinnati.

Benjamin came of a stanch, patriotic breed. The Harrisons belonged to the old Virginia colonists, and a nimbus of the Revolution clung about the name. The boy at North Bend was christened after the great-grandfather who had set his name to the Declaration of Independence, and who served his country loyally in the colonial Congress during the Revolution, and as Governor of the young State of Virginia.

The grandfather, under whose roof Benjamin was born, became, a few years after the boy's birth, ninth President of the United States, so the Harrisons form the second instance within one century where the great office has been bestowed on members of the same family.

Benjamin's father, John Scott, loved his farm, "lying on the peninsula between the Ohio and Miami rivers, just five miles below North Bend, and touching at one point the Indiana boundary line," better than he did all the honors and high places of the world. He was twice sent to Congress, but the political arena was not suited to his temperament. He returned to his family and his farm. He belonged there. He will always stand a quiet, unpretentious figure between his famous father and his distinguished son.

Benjamin was the second boy of the household. His first school house was a log cabin, a short distance from his own very simple home. His father, who could leave his boys no fortune, was resolved they should be started with a good education. When the log cabin went to pieces with age and the weather, private teachers were secured for the boys at home. Afterward Benjamin went for two years to an academy, Farmers' College, a few miles from Cincinnati.

After two years at Farmers' College, the boy entered Miami University. He was, at this time, a slight-framed, rather undersized youth, a little grave and serious, one imagines, for his years. He showed a decidedly studious bent and made the most of his advantages; he was fond, too, we learn, of all the rude, outdoor games of the time and the place.

Young Harrison made a fine record at Miami University and graduated at eighteen, "taking the fourth honors of his class."

The boy reared on the Ohio farm had now to face life for himself. Things had gone from bad to worse with the estate which his father had inherited, and stripped of everything else, the owner was barely able, through the interposition of relatives, to retain possession of his farm.

He was barely twenty, his studies were not yet completed, when he took to wife Miss Caroline W. Scott, the daughter of the president of an academy, which "stood in a town overlooked by Miami University."

The bright, intelligent, attractive girl had won the heart of the young student. That early marriage must have seemed a very imprudent step to their older and wiser friends. The young husband had no fortune, no assured means of support.

Young Harrison completed his studies and resolved to enter the Indianapolis bar. It seemed a godsend that he had inherited a few hundred dollars from an aunt, but the sum was too small "to admit of his renting a house, or even an office." He had no influential friends in that young Western city, where the grandson of the President resolved to make his brave struggle with fortune.

The struggle, for the first years, must have taxed every energy and strained every fiber. Alluding to that hard time long after it was over, Benjamin Harrison has said, "A five dollar bill was an event."

Times brightened slowly but steadily. After the birth of the first son the young people went into housekeeping. The home—a one-story house, with three rooms—was the humblest imaginable.

In due time a law partnership opened to young Harrison. His ability and integrity began to make their mark. In 1860 he was nominated by the Republican Convention for Reporter of the Supreme Court. He stumped the State, and his speeches—particularly one at Rockville, where he was opposed to Mr. Hendricks—gained him a lasting reputation. Harrison was at this time elected to his first political office.

From that time, the record of the Indianapolis lawyer is one of constantly ascending fortunes. He was not long in proving that he had chosen the profession for which nature had designed him.. His arguments were marked by a clear, concise, vigorous style—a style which could on occasion rise into passionate indignation or into earnest eloquence.

Benjamin Harrison was not twenty-eight years old when the Rebellion broke out. In that spring of 1861 he had won his place at the bar, and the future must have stretched ample and promising before him. In 1862, when the times were gloomiest, and the Northern cause had reached its nadir, Benjamin Harrison made up his mind that his country had a supreme claim on him, and resolved to go to the war.

With characteristic promptness he set about drilling and recruiting a company. In a little while other companies joined it. Harrison was commissioned Colonel of the 70th Regiment Indiana Volunteers. He marched with his men to Bowling Green. He remained with his regiment until it was mustered out at the close of the war.

His men called their valiant, small-framed leader, "Little Ben."

When the war closed General Harrison—he had been promoted to the rank of brevet brigadier general—returned to Indianapolis. He now resumed his law practice. He had, however, won his first political honors before he went to the field, and in 1864 he was re-elected to the office of Reporter of the Supreme Court.

Three years afterward he declined a third nomination, as his official duties interfered seriously with his professional work. But his experience during the war had, no doubt, intensified his Republicanism, for he took a prominent part in both the Grant campaigns, and at that time addressed frequent and large audiences throughout the State.

In 1876 he absolutely declined the nomination for Governor of Indiana. But the times were critical. The Republicans regarded it vastly important to carry the State for their Presidential candidate, Rutherford B. Hayes. A great pressure was brought to bear on General Harrison, and he was at last forced to accept the nomination. The Democrats, however, won the election.

In the famous National Convention of 1880, at Chicago, General Harrison's name was suggested for nomination to the Presidency, but he positively declined to enter the lists and threw all his influence into General Garfield's scale.

Honors and fame now fell rapidly to General Harrison. He was offered a seat in the Garfield Cabinet, but declined that, because he had, after the Presidential election, been unanimously chosen to the United States Senate, where he served his country for the next six years with conspicuous ability.

In 1884 his claims to the Presidential office were again discussed. The National Republican Convention, which met in Chicago on June 19th, 1888, nominated General Harrison for the Presidency. He was, after a campaign conducted on both sides with a quiet and good taste in marked contrast to the stormy ones which had preceded it, elected in the following November.

On the 4th of March 1889 General Harrison took the same sacred oath of office which his grandfather took forty-eight years before. His administration saw six new States admitted to the Union. They were North Dakota, South Dakota, Wyoming, Montana, Idaho and Washington. In the Winter of 1889–90, at the instance of James G. Blaine, Secretary of State, an invitation was extended to Haiti and the South American governments to meet representatives of the United States at Washington to consider questions regarding trade and commerce between these countries. It was called the Pan-American Congress.

Legislation during General Harrison's administration was principally along currency and tariff lines. The McKinley Tariff was passed in 1890.

This increased import duties on some commodities and abolished them on others and was largely effected by the signing of reciprocal trade treaties with other countries. These treaties permitted importations to come in at low tariff rates provided our exports would be similarly accepted overseas.

In January 1893 a commission arrived from the Hawaiian Islands to ask for annexation to the United States. President Harrison favored this move and sent a treaty to effect it to the Senate a few days before the termination of his term of office.

Grover Cleveland defeated Benjamin Harrison for re-election in 1893, whereupon Harrison retired to his home in Indianapolis. He was soon called from his retirement, however, to serve as chief counsel at Venezuela in the settlement of a boundary dispute. He was also a delegate to the peace conference at The Hague in 1899. Returning to Indianapolis, he died on March 13, 1901 at the age of sixty-eight.

WILLIAM McKINLEY

IN THE town of Niles, Ohio, in a small, two-story house, was born on January 29, 1843, William McKinley, the twenty-fourth President of the United States. In his veins ran mingled the blood of the Puritan and the Scotch coventer. Industrious, pious, not liberally endowed with this world's goods were his parents, but yet for the education of their children they were ready to make any sacrifice. It was this self-denial that forced the father and mother to move to Poland, a town in the southwestern part of the Western Reserve, when William was but a child; for there was an academy in which the ambitious parents could educate their children.

The boy, William, was not a prodigy, neither was he an "impenetrable dunce." He was simply a boy of gentle manners, industrious, working during his vacation to relieve his father of the burden of his tuition and maintenance. At the age of sixteen he was a member of the Methodist church and at seventeen was attending a college at Meadville, Pa. Unfortunately illness forced him to leave the college, and before he was able to return, the war clouds that were hovering over the country during the winter of 1860 and '61 broke. In June this lad of eighteen years, then "pale faced, slender, scarcely medium height," left books and home to die if need be that his country might live. The company, in which he was a private, was joined to the Twenty-third Ohio regiment, of which W. S. Rosecrans was the first colonel. This regiment was principally engaged in western Virginia, and it remained in the field to the end of the war. It was a fighting regiment, and the lad remained with it to the end, rising from a private to the position of a major. He was mustered out of the service on July 26, 1865.

The boy returned to his home a man, but a poor man. Eager to be at work, he entered the office of Judge Charles E. Glidden, a prominent attorney, and began the study of law. His father could help him very little, and, although he was sometimes tempted, because of his straitened circumstances, to abandon the law and enter upon business pursuits, he kept on with dogged persistency, studying and reading day and night, until after two years of great labor, he was admitted to the bar—"a lawyer without a brief." After a little delay, he concluded to settle in Canton, a town of some 5,000 inhabitants. Major McKinley, as he was known then and afterwards, pushed himself to the front, not only in the affairs of the town, but the county. Three years after this he was elected prosecuting attorney for the county. In 1876 he was elected to Congress by a majority of over 3,000. Among those who entered Congress at the same time was Thomas B. Reed, of Maine. It was in 1888 that the House of Representatives was elected which passed the McKinley Tariff Bill. Major McKinley was then Chairman of the Committee on Ways and Means. In 1892, however, the people elected a Democratic President, and the Senate and House were also Democratic. Major McKinley had been elected Governor of Ohio the previous year by a plurality of 21,000 votes; and two years afterward he was again elected by a plurality of nearly four times that number.

It was while Governor of Ohio that an event occurred by which McKinley's reputation as an honorable gentleman was greatly enhanced. He had succeeded in accumulating a modest fortune by means of his business, but this was entirely swept away by the failure of a friend whose notes had been endorsed by him, but who had manipulated those notes in an unjustifiable manner. Although the debts that thus fell upon him far exceeded his modest savings, he insisted upon paying them to the last penny.

In 1871 McKinley had married Miss Ida Saxton of Canton, and his wife now courageously offered her private fortune to her husband's creditors. This was eventually deeded back to her, but the Governor of Ohio had now the respect of the whole country by his action at this crisis.

As early as 1880 McKinley's name had been mentioned in connection with the Presidency, but he had refused for various reasons to become a candidate. In 1896, however, the issue turned on the tariff, and McKinley's prominence in Congress as an expert on tariff measures made him the natural choice of the Republican Party. A spirited campaign followed, but it was carried out on novel lines, for McKinley, instead of canvassing the country in person, remained quietly in his own home. His front porch was converted into a rostrum, and here he received delegations of voters and delivered a series of addresses which stamped him as master of the political situation.

The election proved a triumph for the Republican Party and Protection, and the new President was inaugurated in 1897. His first act was to call an extra session of Congress to revise the Wilson Tariff Law under which the country had been suffering serious business difficulties. The result of this session's work was the Dingley Tariff, which was passed with a notable absence of scandal, and under which, whether for this reason or not, the business prosperity of the country revived.

For some time past, this country had been watching with interest the relations between Spain and her Cuban dependencies. The Cubans had for a long time been engaged in fruitless efforts to shake off the oppressive rule of Spain, and the Spanish methods of warfare in the island had excited the indignation of all observers. The President made some fruitless efforts in the early part of 1897 to secure a settlement of the difficulties, but he advocated a strict neutrality on the part of this country.

Events soon occurred, however, that made neutrality very difficult. Sympathy for the oppressed and starving Cubans had been growing steadily, when on February 15, 1898, news reached the United States which acted like a spark upon powder. The United States battleship *Maine* was lying in Havana harbor on a mission of good will and courtesy. On February 15 the ship was entirely destroyed by a submarine mine. The public was naturally excited by such a suspicious accident, but the President acted with all possible moderation. A naval board of inquiry was instituted, which declared that the catastrophe was caused by a mine, but could obtain no evidence for fixing the responsibility.

It was evident, however, that the relations between Spain and this country could no longer continue on a friendly footing and Congress voted an appropriation of fifty million dollars for national defense. McKinley still hoped for a peaceful settlement with Spain, and made various proposals to Spain for the relief of Cuba. Not until all negotiations had proved useless did the President recommend more active measures, and on April 25, Congress declared war.

Volunteers were at once called for, coast defenses provided from Maine to Texas, and troops shipped to Cuba. The first notable event of the war was the capture of Manila by the Pacific squadron under Admiral Dewey. This fleet, while at Hong Kong, had received orders to capture the Spanish fleet then assembled at Manila. On the 18th of May the American fleet reached the Philippine Islands and completely wrecked the Spanish ships after a few hours' engagement.

This victory greatly encouraged the troops in Cuba, especially since it had been attained without loss of life. A powerful Spanish squadron under Admiral Cevera had assembled in the harbor of Santiago de Cuba. It was necessary to attack this point both by land and sea. The entrance to the harbor was blocked by the sinking of the *Merrimac* by Lieutenant Hobson and a brave band of men who escaped death only by a miracle, and troops were landed at Baiguiri, fifteen miles east of Santiago. These advanced rapidly, and after a severe battle, the outworks of Santiago were taken. On the 2d of July, El Caney and San Juan were taken after a hard struggle, and the city was occupied.

The following day the decisive battle of the war took place. The Spanish fleet attempted to leave the harbor secretly. Its movements, however, were quickly detected and met by the American ships. In less than three hours every Spanish ship had been destroyed or driven ashore, and the Admiral and thirteen hundred men taken prisoners. Only one American was killed and one seriously wounded.

On the 17th of July, Santiago capitulated and the war was virtually at an end. The island of Puerto Rico was occupied with little difficulty, and Manila surrendered after a long siege on August 15. After an absence of only two months, the land troops were recalled to the United States, and the Spanish government made overtures of peace. A protocol was agreed upon by which all hostilities were suspended and peace commissioners were chosen to draw up a treaty.

They met in Paris on October 1, and by the terms agreed upon Cuba, Puerto Rico and the other Spanish islands in the West Indies, as well as the Philippines, became possessions of the United States.

No act in McKinley's administration created so much opposition as the annexation of the Philippines, which were in a state of insurrection, and could only be made peaceful and prosperous at a great expense of money and possibly life.

The people, however, showed their approval of this policy of territorial expansion two years later at the polls.

The last two years of the administration were occupied chiefly with affairs in China and this country won much prestige among the allied powers by its moderation and firmness. By the President's efforts, also, the right to build and control the Panama Canal was secured for the American people, and is a brilliant example of his diplomatic skill.

The readjustment of our trade relations with our new dependencies was a question that pressed for solution. President McKinley favored a liberal system of reciprocity not only with these colonies but with other nations. He was still occupied with such questions when his term of office closed. The people showed their confidence in his ability and their approval of the unlooked-for events of the past four years by emphatically calling McKinley to a second term. He himself took no part in the election, but remained quietly at Washington, doing his work as if nothing were happening.

He was inaugurated for the second time on March 4, 1901 and soon after made an extensive journey through the South and West. Indeed, it is said that he was known to more of his countrymen by actual sight and hearing than any other President of the United States in his day and generation.

This was the year of the Pan-American Exposition at Buffalo. President's Day had been appointed for September 5 and Mr. and Mrs. McKinley had accepted an invitation to be present.

On the following day, September 6, the President held a reception in the Temple of Music at four o'clock. Here a great crowd of people had gathered to shake hands with him, and the people had just begun to file in front of the platform where the President stood when two shots rang out and he fell back into the arms of those who stood about him. In an instant twenty men had sprung for the assassin, Leon Czolgosz, whose weapon had been concealed beneath a bandage bound about his hand, and he would have been killed by the crowd if McKinley had not interfered by exclaiming, "Let no one hurt him." The man subsequently proved to be an anarchist.

The wounded President was carried to the house of Mr. Milburn, president of the Exposition, and everything was done for him that science could suggest. For a few days his condition was hopeful. His great personal courage and the natural strength of his constitution made the chances of recovery in his favor. A sudden change for the worse, however, occurred, and on Saturday morning September 14, 1901, the President quietly died.

THEODORE ROOSEVELT

WHEN William McKinley lay dying at Buffalo, the Vice-President, Theodore Roosevelt, was vacationing in the Adirondacks for the summer. When the change for the worse occurred, he was summoned in haste to Buffalo, but before he could reach the city, his Chief was dead. There was a hurried cabinet meeting and it was decided that Roosevelt must take the oath of office at once. They met in the parlor of the Wilcox house, and here, the new President repeated the solemn oath: "I do solemnly swear that I will faithfully execute the office of the President of the United States, and will, to the best of my ability, preserve, protect and defend the Constitution of the United States."

The man thus suddenly thrust into the highest office of the nation was, at that time, the youngest President who ever presided in the White House. He was born in New York City on October 27, 1858, of a Dutch family whose members long were prominent citizens of New York. He was not strong as a boy and most of his early life was spent in the country where he gained that love of outdoor life and exercise which was one of his distinguishing traits.

After a successful career in Harvard College, where he became a member of Phi Beta Kappa and an editor of the *Advocate,* he spent a year in foreign study and travel. On his return to New York he began the study of law, but the field of politics soon attracted him. His charm of manner soon won him many friends, and at the age of twenty-three he became a member of the New York Assembly. Here his fearless attacks on the corrupt methods of city government in New York City soon made him well known outside of his own State and opened the way to the famous Lexow-Parkhurst investigation.

In 1881 Mr. Roosevelt married Miss Alice Lee of Boston, who died three years later, leaving him one little girl. Soon after, he lost both his parents in one week, and these heavy sorrows, added to his strenuous political life, for a time broke down his health and made rest necessary.

His way of taking a rest was very characteristic. He built a log house on the desolate reaches of the Western plains, took a rifle, bought a herd of cattle, hired several cowboys to care for them, and set about recuperating his broken health.

Such rigorous treatment soon restored his health and in 1886 he returned to civilization once more. Again in New York, he soon distinguished himself in a contest on the Mayoralty and was appointed National Civil Service Commissioner. While in this post he succeeded in increasing the number of positions on the civil service list from 1400 to 40,000. During this same year Roosevelt married Miss Edith Kermit Carow in London, England.

When Mayor Strong, the reform candidate, was elected, Roosevelt, somewhat to his friends' surprise, accepted the position of Police Commissioner of New York City, attracted to the office by the opportunity which it offered for improving the efficiency of the police force.

From this post he was called to that of Assistant Secretary of the Navy in 1897, a position in which he brought about great improvements in the efficiency of the navy which, he insisted, "must be ready for war at all times."

When the Spanish-American War was declared, Roosevelt became lieutenant colonel of a cavalry regiment and embarked for Cuba. Here his regiment, the Rough Riders, distinguished themselves in the battle of San Juan Hill, and Roosevelt himself led the famous charge up the hill, which led to the capture of the town of Santiago.

On his return, Colonel Roosevelt was received with great enthusiasm, and immediately elected Governor of his State. During his term of office he proved himself an efficient and absolutely fearless executive, and so won the admiration and confidence of the people that he was placed on the Republican ticket as Vice-President when McKinley was nominated for a second term.

Destiny seemed to have marked him for higher things, however, for he had hardly entered upon his new office when he was called to the White House on September 14, 1901. He was re-elected in 1904, the first Vice-President to be so chosen. His administrations were characterized by his sweeping reforms which included his successful opposition to gigantic mergers of monied interests, passage of the Interstate Commerce Act, the Pure Food Laws, establishment of the Department of Commerce and other far-reaching measures. In addition, he commenced the building of the Panama Canal, effected a peace between Russia and Japan and was awarded the Nobel Peace Prize in 1906.

At the end of his second term Roosevelt found himself able to fulfill one of his fondest dreams. Within two weeks after leaving the White House he was off on a big game expedition to Africa which lasted almost a year. His return to America followed a triumphal tour of Egypt, Europe and England.

If Roosevelt's European tour seemed to imitate Grant's, then Roosevelt's supporters sought also to copy the friends of the Civil War General. His name was submitted in nomination for a third Presidential term but, again, like Grant, he was defeated. The newly formed Progressive Party, however, nominated him in 1912 but he was defeated by William Howard Taft.

He retired from public life only to emerge again to run against Taft for the Presidency. This split the Republican ticket and Woodrow Wilson, a Democrat, was elected.

With the start of the first World War, he offered to organize a regiment for active duty overseas but the government could not accept his offer, and he devoted himself instead to writing and speaking for the Allied cause until his death at his home at Oyster Bay, N. Y., on January 6, 1919.

WILLIAM HOWARD TAFT

THE twenty-seventh President of the United States was born in Cincinnati, Ohio on September 15, 1857. His father, Alphonso Taft, was a wealthy lawyer who had served as Secretary of War in President Grant's cabinet and was later appointed Attorney General during the same administration. When Chester Alan Arthur succeeded Grant in the Presidency, he sent the elder Taft to Austria and later to Russia as this country's Minister.

William Taft graduated in 1878 from Yale University where he distinguished himself on the athletic field as well as in the classroom. Two years later he graduated from the Cincinnati Law School and was admitted to the bar in the same year. He did not, however, begin the practice of law immediately but became a law reporter for the Cincinnati newspapers. This training was invaluable for it enabled him to learn much concerning human nature in relation to the law.

Amiable and jovial, young Taft was liked by everyone and the end of his first year as law reporter saw him, at the age of twenty-four, elected to the office of assistant prosecuting attorney of Hamilton County, Ohio. But he had been at his new task scarcely a year when he was appointed collector of internal revenue. Although his new position paid him far more than he could hope to make, at first, in private practice, he was so discontented that he resigned his post and returned to Cincinnati where he began the practice of law in partnership with one of his father's former associates.

At that time the law courts of Cincinnati were foully corrupt. Taft had had an inkling of this as a law reporter. He was twenty-six years old when he began his investigation of corrupt legal practices and, with his characteristic vigor and thoroughness, he soon exposed the evils that had made law and order in Cincinnati a mockery, and was largely instrumental in instituting sweeping and lasting reforms. Four years later William Taft was appointed judge of his city's Superior Court.

From then on his rise was rapid. When he was only thirty-three years of age, President Harrison gave him the post of solicitor general of the United States and two years later he became judge of the United States Sixth Circuit Court, at the same time becoming professor and Dean of the law department of the University of Cincinnati.

In 1886 he married Helen Herron, daughter of a Cincinnati judge who had been a law partner of Rutherford B. Hayes. Herself a musician, she founded the Cincinnati Orchestra and later, as mistress of the White House, the soothing strains of her music must have eased the troubled soul of her husband during those trying days when he fought so desperately against petty factionalism in his administration. Of their three children, Robert and Charles were lawyers, and the daughter Helen, who married professor F. J. Manning of Bryn Mawr College, was Acting President of that institution.

In the meantime the United States which had itself been a colonial possession, now found itself with colonies of its own. At the end of the war in Cuba, Spain had ceded the Philippine Islands to the United States. The greater majority of the natives were half savage, diseased and badly frightened. Torn by internal rebellion, bewildered and confused at the sight of the stars and stripes replacing the old Spanish flag, the entire population of the islands was in the wildest state of disorder imaginable.

A steady hand, a kind heart, and a keen mind was needed to bring order out of this chaos and so in 1901 President McKinley appointed William Howard Taft as first governor of the Philippine Islands.

The great services he performed there are too well known to require repetition here. He established free schools, improved the sanitation, reducing the dreadful toll of disease, and introduced a system of postal savings banks; he also set up the first real courts of justice the islands ever had. Then, to insure the permanence of his reforms, he selected and trained the most intelligent and responsible natives in all matters pertaining to modern government so that they could continue for themselves the work he had begun.

When Theodore Roosevelt assumed the Presidency of the United States following the death of McKinley, he called Taft home from the Philippines and made him Secretary of War. And so Taft went to Cuba to assume control of the government there. He had barely straightened matters out in the new republic when some difficulties arose over the construction of the Panama Canal. Again it was William Howard Taft who soon had matters going smoothly. In the midst of all this, the Japanese government became highly alarmed over the strong anti-Japanese feeling that had developed on the American Pacific coast. Once more William Howard Taft's calm judgment and scholarly statesmanship poured oil on troubled waters. He went to Japan and succeeded in allaying the fears of the Nipponese government.

By now the people of America knew what McKinley and Roosevelt had known long before; that William Howard Taft, quiet and efficient, was a man to be trusted.

The Republican Party nominated him for the Presidency at their convention in 1908 and on March 4, 1909 he took the oath of office. Factional politics, however, weakened his party support and much of the good he had hoped to accomplish was lost in political wrangling.

But a man of Taft's determined nature and deep insight into the needs of his country and the necessity for further helping the Philippines, was above party politics and disputes. Almost single-handed he compelled Congress to accept at least some of his measures, even though in the end he remained unsatisfied. Adoption of an annual budget for the United States, tariff reforms and other measures were suggested by him but were bogged down in the political factionalism of his administration, but many of them, like the budget, were so obviously necessary that they were later adopted. He enforced the Sherman Anti-trust Law, pushed railroad regulation through the Interstate Commerce Commission and recommended, among other things, the establishment of postal savings banks. His foreign policy, which was one of diplomacy and arbitration, was completely wrecked by Congress but nonetheless he lived to see his ideas and theories used with good effect as a basis for successful negotiations in succeeding administrations.

President Taft's impartial nature did not permit him to retain men in office whom he believed unfit for the task, or to appoint officeholders merely on a basis of political patronage. Such an attitude, sincere and honest though it was, did not help to heal the breach between his party and himself and when this policy disposed of some of Roosevelt's appointees, the friendship that had existed between the two men waned. As a result, the Republican Party split over the two men and while Taft was nominated by the Republicans and Roosevelt by the Progressive, or Bull Moose Party, both were defeated and Woodrow Wilson, a Democrat, was elected.

But Taft's public career was not yet done. He gave his wholehearted support to Wilson during the trying years of the World War and after.

In the meantime he became professor of law at Yale University and again began the practice of his profession. On June 30, 1921 the fondest dream of his life was realized when President Warren G. Harding appointed him Chief Justice of the United States Supreme Court. He continued to serve in that capacity, the highest honor ever to be bestowed on an ex-President, until February 3, 1930 when he became seriously ill at Asheville, North Carolina and resigned his post.

He never recovered from his illness and died in Washington, D. C. on March 8, 1930. So ended the career of the man whose kind heart and jovial good humor coupled with a deep-rooted sense of honesty and integrity, made him loved by all.

In 1940, Taft's eldest son, Robert Alphonso Taft, then a Senator from Ohio, sought the Republican nomination for President, but was defeated by Wendell L. Willkie, a lawyer and former utilities executive.

WOODROW WILSON

Thomas Woodrow Wilson was born at Staunton, Virginia on December 28, 1856. His father, Rev. Joseph R. Wilson, was a Presbyterian minister, and his mother, who was before her marriage Janet Woodrow, was the daughter of a Scottish-Presbyterian minister.

Young Wilson earned degrees from three institutions of higher learning before he started the practice of law. After his graduation from Princeton University in 1879, he continued his studies at the University of Virginia, from which he graduated in 1881 and then, in 1886, took his Ph.D. degree at Johns Hopkins University.

He entered upon the practice of his profession at Atlanta, Georgia and three years later married Ellen Axson. Mrs. Wilson died in 1914. A year later the President married Mrs. Edith Bolling Galt. She was his constant companion during the last five years of his administration, accompanying him to Versailles for the Peace Conference after the World War, and was his faithful and vigilant nurse during the long years of his ultimately fatal illness.

Although Woodrow Wilson had strong political ambitions, he did not enter active politics until thirty years after his graduation from Princeton. During those years he devoted his time and brilliant talents to scholarly pursuits, teaching history and political economy at Bryn Mawr College and later at Wesleyan University in Connecticut. He resigned the latter post in 1890 to become professor of jurisprudence and political economy at his old alma mater, Princeton, and in 1902 he was chosen President of that institution, an office he held until 1910 when he was elected governor of New Jersey. As Chief Executive of that State, he entirely revised and improved its public utility, labor, corporation and election laws, putting a successful end to widespread, corrupt practices.

So well did he perform his task and so cleverly did the quiet, brilliant scholar meet and match wits with the rough-and-tumble practical politicians, that in 1912 the Democratic Party nominated him for the Presidency of the United States.

Woodrow Wilson stepped into the White House more fully

equipped to assume the helm of government than perhaps any of his predecessors. He was a recognized and respected authority on the science of government and his years as president of Princeton and governor of New Jersey had given him invaluable practical experience. No man could have been better fitted for the role he was destined to play.

Wilson served two terms as President of the United States. The first administration under his energetic leadership saw more economic reforms than were ever put into effect in so short a time. To him goes credit, in a large measure, for the enactment of the Federal Reserve Act, conceded to be one of the greatest and most progressive legislative measures ever enacted. Other brilliant reforms and new measures followed among which were the Child Labor Law, creation of the Federal Trade Commission, and the purchase of the Danish West Indies, later re-named the Virgin Islands.

In the meantime the clouds of war hung heavy over Europe. England and France were at war with Germany and powerful interests were drawing the United States closer and closer to the battlefields of Europe. Wilson battled those forces successfully for two and one-half years and, in fact, was re-elected because of that effort. But he could hold out no longer and on April 2, 1917 he asked Congress to declare war against Germany. And so Woodrow Wilson, the quiet, mild-mannered, brilliant scholar who abhorred war, found himself in the distasteful role of man of destiny, commander in chief of over two million men whose duty it was to destroy their fellow humans.

Able statesman though he was, Wilson's knowledge of military matters was limited and he therefore agreed to the organization of a staff of trained military experts under the leadership of General John J. Pershing to decide all military questions.

Fully realizing all the horrors of modern warfare, with its attendant disease, famine and destruction, Wilson cast aside all party lines and selected the best men in their fields for important wartime posts. One of these men was Herbert Clark Hoover who became the most successful relief administrator the world has ever known.

With the timely intervention of the United States, Germany was soon vanquished and Wilson, the scholar and statesman, went to the Peace Conference at Versailles with the eyes of the entire world upon him. Here his famous fourteen points became the foundation on which the structure for an earnestly desired, permanent world peace was to be built. That that peace finally failed was not so much the fault of the former law professor who fought to bring a dream into being, as it was of the practiced diplomats and international politicians of the foreign powers who made the mistake of browbeating the conquered nation. And Wilson yielded step by step and point by point, all to bring into realization the one thing he hoped would insure lasting world peace. His fourteen points were accepted and their acceptance breathed the breath of life into his most cherished hope for world peace, the League of Nations.

His return to America from the conference tables of Versailles was greeted by a storm of controversy over the terms of the peace treaty and the entire question of the League. Despite stiff political opposition, Wilson fought determinedly and by agreeing to certain changes in the Covenant of the League of Nations, he finally won its acceptance from Congress. He returned to Paris to submit those changes for approval to the European powers and, in order to have them accepted, he had to agree to further changes made by them which subsequently were rejected by Congress.

By this time Congress was strongly Republican and despite anything Wilson could do, the United States never became a member of the League although most of the European and some of the South American and Asiatic countries did so.

Disappointed but determined, Wilson started to tour the country to appeal for popular support of the League of Nations but his health broke under the strain.

Despite the fact that his own country never became a member of the world-wide organization he created, he was awarded the Nobel Peace Prize in 1919.

Partly paralyzed by apoplexy, Wilson retired from public life at the close of his second term, a broken and heartsick man. He never again spoke publicly concerning his, for him, shattered dream, the League of Nations, nor did the Senate ever ratify the Treaty of Versailles.

Wilson lived secluded in Washington, D. C., a helpless invalid until his death on February 3, 1924. He was sixty-seven years old. Had he lived another ten years he would have seen the broken fragments of his dream crushed under the military heel of a vindictive Germany.

WARREN GAMALIEL HARDING

THE man who was to become the twenty-ninth President of the United States was born November 2, 1865 in the same little homestead cabin in which his father, Dr. George Harding, was also born.

When, in the eighteenth century, a hardy group of pioneers crossed the Alleghenies from Pennsylvania into Ohio, the Harding family formed no small part of that group. Warren Harding's grandfather led his little band to a place in Morrow County, Ohio where, near the settlement of Blooming Grove, he cleared his land and built the cabin in which his son and grandson were born.

The settlement of Blooming Grove later became known as the town of Corsica, Ohio, but it is the city of Marion, Ohio that is most closely identified with the early beginnings of Warren Harding. His father was a country doctor and when Warren was ten years old, his father transferred his practice to Marion, and Warren rode into town on the back of a mule.

Warren Harding's chief ambition was to be a newspaper editor and as his first step toward achieving that goal, he left Ohio Central College at the age of sixteen to accept a position as cub reporter and printer's apprentice on the Marion *Star*. Three years later he was editor of that paper and so marked was his success that by the time he was thirty-five he was its owner and publisher.

In 1900 with the backing of Senator Joseph B. Foraker he ran for, and was elected to, the Ohio Legislature where he served two terms. At the end of his second term in 1904, Myron T. Herrick was Republican candidate for Governor of Ohio with Warren G. Harding as his running mate. Herrick was elected and Harding became Lieutenant Governor of Ohio. Many years later Harding remembered his old friend and former chief by appointing him American Ambassador to France.

Defeated for the governorship in 1910, Harding for a time considered abandoning politics altogether, but in 1912 the lure of political controversy overcame him and he made the opening speech for Taft's renomination as President. In 1914 he proved the power and charm of his personality by running against and defeating his friend and former patron, Joseph Foraker, for the post of United States Senator without allowing the political battle to interfere in the slightest with their friendship.

Throughout his entire political career, Harding's constant companion and never failing source of inspiration was his wife. Florence Kling DeWolfe had been divorced from Henry DeWolfe and was the mother of Marshall DeWolfe when she met and married the twenty-six-year-old editor in 1891. She was thirty-one years old.

Warren Harding went to Washington as United States Senator from Ohio while the clouds of war were gathering over the country. From 1915 until his election to the Presidency in 1921, he served his country in the Senate by throwing the full weight of his support behind President Wilson's war policies, withdrawing it only after the war, in the matter of the League of Nations.

In the Senate he favored the Prohibition Amendment and the antistrike clause of the Cummings Railway Bill and while he never distinguished himself as an orator or a champion of any cause, his views and opinions were so well known and acceptable to his party that his name was placed in nomination at the Republican National Convention in Chicago in 1920 and he was nominated on the tenth ballot with Calvin Coolidge as his running mate.

Harding was not a nationally known figure. In fact, outside of the political circles in Ohio and at the nation's capital, he was practically unknown. But he had friends, powerful and influential men who saw to it that the Republican nominee became well known.

Harding himself borrowed a page from history and, like McKinley, conducted his campaign from the wide, cool porch of his home at Marion, Ohio. Promising, if elected, to return the country to its old peaceful and prosperous way of life, Harding was elected by an enormous majority and was inaugurated March 4, 1921. In his cabinet were Charles Evans Hughes as Secretary of State, Herbert Hoover as Secretary of Commerce and Andrew W. Mellon as Secretary of the Treasury. These men he selected for their known, high ability but, unlike Taft, and before him, like Andrew Jackson, other appointees were selected merely to pay off old political obligations.

Harding was the first President who came to the White House from the business life of the country. Confronted with almost complete national disorganization following the World War, he kept

Congress in session for almost two years in an effort to bring some order into being. Much of the legislation enacted during his administration staved off, for a time, the impending financial depression. The War Finance Corporation was revived, immigration restricted, and an emergency tariff law was put into effect. Taxes were sharply reduced, and the emergency tariff law was made permanent to protect the home markets.

In spite of all President Wilson's efforts, the Senate had never ratified the Treaty of Versailles, and so a separate peace, during Harding's administration, was signed between the United States and Germany. But Harding intended to do even more to fulfill his campaign promise of insuring world peace and so, at his invitation, representatives of most of the European powers met in Washington on Armistice Day, November 11, 1921, for the first International Conference on Armament Limitations. Although the conference produced nothing concrete, it established, for the time being at least, a feeling of good will.

But Harding's administration was not all smooth sailing. Like General Grant, he had been duped by those he had trusted. When the scandal broke, the blame fell on his shoulders. He was accused of having known of the dishonesty of his friends and was censured by the public for not taking measures against them. With his characteristic directness, Harding went to the people to plead his cause. He left Washington for the Pacific coast and Alaska, the first President to visit that possession. On his return he became ill at Vancouver, B. C., and was taken to San Francisco, where he died three days later on August 2, 1923 at the age of fifty-seven.

CALVIN COOLIDGE

In 1630 a hardy band of Puritans braved the long perils of an ocean voyage and set sail from England for the New World. Among them was John Coolidge and his wife Mary. They landed at the Puritan Colony of Massachusetts Bay and settled at Watertown, a tiny settlement that was later to become the city of Cambridge. With the restlessness of pioneers, the family of that early Puritan colonist pushed on through the wilderness, some of them finally settling, many years later, in Vermont. It was here in the little town of Plymouth on the day some of those ancestors had helped to make famous—July 4—that Calvin Coolidge, destined to become the thirtieth President of the United States, was born in 1872. His father, Colonel John Calvin Coolidge, was an unassuming farmer, proprietor of a country store, and the local Justice of the Peace.

True to their stern New England heritage, the Coolidge's were a laconic, unemotional, frugal people and Calvin, even in his youth, was no exception.

His boyhood was no different from that of any other of the thousands born and brought up in small country towns and his interests were the normal interests of a small boy. He helped on the farm, or in the store, as the occasion required, and in the winter attended the little stone schoolhouse where he learned to read and write and figure and remained as undistinguished in mastering these achievements as anyone else of his age who was learning the same things. But all was not work for the New England farm boy. Calvin had his normal share of fun along with the others. The simple pastimes of a country community, husking bees, county fairs and that event of events, the circus, all gave the young New Englander his share of enjoyment. And then there were the holidays. The New England farm must have been a perfect setting for the observance of the traditional Thanksgiving and Christmas and the Fourth of July had a double significance since it was not only the birthday of the nation but also of the boy who someday would grow up to be its Chief Executive.

When Calvin was thirteen years old he was sent, as his father and mother before him had been sent, to Black River Academy. The school was only twelve miles away from his home but twelve miles in a Vermont winter presented a serious transportation problem and so, when the roads were impassable, as they so often were, Calvin remained in town over the week end instead of risking the perilous trip home. With his characteristic New England thriftiness and credo of hard work, Calvin did not remain idle during those week ends. On Saturdays he found employment in the factories of the town, and his Sundays were spent as he had always been taught to spend them, in earnest study of the Bible.

From Black River Academy it was intended that young Calvin go directly to Amherst College but an illness intervened and he did not enter that institution until 1891. The first two years of college were hard ones indeed for the young New Englander and he despaired of ever completing his education. Dogged determination and an inherited capacity for hard work plus much encouragement from his father finally pulled young Coolidge through, and he graduated in 1891 with high honors. In addition he was Commencement Orator and also won a prize for his essay on the American Revolution.

After his graduation from Amherst, Coolidge chose the law as his profession. Although this meant leaving the farm and the store which his father had hoped to hand down to his son, the elder Coolidge offered no resistance to his son's plans, and Calvin went to Northampton, Massachusetts, where in a lawyer's office, he completed the required course of study in less than two years and was admitted to the bar in 1897. All during his student years, his father paid all of his son's expenses and it was characteristic of the son never to ask for one penny more than he absolutely needed and never, during all that time, did he once run into debt. Whatever money young Coolidge earned at odd jobs during the summer, was, at his father's insistence, put in the bank. And although John Coolidge stood ready to finance his son as long as need be, the young lawyer kindly but firmly refused further aid and at the age of twenty-five opened his own law office and prepared to support himself. This was easier said than done, but Calvin Coolidge was used to frugal living and he must have, in a way, enjoyed the uphill fight.

As his ancestors before him, including his own grandmother, had taken an interest in the politics of Plymouth, so did the rising young lawyer interest himself in the local politics of Northampton and two years after he began his law practice there, Coolidge was elected one of the town's councilmen. From that humble beginning Calvin Coolidge rose through a succession of city, county, and state offices to the highest office in the land.

In 1905 when he was clerk of courts, after having been city solicitor, he married Grace Goodhue who, like himself, was a native of Vermont. She was the daughter of Captain Andrew Goodhue who had been an active Democrat and steamboat inspector under President Cleveland. But romance knows little and cares less for party politics. After her graduation from the University of Vermont, Grace Goodhue taught at the Clarke School for the Deaf in Northampton and after her marriage to Calvin Coolidge, she made a home for the rapidly rising young politician in half of a two-family house in Northampton where they lived until Coolidge went to the White House. Of their two sons, Calvin Coolidge, Jr., who was born in 1908, died in the White House in July, 1924.

Coolidge's political rise, while not spectacular, was rapid. Frugal of words almost to the point of taciturnity, he was, nevertheless, universally liked and believed in letting his actions speak for him. That these actions were more than eloquent is attested to by the fact that without any waste of time, money or effort he not only built up a substantial law practice for himself, but in each of the political offices he held in the twenty years that saw him rise from city councilman to governor of Massachusetts, he discharged his duties honestly, faithfully and efficiently. No matter what position he held, he always effected savings of time, money and effort for the public good.

From the clerkship of the county courts, Coolidge went to the Massachusetts legislature and then returned to Northampton to serve as mayor for two terms. At the completion of those two terms he was sent to the State Senate where he served for three years as Speaker of that body, and then at the age of forty-four became lieutenant governor of Massachusetts for three terms.

In 1919 he was elected Governor of Massachusetts and stood on the threshold of one of the most momentous and important events of his career. In September of that year the police of Boston went out on strike, an almost unprecedented event, because the Police Commissioner refused to allow his men to become affiliated with the American Federation of Labor. Riots followed and disorder and confusion was rife. The Mayor of Boston ordered all near-by state guards into the city and called on Governor Coolidge for aid. Coolidge at once ordered three regiments of militia to Boston, with the result that a general strike appeared imminent. But Coolidge was not a man to be intimidated. He called out the entire military strength of the State and placed the city under martial law. What might have been an uprising with serious consequences was thus nipped in the bud and Coolidge fully supported the Police Commissioner in his refusal to reinstate those policemen who had gone out on strike. This caused a great hue and cry among those who believed themselves in sympathy with the strikers but Coolidge put an effective end to what his opponents might easily have advantageously developed into a sort of mass hysteria in favor of the ousted men by declaring that no one, anywhere at anytime, had the right to strike against and thus imperil, public safety.

His political advisors feared that Coolidge's firm stand and direct action in the matter of the police strike would offend organized labor and thus put an end, if not forever, for at least a good number of years, to his political career. With his characteristic calmness and detachment, Coolidge replied that it did not matter. He did his duty as he saw it and, right or wrong, was ready to take the consequences.

But far from injuring him politically, his action in the Boston police strike brought him into national prominence. The people liked and approved what he did. He was re-elected to the Governorship by a large majority.

By the time the Republican National Convention met in Chicago in 1920, Coolidge was well known and respected by his party and so, when Warren G. Harding was nominated for the Presidency, Coolidge easily won the Vice-Presidential nomination. With his unfailing loyalty and quiet determination, he supported the President and presided over the Senate without any thought or effort to use the influence of his position for any purpose or cause whatsoever. Quietly, faithfully and with fitting respect for the office he held, he served as Vice-President for two years until Harding's death in the summer of 1923 called him from his home in Vermont to the White House.

Coolidge had been spending the summer with his father when

the news came and it was his father who received the message early in the morning of August third. Informing his son of the great responsibility that had fallen to him, John Coolidge, by the light of a kerosene lamp in the little homestead cabin in Plymouth, Vermont, administered the oath of office to his son, making him the 30th President of the United States.

Without the slightest show of emotion, Coolidge dressed, said a brief prayer for guidance in his new office, sent a message of sympathy to Mrs. Harding and even took time to write a message of assurance to the nation. Then he went to Washington to take up his new duties. From August until December he maintained that silence that the nation was later to accept as part of him. Then he made his first speech. Without any show of oratory, without any high-sounding words, but in a simple, direct and straightforward manner, he told the nation what was in his mind, what he approved and what he disapproved. When he finished there was no doubt in anyone's mind that he meant to maintain the tariff, that he frowned on Government relief for the farmers and the soldiers' bonus, and that he stood for peaceful foreign co-operation and the World Court but without involving the United States in the League of Nations.

But his political surroundings in Washington were not of the best. Dissension in the Republican ranks grew greater and bills vetoed by Coolidge were passed over that veto, although he himself broke all precedent in the number of times he vetoed measures. The reverberations of the oil scandals that had broken during Harding's administration were still shaking the nation and for a time threatened to destroy the entire Republican Party and Coolidge's administration with it. With his native, unruffled calm and impartiality, Coolidge refused to listen to anyone or anything until he had all the facts. He therefore appointed a special body to investigate the matter thoroughly and then, when he had all the facts and evidence as presented by that body, he acted with the same force and directness that had brought him national recognition in the Boston police strike, and once and for all, he settled the matter of the Teapot Dome oil scandal.

So greatly did the public admire this silent and swift-acting New Englander that in spite of internal party strife, Congress could do nothing but obey the voice of the people and put aside their differences to support Coolidge. He was nominated for the Presidency and elected in 1924, the second of the six Vice-Presidents to receive that honor after having served the unexpired term of a deceased President. During his administration, a system of war reparations was instituted, the national debt was reduced by an estimated $750,000,000 annually, effective operation of the budget system was begun, and the famous and later disregarded Kellogg-Briand Pact to renounce war as a means of settling international disputes was signed at Paris in 1928 by the United States and fourteen other nations.

Whenever possible he turned over matters which he felt himself incapable of handling, to recognized experts. He thus established a board of experts for flood control, he left all matters pertaining to the treasury to Andrew Mellon and gave Herbert Hoover free rein in the Department of Commerce. Secretary of State Kellogg ably sustained his foreign policies and matters ran so smoothly that the Senate even, in 1926, voted to enter the World Court but with so many reservations that the plan was not acceptable to foreign powers. In 1927 the United States, with Coolidge's approval, took part in an arms limitation conference at Geneva, Switzerland. Not much was accomplished, but it was a step in the right direction, and with our foreign relations progressing so satisfactorily, and definite steps toward continued peace and prosperity being made throughout the United States, Coolidge's popularity was at its peak. With all signs pointing toward easy renomination and almost certain re-election, Coolidge put an end to further speculation concerning a third term by his characteristically terse remark: "I do not choose to run." And despite the pleas of political leaders and the advice of his friends, he remained firm, as was his nature when once he had reached a decision, not to seek re-election.

He retired to his old home in Northampton and lived in his half of the two-family house with his wife until he was persuaded to move to a larger home on an estate where he could more comfortably enjoy the peace and quiet he so loved. He traveled often to his old home in Plymouth. His father had died in 1926 but there were friends, memories and dearly loved associations to call him back. And then, on the morning of January 5, 1933, he returned home unexpectedly from his office and died suddenly while alone in the house. He was sixty-one years old.

HERBERT CLARK HOOVER

WITH very few exceptions, the United States has recruited her Presidents from the ranks of the legal profession. Herbert Clark Hoover, thirty-first President of the United States was one of those few exceptions. Realizing his boyhood ambition to be a mining engineer, Herbert Hoover answered his country's call for trained executives during the first World War and thereby found himself on the brink of a political career that was to carry him to the White House.

When George Washington was only six years old, Andrew Hoover came to America from his native Germany. He settled in Pennsylvania but perhaps embued with the restless spirit of the other pioneers in whose company he found himself, he too pushed on through the wilderness, moving first to Maryland and from there to North Carolina. His son John, setting out later to make his own way, went from the home in North Carolina to Ohio from where the grandson of the German immigrant, heeding the call of the West, settled at West Branch, Iowa in 1854. Here on August 10, 1874 Herbert Hoover was born. His father was a blacksmith but the boy was left parentless at the age of ten and was sent to live with an uncle on an Iowa farm. Later he was put in the care of Laban Miles, another uncle who was Osage Indian Agent in what was then Indian Territory. A third uncle, Dr. John Minthorn, then took the boy to live with him at his home in Oregon. Here he continued in the public schools and went to Pacific Academy, in the meantime working as office boy in his uncle's real estate office.

Young Herbert was an avid reader and a good listener. It wasn't long before the office boy knew as much, if not more, about his uncle's business as Dr. Minthorn did, himself. Prominent among young Hoover's books were those dealing with mathematics but he probably never thought of following his natural bent for that science until the day an engineer happened into his uncle's real estate office. At first the boy listened to the conversation of the men in the office and then his boyish curiosity could be curbed no longer. He knew what they were talking about. He had full knowledge of his uncle's business and his grasp of mathematics was sufficient to enable him to understand the engineer. He edged into the conversation. He asked questions and soon he and the engineer had the conversation to themselves, and thus the road that was to lead him to fame and fortune was opened out to the sixteen-year-old orphan.

In the fall of 1891 Leland Stanford University was to open in California. Among its courses were reputedly good ones in mining and geology and Herbert Hoover meant to be a mining engineer. But much preparation was necessary before he could hope to enter the new school. He went to night school to study mathematics; then he went to Portland to take an examination in the subject and failed. The instructor under whom he took the examination was so impressed, however, with the thoroughness of the paper the boy handed in, that he believed he would succeed if given another chance. Young Hoover eagerly grasped the new opportunity and this time passed the examination that allowed him to go to Stanford to take his entrance examinations. There he passed the mathematics requirements easily. History and literature were more difficult for him but he managed to get through. His stumbling block, however, was English composition and his efforts in that direction fell far short of entrance requirements. But Herbert Hoover wanted to be an engineer, not an author, and so because of this and his excellent showing in mathematics, he was allowed to matriculate on the condition that he make up his English requirements later.

Herbert Hoover was now embarked on his chosen career but he faced the necessity of earning his living in addition to devoting long hours to study. He seized every opportunity for making money that he could. He was campus agent for a laundry and for the San Francisco newspapers. He served as secretary to his geology professor and managed lectures and concerts for the University, and during the summer vacations he worked for the United States Geological Survey and the geological survey which was then being conducted by the State of Arkansas. But even though his time was fully occupied between working and studying, he still found time to enjoy a normal amount of fun with his fellow students. He became active in campus politics and immediately showed that ability for leadership and organization that later was to make him an outstanding figure in a field where leadership and organization ability were of vital importance. He graduated from Leland Stanford in 1895 and, faced with the prospect of having to earn money immediately, he went to work as an ordinary miner in California, receiving $2.50 for a day's work. Twenty years later his fame as a mining engineer was world-wide.

But young Hoover just then wasn't satisfied with being an ordinary miner. He had worked long and hard to get a good technical education and he meant to use it. While listening to the talk of the men around him, Hoover heard one name frequently repeated in the men's conversations. That man was a prominent mining engineer in San Francisco and Herbert Hoover decided that some day he would pay that man a visit. Not long afterward Hoover counted over his savings and found he had enough to pay his way to San Francisco. Arriving in the city, he went straight to the office of the man whose name he had so often heard, and applied for and was given a job. But it was not the kind of job Herbert Hoover wanted. He wanted to use his technical training for something better than a mere clerkship. That opportunity came one day when a confused jumble of miscellaneous papers were thrust upon him and he was told to find out what they contained and submit a report. The documents pertained to some mining matter and Herbert Hoover at last had his chance to prove whether that hard-won training at Leland Stanford University was to stand him in good stead or not. In bringing order out of that chaotic mass of papers, Hoover was even thankful for the experience he had gained as a common miner, but when the task was done, he knew that those four University years had not been wasted.

The young engineer worked long and hard over his report, putting everything he had into it. The result was that he was entrusted with more such work and was even sent as technical advisor to mines in New Mexico, Colorado and Arizona. He was twenty-three years old and earning $150.00 a month. Two years later he was offered an opportunity that most young men dream about but few ever realize. At the recommendation of his employer, a company in England offered him the job of developing a gold mine in western Australia. It was the chance of a lifetime and after cabling his acceptance, Hoover could barely wait to get out of the office.

Hoover did not leave at once for Australia. It was necessary that he go to London first for a talk with his new employers. He stopped at his former home in West Branch, Iowa on his way across the country and while there, must have received some sound advice for when he arrived in London, he was wearing a beard in order that his employers might not be too dismayed at his youthful appearance.

So began the first of a long series of trips that were to carry him to the far-off places of the globe. Reaching the Australian mining camp, he found it a confusion of disorganized men and machinery. If the young engineer was awed by his new surroundings and responsibilities, he did not show it. He plunged immediately into his work, imported more men and machinery from the United States and soon had the ten mines he was sent to develop running on a profitable basis. So well did he do his work that his name reached the ears of the Chinese Government and in 1899 he was invited to assume full charge of its newly established Department of Mines. Herbert Hoover accepted, but instead of proceeding directly to China from Australia, he went back to California to marry Lou Henry whom he had met when both were students at Leland Stanford University. Perhaps they were first drawn toward each other because Lou Henry, too, had been born in Iowa. Her father had been a wealthy banker in Iowa but due to his wife's poor health, he moved his family to Whittier, California and then later to Monterey in the same State and it was in Monterey that Herbert Hoover married Lou Henry and took her to China.

It must have been a strange and wonderful honeymoon for the young couple, exploring ancient China for indications of the mineral wealth that lay under her historic soil. Rich coal veins were known to exist in the northeastern section of the country, and it was decided to begin the operation of the new Department of Mines by opening these. The Hoovers went to live in Tientsin to be near the field of operations and they were in that city when the Boxer Rebellion shut them off from all communications with the rest of the world for almost a month. Hoover and his staff of engineers immediately erected a defensive wall and held it against the onslaughts of attack. It was at this time, too, that Hoover gained his first experience in saving and apportioning food and medical supplies, a task of world-wide proportions that he was later to assume.

With the Rebellion in full swing it was impossible to continue mining operations but Hoover knew that the war would not go on forever. The Rebellion had destroyed the newly created Department of Mines and Hoover's job with it but he knew that the war could not destroy the vast mineral wealth that lay underground. He went to Europe, therefore, and obtained financial backing to exploit the Chinese mines. Again he imported men and machinery from the United States and again, in China, as he had done in Australia, he began to make his mines show profits. But the country was still in the grip of the Rebellion and Herbert Hoover was forced to yield to the Gods of War and returned to the United States in 1901.

Home again in California, he set about the work of establishing his own business. He was only twenty-seven years old but he soon had branch offices all over the world. He made a fortune for himself and for others and he traveled throughout the world making mines pay where they had failed before. He wrote his book *Principles of Mining,* and, with the help of his devoted wife, translated from the Latin Agricola's classic work on mining and smelting.

And then Germany invaded Belgium. Herbert Hoover was in London where he had gone after a tour of Europe, to interest foreign governments in participation in a celebration in connection with the opening of the Panama Canal. Thousands of Americans found themselves caught by the outbreak of war and its resultant confusion. Herbert Hoover stepped quietly into the picture and, with the aid of his friends, he obtained money and transportation for 150,000 distracted but grateful men and women.

Herbert Hoover's reputation was world-wide and in her hour of need the Belgian government called upon him to assume the stupendous and almost impossible task of feeding and clothing its 10,-000,000 homeless, hungry, war-torn population. To these destitute millions Herbert Hoover was a worker of miracles for he brought them and distributed among them five million tons of food and a comparable amount of clothing and medicines through the enemy's lines without once ever antagonizing the enemy commanders. But as the war spread across Belgium and deep into France, Hoover's task and responsibilities grew heavier and more burdensome, but he kept on. He served without pay and even sacrificed part of his own fortune to alleviate the sufferings of the innocent victims of war.

When the United States entered the struggle in 1917, Herbert Hoover was called home to take over the duties of Food Administrator for his own country and again he plunged into the almost overwhelming amount of work and mass of detail necessary to teach the American people to conserve their food so he would have a surplus to send across the seas, not only to our own soldiers but to the millions of hungry and homeless refugees of Europe. It is known that he supplemented with funds from his own pocket the salaries of many of those who worked with him at that time, since he believed that those people were not being paid enough for the work they were doing.

And at last, on November 11, 1918, the Armistice was signed and the first World War came to an end. But while it brought the fighting to an end, it did not end Herbert Hoover's work. There were still millions of starving, homeless people in Europe who must be cared for. Congress appropriated $100,000,000 and put Herbert Hoover at the head of a Relief Commission. This sum was subsequently increased by additional loans from the United States and other governments, and the much needed work of relief went on. When those funds were depleted, Hoover organized and administered the European Children's Fund and he continued to give aid to the millions of Europe's needy until their own governments were able to care for them.

Such a man was too valuable to be ignored by his own country and President Harding lost no time in appointing him Secretary of Commerce and Coolidge retained him in that post. Much of the prosperity, temporary though it was, that this country enjoyed during the Coolidge administration was largely due to the efforts and ceaseless labor of Secretary of Commerce Hoover.

Despite his long and close associations with governments and their leaders and his even closer association with politics as Secretary of Commerce, Hoover had little or no desire for a political career. It is not strange, therefore, that he protested when his friends sought to nominate him as the Republican candidate for the Presidency in 1924 and it is understandable that he was perhaps secretly glad when that attempt failed.

By 1928, however, the country had begun to understand that the encouraging upward trend of business was, in a large part, due to Hoover's efforts and so, despite his protest, he was nominated and elected by a popular majority of 6,000,000 votes and an electoral majority of 357 votes, one of the greatest majorities any President had received up to that time.

Herbert Hoover was the first so-called "big business" man and engineer to be sent to the White House. His experience in organization and administration was vast. He had handled many a grave situation and had come through with flying colors. When he took the oath of office in Washington on March 4, 1929, it might have seemed a bit amusing to some to see the most successful relief administrator the world had ever known take charge of a country in which increasing prosperity would make the new President's humanitarian genius totally unnecessary.

Hoover had plans, great plans, for continuing his country's prosperity and insuring world peace and harmonious foreign relations, but in the midst of these plans, even while many of them were being put into effect, a terrific blow shook the country and the world.

The prosperity that Coolidge had begun and that Hoover had hoped to continue was too slow in developing for some. A wave of speculative investment swept over the country. Prices soared and fortunes were pyramided but it was an inverted pyramid and in October, 1929, that pyramid tumbled and crashed of its own weight. Fortunes and life savings were lost overnight. Business concerns, many of them of sound reputation and long standing, failed. Unemployment became widespread and pitiful breadlines began to grow throughout the land. The country was plunged into the first depths of a long depression. Nor was the depression confined to the United States alone. It spread over the world like fire eating through dry tinder.

With all his years of experience, particularly the war years, in meeting emergencies and crises, Hoover fought valiantly to stem the tide of the depression. In the summer of 1931 he announced his famous moratorium—a suspension of payment on all war debts for a year. But banks were closing and foreign nations were taking their gold out of this country. To offset this, he recommended to Congress the creation of the Reconstruction Finance Corporation with a capital of $500,000,000 and authorized power to borrow $1,500,000,000 more. He created the Farm Board to aid the farmers whose need of relief was desperate but while these measures did some good and alleviated some suffering, the momentum gained by the swift descent of the world's markets could not be checked.

At Hoover's suggestion the American Red Cross appropriated $5,000,000, and began a collection of $10,000,000 more for direct relief, but despair and gloom had settled over the once prosperous land and the most herculean efforts of one man could not lift it. He vetoed the bill for Philippine independence. But all the other measures that

Hoover had hoped to put into effect for the relief of his country were blocked in Congress.

He was defeated for re-election in 1932 but he invited his successful opponent, Franklin Delano Roosevelt, to the White House before his inauguration to discuss the state of the country and international affairs. He offered the new President his fullest co-operation and then retired to his home in Palo Alto, California to re-establish his business and engage in the furtherance of child welfare work.

After leaving Washington and the political scene, Hoover remained in comparative retirement, devoting his time to his business, appearing publicly only twice, once at the Republican National Convention in Cleveland in 1936 and again at that party's convention at Philadelphia, in 1940.

By the time the second World War was a year old, in September of 1940, Herbert Hoover had again professed his willingness to reassume his old role of Relief Administrator for the devastated countries of Holland, Belgium, Norway and France which had fallen under the hammer blows of Nazi Germany.

FRANKLIN DELANO ROOSEVELT

THE economic collapse that made a nightmare of Hoover's administration gave the Democratic Party and Franklin Roosevelt ample material for a successful political campaign. The financial structure of the nation lay in ruins and it required very little encouragement from political leaders to convince the people that the "New Deal" promised by the President-elect would be everything its name implied.

Franklin Delano Roosevelt, fifth cousin of Theodore Roosevelt, was inaugurated thirty-second President of the United States on March 4, 1933, during the darkest days of the longest financial depression this country had known up to that time. This depression was the political heritage of the man who had never known the pinch of poverty or the desperate need of employment.

Franklin Roosevelt was born January 30, 1882, on his father's estate at Hyde Park, N. Y. He was a direct descendant, in the eighth generation, of Claes Martenszan Van Roosevelt who came to the New World from Holland in 1649. A branch of the Roosevelt family have been residents and political figures in New York State ever since.

Young Franklin had the typical boyhood and education of a rich man's son. He attended Groton School at Groton, N. Y., and then entered Harvard University and graduated in 1904, completing the regular four-year course in three years. He subsequently became a student at Columbia Law School and was admitted to the bar in 1907. Two years before that date, on March 17, 1905, he married his fifth cousin, Anna Eleanor Roosevelt, daughter of Theodore Roosevelt's brother, Elliott. The wedding was a brilliant social affair and took place in the White House where the bride was given in marriage by her uncle, who was then President of the United States.

No other mistress of the White House had, until then, taken the keen and active interest in political and sociological matters and affairs of the day that Eleanor Roosevelt did. She traveled widely, giving her time as freely as she could to any cause that she deemed worthy. She taught English and American history in a girl's school and wrote and lectured extensively. When widespread unemployment gripped the nation as a result of the depression, Mrs. Roosevelt took an active interest in the problems of youth that arose as a result of that unemployment. She served on innumerable committees and held important posts in organizations created for the betterment of the underprivileged. Despite these interests and her position, she never used one to further the aims of the other.

Five children were born to the Roosevelts, four sons and a daughter. Of these, James, the eldest, was the only one who was given a political appointment by his father, and that was a minor, temporary post which he soon left to enter private business.

Franklin Roosevelt was the only child of James and Sarah Delano Roosevelt. His mother's ancestors were among the first of that hardy group of Pilgrims who landed on the shores of Massachusetts in 1621. Rarely having anyone of his own age to play with, young Franklin early formed the habit of listening, and later asking questions, when his father, who was a railroad executive and village supervisor of Hyde Park, filled his home, as the occasion required, with business associates or neighbors and local politicians for the discussion of whatever problems were then pertinent.

And so, brought up though he was in the lap of luxury, he early developed that freedom of class distinction that became so characteristic of him in his later years. Nor was his boyhood confined entirely to the narrow limits of his own social sphere. His father's health was delicate and at the early age of three, Franklin was taken abroad by his parents while his father tried first one and then another of Europe's health resorts. Thus, until he was fourteen, young Franklin had made eight trips back and forth across the ocean, but despite the staff of tutors and servants employed to see that his education was continued and to minister to his every want, the young American delighted in nothing more during his stays in Europe than to slip away from his guardians and mingle with the natives of the little villages near any one of which the family happened to be staying at the time.

With such a wide and varied background of study and travel, young Franklin entered the exclusive Groton school where class distinction was accepted as a matter of course. But the social aloofness that existed there failed to make any impression on the boy and he completed his four years eager and ready to accept the hand of friendship, be it toil-hardened or not, as long as he felt in his own heart that it was offered with honest sincerity. This was a characteristic that identified him throughout his entire life.

He was eighteen, tall, handsome and broad-shouldered when he entered Harvard University and plunged with his boundless energy and enthusiasm into every phase of college life. His major studies were government and history but he did not attempt to specialize in any particular study. He did, however, spend a good deal of time protesting loudly and vehemently against any course of study that he felt was impractical and not calculated to be of use later on in life.

Muscular and athletic though he was, young Roosevelt cared little for college sports. He played football for a while and rowed on the freshman crew, but aside from these activities, he seemed to prefer the more mentally stimulating pursuits of campus politics, and writing. He joined the staff of the Harvard *Crimson,* and devoted his time and energies to it with such success that the freshman reporter rose, through various promotions, to senior president of the paper.

It was during his college years also that young Franklin's strong dislike of the social caste system manifested itself with concrete results. As the son of a rich man and a member of one of the most socially prominent families in the country, young Franklin was naturally accepted as a member of the exclusive and snobbish clubs in existence on the campus. He was a well-liked and popular member of those clubs, but he thoroughly disliked their rigid exclusiveness. He had made friends with, and had grown to know and admire, many of his fellow students who were excluded from those clubs merely because their families were not recognized by the arbitrary social rules of the day. Roosevelt did not like the system that gave responsible positions in student organizations to members of these exclusive clubs only. He knew many students outside the social pale who were every bit as worthy and capable of filling those positions as were members of his own set. And so, while still an undergraduate at Harvard, Roosevelt began the first of a long series of bold and daring strokes that were to earn for him the reputation as a destroyer of precedent whenever that precedent stood in the way of real, progressive achievement.

So, while his cousin, Theodore, was pursuing almost the same tactics in the White House, young Franklin threw the weight of his support on the side of the underprivileged. He rallied a few friends from his own group to his support and presented a ticket for the election to the various student offices that contained names that were not found in the Social Register. This was, of course, contrary to all tradition but so well did Roosevelt conduct his campaign, so sincere and understandable was the force of his arguments, that ancient tradition was upset and his candidates, recruited from among those undergraduates who were not members of any socially exclusive group, were elected.

A year after his graduation from Harvard, Franklin Roosevelt married Anna Eleanor Roosevelt and then went on to Columbia Law School to prepare for his chosen career. He graduated and was admitted to the bar in 1907 and then settled down to the practice of his profession with a firm of well-known New York lawyers. But young Roosevelt's spirit was too restless to be content with the routine matters of a law office and in 1910 he became Democratic candidate for State Senator from his home district of Dutchess County, N. Y. That area was traditionally and solidly Republican but nothing daunted, young Roosevelt bought himself an automobile which, in those days, was something of a curiosity, and launched his campaign. At first, even his own party didn't concern itself much over the young Democrat in the bright red automobile who went campaigning up and down the county frightening horses and awing farmers with what they called his "contraption." It is possible that people came to hear him speak, drawn only by their curiosity to see one of the "newfangled horseless carriages." It is certain, however, that having come, they remained to listen, surprised and completely won over by the warm friendliness and honest sincerity of the young politician. At the end of that campaign, Franklin Roosevelt had upset another tradition by being the first Democrat to be elected in that district in twenty-eight years.

Having arrived in Albany, young Roosevelt met and accepted another challenge. The powerful Tammany organization held New York State in an iron grip. Its leaders had smashed or weakened all opposition, employing methods that the new State Senator did not consider ethical. He also knew too well the unsavory record of that organization's candidate for the United States Senate and young Roosevelt, with his characteristic straightforwardness, immediately went into action. The Tammany organization was all powerful. It could make or break politicians and many were the fearless young crusaders who had been crushed by this relentless machine. Franklin Roosevelt knew all this. He knew that the iron hand of Tammany could break him as easily, politically, as he could snap a stick between his fingers. But a wrong was being perpetrated. Vested interests sat in high places and young Roosevelt could not and would not sit idly by while he had a voice to raise in protest.

Boldly the young State Senator rallied a small group to his cause and with swift, lightning strokes, backed the Tammany Tiger into a corner and brought about a compromise on a candidate acceptable to his group as well as to Tammany. Thenceforward, the once ferocious Tammany Tiger became as a lamb as far as Franklin D. Roosevelt was concerned. Its tail had been twisted and it respected the man who had twisted it.

After the Tammany episode young Roosevelt settled down to the routine business of his first term as State Senator. In the meantime, however, his vision saw beyond the political horizon of Albany to the National Democratic Convention in Baltimore. It was 1912. His cousin, Theodore Roosevelt, was in the thick of a three-cornered fight for the Presidency with Taft and Wilson as his opponents. Young Franklin was, of course, a Roosevelt, but he was also a Democrat. He had met and liked the Princeton professor and so alone, and without any official authority, he went to Baltimore as chairman of a committee which consisted only of himself and a few friends, and made a speech to the convention expressing the preference of New York State for Wilson. Upon Wilson's nomination, young Franklin went to New York and plunged into the work of organizing a campaign committee for the Democratic nominee. He was re-elected to the New York Senate during the same year but before he could resume his duties at Albany or get his work for Wilson well under way, he was stricken with typhoid fever and forced from the political arena. But rather than let matters go until the time when he would be well enough to resume his old activities, he entrusted the fulfillment of his plans to his friend, Louis McHenry Howe, a newspaperman who saw in Franklin Roosevelt a man of promise and future greatness. Later, when Roosevelt became President, Howe was the first member of Roosevelt's famous "Brain Trust."

And so, while young Roosevelt lay ill, faithful Louis Howe put into execution those plans that his friend formulated before his illness. Wilson was elected President of the United States and polled a big New York vote.

His first taste of national politics left Roosevelt with a desire for more. He recovered from his illness and plunged into the work of his second term at Albany but Washington called irresistibly. Political leaders were gathering in the nation's capital for the inauguration of the new President and Roosevelt could resist the call no longer. He went to Washington to witness the induction of the new President into office and, with an eye to the future, to further political friendships begun at Baltimore.

His work for Wilson had not been in vain. Political leaders remembered and liked the energetic New York Senator who, almost alone and, certainly unasked, had gone to Baltimore and boldly but sincerely offered his State's support.

The political leaders decided to reward him and offered him the post of Collector of the Port of New York. The position was a political sinecure and Roosevelt knew that if he accepted it, he would have a good job but his political career would come to a standstill. The smoke of political battle was too keen in his nostrils and he enjoyed the fight far too much to give it up, no matter how rich the reward. He declined that post with the same affable good humor with which he also refused the Assistant Secretaryship of the Treasury when it was offered to him later. But, when his party leaders, intent on putting a man of his known and proved ability in a place where it could be used and developed, offered him the post of Assistant Secretary of the Navy, Roosevelt's eyes grew bright and his infectious smile grew broader. His boyhood ambition had been to be a sailor, and all his life he carried with him a love of the sea and things nautical. It is small wonder then, that the man whose collection of ship models was nationally famous, could not refuse such an offer. Roosevelt's knowledge of ships and sailing was not, however, confined to the armchair pursuit of collecting models and pictures of ships. He owned a summer home on Campobello Island in New Brunswick on the Atlantic coast of Canada, and whenever time and the opportunity afforded, he would sail his own boat up the coast to this island retreat and spend as much time as he could fishing and sailing in the waters around the island. Franklin Roosevelt would have needed superhuman will power to have refused the post of Assistant Secretary of the Navy. His cousin, Theodore Roosevelt, had held the post before him and, like him, young Franklin gave all his enthusiasm and energy to the task. When Franklin Roosevelt left Albany and went to Washington in March, 1913, to begin his new duties, he was the youngest man, up to that time, to fill his post. He held that post for seven years, many of which were momentous years, for they were the years of the first World War. Ordinarily, as Secretary of the Navy, Roosevelt's duties were concerned with economic management, reorganization and revision, the purchase of supplies and similar duties. During the war, however, these duties were supplemented by the responsibility for the construction of barracks, obtaining small merchant ships to be refitted and used as auxiliaries and organizing, and causing to function, a service for the operation of cargo carriers for the government. In addition to this, the task of organizing and bringing into being the first beginnings of the War Labor Board fell to him.

Despite these manifold duties, Roosevelt found time to formulate, and push through the stubborn bureaucracy of the Navy Department, a plan for effectively bottling up enemy submarine chasers in the North Sea behind a line of explosives planted undersea between Scotland and Norway.

He was in charge of the inspection of United States Naval forces in European waters in 1918 and the following year, after the Armistice had been signed, he was in charge of the demobilization of United States troops in Europe and while overseas on this mission, was put in charge of the postwar work of salvaging or demolishing, as each case required, naval supplies and equipment.

When he returned to the United States, Roosevelt again threw his hat into the political ring and at the Democratic National Convention at San Francisco in 1920 he was nominated for the Vice-Presidency with Governor James M. Cox of Ohio as the Presidential nominee. Governor Alfred E. Smith of New York, made the speech seconding Roosevelt's nomination. The Democrats lost the election, however, and Roosevelt went back to New York to resume the practice of law.

In 1921 he began what promised to be an enjoyable summer vacation. Aboard a friend's yacht, Roosevelt took the helm and plotted his course for Campobello Island. There the party found a forest fire raging which endangered the camp. Roosevelt, along with the others, rushed ashore and battled the blaze until it was under control.

Then followed a refreshing swim before the return to camp. Two days later he was paralyzed from the waist down, a victim of poliomyelitis, or infantile paralysis.

Long months of illness followed during which his life was despaired of. Then came convalescence and the terrific uphill climb back to health. And Franklin Roosevelt made that climb with all the grit and determination that later, when he faced national and international crises, was to stand him in such good stead. He went to Warm Springs, Georgia, where he exercised his wasted legs in the warm waters that gave the little place its name. Satisfied with the results obtained there, he organized the Georgia Warm Springs Foundation, risking his own fortune to do so, and later making the Foundation the beneficiary of a $500,000 insurance policy on his life. Warm Springs and Franklin Delano Roosevelt's indomitable courage had won through for, in taking out that policy, physicians of more than twenty insurance companies had examined him and accepted him as a good risk.

Franklin Roosevelt was thirty-nine years old when he was stricken with infantile paralysis but despite the loss of time, and his absorption in the task of winning back his health, he still maintained his keen interest in politics.

When the Democratic National Convention was held in New York City in 1924, Roosevelt was there to nominate his friend Governor Alfred E. Smith of New York for the Presidency but the choice fell, instead, to John W. Davis, a New York lawyer and the Democratic Party went down to defeat in the November elections. But with his same high courage, Roosevelt kept his watch fires burning and, in 1928, at the convention in Houston, Texas, he again put Smith's name in nomination, referring to him as the "Happy Warrior," a name that soon became as closely identified with the battle-scarred old campaigner as his famous brown derby hat. Smith won the nomination but failed in the elections which, that year, put Franklin D. Roosevelt in the executive mansion at Albany. He served two terms as Governor of New York and then the nation, beaten and heartsick by the economic debacle that Hoover had been unable to check, turned to Roosevelt in 1932. Alfred E. Smith was making his third bid for the Presidency and William McAdoo, Secretary of the Treasury under Wilson, was also a candidate for nomination. The convention was deadlocked until the California delegation, headed by McAdoo, withdrew his name at his insistence, and gave their votes to Roosevelt, insuring his nomination.

Listening at his radio in Albany, Franklin Roosevelt heard himself selected as the Democratic choice for President and straightway upset another tradition. He did not wait to be officially notified. He telephoned the convention leaders instead and told them he would arrive in Chicago to accept the nomination in person the next day. He flew from Albany to Chicago and brought the weary delegates to their feet, singing and cheering. His vast personal charm and magnetic personality almost at once injected new life and hope into a discouraged nation. He campaigned for the "Forgotten Man," the ordinary citizen whose needs and privileges seemed to have been almost submerged by the collapse of the world's markets and the mad scramble by political leaders to save what they could for themselves and the vested interests. Roosevelt promised a "New Deal," an appellation that characterized and identified his administrations, and immediately after taking the oath of office in March, 1932, he set about putting that New Deal into effect. He closed all banks, to allow the Government a chance to step in and help bring order out of their financial chaos, he set up an embargo on gold and in a series of swift, breath-taking, unprecedented moves, struck boldly and fearlessly all about him wherever and whenever the Monster of Depression reared its loathsome head.

At his own insistence, Congress voted him the greatest and broadest emergency powers ever accorded a President in time of peace. And Franklin Roosevelt used those powers wisely and with telling effect. Millions of unemployed young men were given work in the Civilian Conservation Corps, rehabilitating depleted timber lands, combatting soil erosion and aiding in flood-control work. Other millions were put to work first under the Civil Works Administration, then under the Public Works Administration and finally under the Works Progress Administration, improving public property, building bridges and in government-sponsored cultural projects.

Few Presidents have ever had the united support of Congress in all measures that Roosevelt had during his first term. Order and financial stability began to rise out of the ashes of the old economic ruins, the hated Prohibition Amendment was repealed. Banks reopened. Gold hoarders were made to release their hidden treasures and one of the largest government-sponsored projects began to take shape. Under the work relief acts, the United States had built gigantic dams but the largest undertaking of this kind for the production of power was the Tennessee Valley project, embracing an area of 440,000 square miles. Throughout this area, stretching out over Tennessee, Ohio, Virginia, North Carolina, Alabama and Mississippi, the Roosevelt administration brought electric power cheap enough to be available to the poorest farmer and electrical equipment priced low enough to enable those farmers and villagers to use that power.

The country was slowly but surely getting back on its feet. The first feelings of fear, uncertainty, and panic had passed. Farmers were given government funds with which to reclaim their drouth-parched lands and investments were brought under government control to abolish unscrupulous market manipulations. The National Industrial Recovery Act came into being to aid in the recovery of business through the regulation of wages and hours.

So heartened and encouraged were the people of America by the fearless boldness of the man who was leading them out of the depths of the depression, so completely had he won their hearts by the warm friendliness of his radio talks in which he periodically reported to the people on the state of the nation that, in 1936, he was re-elected by a hitherto unprecedented majority, receiving the pluralities of forty-six of the forty-eight States.

During his second administration the opposition rallied their forces, now that they no longer faced financial ruin, and began severe criticisms of Roosevelt's lavish spending, forgetting, perhaps, that it was just that spending that saved them from annihilation. But Roosevelt kept on, in the face of the harshest condemnation, to push through his plans for the security of the country.

World-shaking events in Europe found Roosevelt in the role of peacemaker. That those efforts failed was due only to the blind greed of European dictators and when the flames of war again ravaged Europe, Roosevelt immediately began the work of preparing this country for any contingency. He asked for and received the largest peacetime appropriation of funds for military purposes ever given, up to that time, by Congress. He set up an emergency Advisory Board of business executives to co-ordinate and facilitate the procurement of supplies and, for the first time in the history of the country, universal compulsory military training while the country was at peace, was instituted.

The Democratic National Convention took place at Chicago in July, 1940. Roosevelt had never publicly stated his views on the much-discussed issue of a third term but when his party almost unanimously renominated him on the first ballot, the President, that same night, accepted the nomination in a nation-wide radio speech. His running mate was Henry A. Wallace, Secretary of Agriculture and his Republican opponent was Wendell L. Willkie, former head of a utility company who had challenged the authority of the Government's Tennessee Valley power project to compete with private business. Willkie had been a Democrat until the Tennessee Valley project had, or so he feared, encroached on his private domain. Both Roosevelt and Willkie were men of outstandingly charming personalities and exceptional abilities, and the fight for the Presidency promised to be a close and interesting one.

But when the election was over, and the ballots counted, Franklin Delano Roosevelt emerged victorious, the first and only man in the entire history of the United States, up to that time, to hold the high office of President for three successive terms.

UNITED STATES HISTORY AT A GLANCE

UNITED STATES HISTORY AT A GLANCE

A Chronology of the Most Important Happenings in United States History

YEAR

Unknown—Successive waves of immigration from Asia, over Bering Straits and by sea, peopled the Americas.

A.D.

6th Century—The Toltecs moved down from the North into Mexico.

Before 1000—Recorded voyages by Arabians, Irishmen, Welshmen, Chinese, Japanese and Frenchmen to America.

1000—Leif Ericsson landed in Vinland (Labrador, Newfoundland and Nova Scotia; or Rhode Island; or Massachusetts).

1003—An Icelander, Thorfinn Karlsefni, settled for 3 years in Vinland.

11th Century—The Toltecs largely perished, by drought, famine and pestilence. The remainder migrated into Yucatan and Guatemala.

12th Century—The Chichimecs spread over Mexico.

About 1230—The Incas, or "People of the Sun," settled the Cuzco Valley, Peru.

1325—The Aztecs moved to Mexico, founding Mexico City.

1426—Pachacutic Inca formed the Peruvian Empire.

1430—Mexican Empire consolidated under the Aztecs.

1453—The Ottoman Turks captured Constantinople, and soon closed the overland spice routes to the East. This sent Europe looking for an overseas route to the spice islands.

1486—Bartholomeu Diaz, Portuguese, discovered the Cape of Good Hope, sailing toward the spice lands.

1492—Christopher Columbus, a Genoese sailing under the Spanish flag, discovered America: landing on Watling Island, in the Bahamas.

1493—Columbus discovered other West Indian islands, on his second voyage.

1497—Cabot, an Italian sailing under the English flag, discovered Labrador.

1498—Vasco da Gama, Portuguese, sailed southward and eastward around Africa to India.

—Third voyage of Columbus, in which South America was discovered.

1501—Amerigo Vespucci, a Florentine sailing for Portugal, explored Brazil. (America was named for him.)

1502—Fourth voyage of Columbus, to Central America.

1508—The Spaniards conquered and settled Puerto Rico and Cuba.

1513—Balboa discovered the Pacific Ocean. Ponce de Leon landed in Florida, in search of the Fountain of Youth.

1519–21—Hernando Cortez conquered Mexico.

1519–22—The expedition of Ferdinand Magellan, Portuguese, circumnavigated the globe.

1524—Giovanni Verrazano, sailing under the French flag, discovered New York.

1526—Huayna Capac, the Great Inca of Peru, died.

1529—Cabeza de Vaca travelled from Texas and Mexico to the Gulf of California.

1531–35—Pizarro conquered Peru.

1535—Pizarro founded Lima, Peru.

—Jacques Cartier sailed up the St. Lawrence River for France.

1539–42—Hernando de Soto travelled from the Gulf to the Mississippi River and died there.

1540–42—Coronado travelled northward from Texas, seeking the Seven Cities of Cibola.

1542—Las Casas complained of Spanish treatment of the Indians.

1565—St. Augustine, Florida, settled by the Spaniards—the oldest existing white settlement in North America.

1583—Sir Humphrey Gilbert's expedition to Newfoundland, which failed.

1584—Sir Walter Raleigh named the South Atlantic coastal regions Virginia, after the Virgin Queen, Elizabeth.

1585—Roanoke Island, North Carolina, settled by the English. This settlement lasted nine months, after which the settlers returned to England.

1586—Roanoke Island re-settled. No trace of any of these colonists has ever been found.

1602—Captain Bartholomew Gosnold, English, landed in Massachusetts.

1607—Virginia settled at Jamestown by King James's London Company, under the leadership of Captain John Smith. The Plymouth Company settled Maine. The colony lasted one year.

1608—Samuel de Champlain founded Quebec.

1609—De Champlain discovered Lake Champlain.

—Henry Hudson, an Englishman sailing under the Dutch flag, sailed up the Hudson River in the *Half Moon*.

1614—The Dutch planted a fort at Albany, New York.

—John Smith explored New England for the Plymouth Company.

1619—Wives and Negro slaves arrived in Virginia. The House of Burgesses was founded.

1620—The Pilgrim Fathers landed at Plymouth Rock.

1624—Virginia became a royal province.

1624—The Dutch permanently settled the site of New York.
1630—The Puritans settled Massachusetts Bay.
1634—Lord Baltimore settled Maryland, as a refuge for Catholics.
1636—Roger Williams, driven out of Massachusetts, settled Rhode Island.
—Connecticut settled by Puritans, who founded Hartford, Windsor, and Wethersfield.
—Harvard College established.
1638—New Haven settled by Puritans.
1638–47—Sweden made 6 settlements in Delaware and New Jersey.
1639—Connecticut drew up its "Fundamental Orders," the first constitution drawn up on American soil.
—Sir Ferdinando Gorges made proprietor of Maine.
1640—The *Bay Psalm Book* published, the first book in America.
1643—The New England Confederation established, excluding Rhode Island.
1649—Maryland issued its Religious Toleration Act.
1651—1st English Navigation Act against colonies, by Cromwell's parliament.
1655—The Dutch capture the Swedish settlements.
1656—Anne Hibbins hanged as a witch at Salem, Massachusetts.
1660—Virginia named "The Old Dominion."
1664—New Amsterdam surrendered to the English, under the Duke of York.
1670—North and South Carolina settled.
1673—Marquette and Joliet sail down the Mississippi to about Arkansas.
1675—Bacon's rebellion, in Virginia.
—King Philip's Indian War, in New England.
1682—William Penn settled Pennsylvania.
—De la Salle sails down the Mississippi to its mouth.

1688—1st Protest against slavery, at Germantown, Pennsylvania.

1689—New England, New York and New Jersey united into one royal province, under Sir Edmund Andros. He was ejected by the Glorious Revolution of 1689.

1691—Plymouth Colony united with Massachusetts.

—The first post-office in the United States was organized, under a royal patent granted to Thomas Neale.

1692—The witchcraft persecution in Salem, Massachusetts, in which 16 women and 5 men were hanged.

1693—William and Mary College established at Williamsburg, Virginia, the second college in America.

1701—Yale College founded at New Haven, Connecticut.

1712—Slave insurrection in New York City; 6 committed suicide; 21 were executed.

1713—Treaty of Utrecht signed.

1718—Bienville founded New Orleans.

1720—The Mississippi Bubble, John Law's gambling venture in colonial trading, exploded in England. Law fled to Italy.

1733—Georgia colonized by James Oglethorpe.

1734–35—Trial of Peter Zenger in New York for libel in his newspaper. His acquittal established freedom of the press in America.

1741—Negro slave plot to burn New York City; 13 were burned at the stake, 18 were hanged, 71 transported.

1754—Albany Conference seeking colonial union.

1754–63—French and Indian War in America.

1755—Braddock's defeat by the French and Indians, covered by the bravery of young George Washington.

1759—English General Wolfe captured Quebec; he and its French defender, Montcalm, dying in the battle.

1763—Peace of Paris marks the end of France's colonial empire.

1764—Frenville's laws, taxing the colonists, enacted in England.

1765—The Stamp Act passed by the English parliament.

1766—The Stamp Act repealed.

1767—The Townshend Acts against the colonies enacted.

1770—The Boston Massacre, in which British soldiers killed 3 colonial Americans.

1772—Citizens of Baltimore forced the captain of the *Peggy Stuart* to burn his boat and its cargo of tea, as a protest against the tax on tea.

1773—Disguised citizens of Massachusetts conducted the Boston Tea Party.

1774—First Continental Congress, in Philadelphia.

1775—The Revolutionary War commenced. Battles of Concord and Lexington (April 19th); Ticonderoga (May 10th); Bunker Hill (June 17th).

—Mecklenberg, N. C., Declaration of Independence, May 20th.

—Congress declared war formally against England, July 6th.

1776—Thomas Paine published his *Common Sense*, a powerful pamphlet defending the rights of the colonies.

—Battles of Long Island (Sept. 16th) and Trenton (Dec. 26th) fought.

—Richard Henry Lee of Virginia moved Independence in Congress (June 7th). The resolution was passed on July 2nd. The Declaration of Independence was adopted on July 4th.

—Nathan Hale executed as a spy on September 22nd, accused of having a hand in the burning of New York City the day before.

1777—Battles of Brandywine (Sept. 11th) and Saratoga (Sept. 19th–October 7th) fought.

—The Articles of Confederation and Perpetual Union

were adopted by Congress; the last state to ratify, Maryland, did this in 1781.

1777–8—Washington's troops wintered at Valley Forge.

1778—Franklin negotiated a treaty with France, recognizing American independence.

—Battles of Monmouth (June 28th) and Savannah (December 29th) fought. Wyoming Valley Massacre (July 3rd). English campaign shifted to the south.

—George Rogers Clark explored the West.

1779—Second Battle of Savannah, October 8th.

1780—Battle of King's Mountain, Oct. 7th.

—Bank of Philadelphia, the first bank in the United States, chartered.

—Benedict Arnold tried to betray West Point to the British. Major André, British go-between, was captured and executed as a spy.

1781—Battles of Cowpens (Jan. 17th), Guilford Court House (March 15th), and Yorktown (Sept. 28th and October 19th). At this battle Lord Cornwallis surrendered to the American Army led by Washington and Lafayette, having the French fleet under Admiral de Grasse at his rear.

1782—Preliminary peace agreement signed with England on November 30th.

1783—Peace of Paris signed Sept. 3, 1783, ending the Revolutionary War.

—The Supreme Court of Massachusetts held slavery illegal, because of the words "all men are born free and equal" in the state's Bill of Rights.

1784—John Fitch operated his steamboat on the Delaware River.

1786–87—Daniel Shays' rebellion in Massachusetts, of the debtor class. The attempt to capture the arsenal at Springfield failed.

1786–87—Convention at Annapolis to discuss the commerce of the country.

1787—United States Constitution drawn up at Philadelphia.

—The Northwest Ordinance enacted, to govern the territories in the northwest ceded to the government by the states.

1788—The Constitution became the law of the land on June 21st, when the 9th state ratified it.

1789—First Presidential election held in February. George Washington inaugurated as President, April 30th.

1791—The Hamilton financial policies were adopted.

1792—Washington reëlected as President.

1793—Citizen Genet arrived as French minister, and his arrogance alienated Federalist opinion.

—Washington proclaimed neutrality in the war between republican France and England.

—Eli Whitney invented the cotton gin.

1794–95—Jay Treaty with England negotiated and ratified.

1796—John Adams, Federalist, elected as the 2nd President.

1798—The "X. Y. Z." affair in France.

—A state of war existed between the United States and France until 1800.

—The Kentucky and Virginia Resolutions passed.

1800—Thomas Jefferson, Republican (the name of the Democratic party then) elected as 3rd President.

1801—Peace treaty between Napoleon I of France and the United States.

—John Marshall appointed Chief Justice of the Supreme Court.

1802—The United States Military Academy at West Point was established.

1803—The Louisiana Purchase, by which we bought the Louisiana Territory from France for $15,000,000.

1804—Jefferson reëlected as President.

—Aaron Burr, Vice-President of the United States, killed Alexander Hamilton, ex-Secretary of the Treas ury, in a duel on the Palisades at Weehawken.

1806—Aaron Burr tried for treason, for his plan of western empire, and acquitted.

1806–07—Napoleon's Berlin and Milan Decrees, and England's Orders in Council, harmed American commerce.

1807—Robert Fulton's steamboat, the *Clermont,* steamed from New York to Albany.

—The British *Leopard* fired upon the American *Chesapeake,* killing 3 men and wounding 18. The *Chesapeake* surrendered.

—Congress enacted the Embargo Act against England.

1808—James Madison elected as the 4th President.

1809—The Embargo Act repealed, and a Non-Intercourse act enacted.

1810—Macon's Bill, providing that the Non-Intercourse Act should be revived against France or England, when the other withdrew its offensive orders.

1811—The American *President* forced the English *Little Belt* to surrender.

—William Henry Harrison defeated the Indians at Tippecanoe Creek.

—Earthquakes in the Mississippi River region south of the mouth of the Ohio destroyed small towns, and created Reelfoot Lake, 14 miles long.

—The Republicans refused to recharter the National Bank.

1812—Congress declared war against England.

—Detroit surrendered to the British.

—James Madison reëlected as President.

1813—Admiral Perry's victory on Lake Erie, Sept. 10th.

1814—The British captured Washington, D. C., and burned the Capitol and the White House.

—Francis Scott Key wrote *The Star-Spangled Banner,* during an unsuccessful English attack on Ft. McHenry guarding Baltimore.

—The Hartford Convention, to protest against the War of 1812.

—Peace treaty with England signed at Ghent on December 24th.

1815—Andrew Jackson, American, defeated English General Pakenham at battle of New Orleans, Jan. 8th. Word of the peace had not reached them. Jackson was aided by the pirate Lafitte.

1816—James Monroe elected as the 5th President. His terms called "The Era of Good Feeling."

—The 1816 tariff bill doubled the rates of the 1812 tariff, to encourage infant industries.

—The 2nd National Bank chartered.

1817—Andrew Jackson wrested Florida from Spain.

1818—Connecticut eliminated the religious qualification for holding office.

1819—Religious toleration laws enacted in New Hampshire.

—The *Savannah* was the first steamboat to cross the Atlantic, requiring 30 days to cross from Savannah to Liverpool.

—Florida ceded to the United States.

1820—Monroe reëlected as President.

—Congress passed Henry Clay's Missouri Compromise bill, allowing slavery in Missouri, but not elsewhere west of the Mississippi River north of 36 degrees 30 minutes latitude.

1822—President Monroe recognized the South American republics which had freed themselves from Spain, under the leadership of Bolivar and San Martin.

1823—The Monroe Doctrine announced by President

Monroe, warning the Holy Alliance (Russia, Austria and Prussia) and other European nations to keep hands off American affairs.

1824—Lafayette visited America, touring each of the 24 states.

—John Quincy Adams elected as the 6th President, defeating the leading candidate, Andrew Jackson, and the other sectional "Favorite Sons."

—An increased tariff bill passed.

1825—The Erie Canal opened.

—Panama Congress held, the United States delegates arriving too late to take part—and one of them having died before the Congress met.

1828—Andrew Jackson elected as the 7th President.

—The Tariff of Abominations passed.

—First passenger railroad train in the United States, the horse-drawn Baltimore and Ohio, opened to traffic.

—Vice-President John C. Calhoun presented his *Exposition and Protest* against the tariff bill to the legislature of South Carolina.

1829—The Hayne-Webster debate in the Senate.

1830—The Mormon Church organized by Joseph Smith at Fayette, Seneca County, N. Y.

1831—Nat Turner's slave insurrection in Virginia.

—First steam-drawn train in the United States, Schenectady to Albany.

—First national nominating convention.

—William Lloyd Garrison established *The Liberator.*

1832—The 1832 tariff passed, with rates not lowered.

—South Carolina passed its Nullification Act of the tariffs of 1828 and 1832.

—Jackson reëlected as President.

—Jackson vetoed the bill rechartering the National Bank.

1833—Compromise tariff bill of 1833 passed.

1833—South Carolina accepted this.

—Secretary of the Treasury Roger B. Taney of Maryland withdrew the government's deposits from the National Bank, appointed for the purpose after successive secretaries McLane and Duane had refused to do so.

1834—McCormick reaper invented.

1835—Taney named Chief Justice of the Supreme Court, succeeding John Marshall.

1836—Massacre of the garrison at the Alamo, San Antonio, Texas, by Mexicans, 180 being killed, including Davy Crockett and James Bowie.

Martin Van Buren elected as the 8th President.

—"Gag resolutions" passed in Congress, forbidding petitions against slavery to be read.

1838—Business panic.

1840—William Henry Harrison, Whig, elected as the 9th President.

1841—On the death of Harrison a month after his inauguration, Vice-President Tyler, a Virginia Democrat, became the 10th President.

—President Tyler vetoed the Whig bill rechartering the National Bank, and his Whig cabinet resigned, except Webster, Secretary of State.

1842—On completing the Webster-Ashburton treaty with England, Secretary of State Webster resigned.

1843—England refused our offer to make the line of 49 degrees north the boundary between the United States and Canada, in the Oregon region.

1844—1st telegraph line in the United States, Washington to Baltimore.

—James Polk, Democrat, elected as the 11th President.

1845—United States Naval Academy at Annapolis opened.

—The United States admits the Republic of Texas to statehood.

1846—War between the United States and Mexico.

1847—Mexico City captured.

1848—The treaty of Guadalupe-Hidalgo closed the Mexican War.

—Zachary Taylor, Whig, elected as the 12th President.

—Gold discovered in California, and the gold rush began.

1849—Riots in Astor Place, New York City, against the English actor Macready, in favor of the American actor Edwin Forrest, cost 34 lives.

1850—Clay's Omnibus Bill, the Compromise of 1850, enacted into law. Webster's support of it caused him to be execrated by the anti-slavery group.

—On the death of President Taylor, Vice-President Millard Fillmore became the 13th President.

1852—Franklin Pierce, Democrat, elected the 14th President.

—Harriet Beecher Stowe's *Uncle Tom's Cabin* published.

1853—World's Fair at Crystal Palace, New York City.

—Commodore Perry opened up Japan to American trade.

1854—The Ostend Manifesto, by which three American ministers to Europe announced the intention of the United States to capture Cuba, if it could not be bought. This was disowned.

—The Kansas-Nebraska Act was passed.

1855—First Atlantic cable laid.

1856—James Buchanan, Democrat, elected as 15th President. The present Republican party, founded in 1854, had its first presidential candidate in this election.

—Pro-slavery men sacked Lawrence, Kansas. John Brown massacred 5 Pro-slavery men by Pottawatomie Creek.

1857—Chief-Justice Taney announced the Dred Scott decision declaring that a man could move his slave into any part of the United States, in spite of State laws forbidding it.

—War between Pro-slavery and Anti-slavery settlers in Kansas.

—Financial panic.

—In the Mountain Meadow Massacre, Indians led by Mormons killed 120 emigrants in Utah.

—Hinton Rowan Helper's *The Impending Crisis* published.

1858—Stephen A. Douglas defeated Abraham Lincoln for the Senatorship from Illinois.

1859—John Brown's raid on Harper's Ferry, Virginia. He captured the United States Arsenal, killing 5 men. He was tried, convicted, and hanged.

—First petroleum well opened in the United States, at Titusville, Pennsylvania.

1860—Abraham Lincoln, Republican, elected as 16th President.

—South Carolina seceded from the Union, December 20.

1861—The Confederate States of America established at Montgomery, Alabama, composed of the 7 leading cotton States. Jefferson Davis of Mississippi elected President.

—Fort Sumter, in Charleston Harbor, was fired on by Confederate troops, April 12th, and surrendered two days later.

—Battle of Bull Run, July 21st.

—Lincoln called for volunteers. North Carolina, Arkansas, Tennessee and Virginia joined the Confederacy, the capital being moved to Richmond, Virginia.

1862—The fight engagement of ironclad naval ships, the

Confederate *Merrimac* and the Union *Monitor*, resulted in a draw.

—Admiral Farragut captured New Orleans.

1863—President Lincoln announced his Emancipation Proclamation, January 1st. On November 19th, he delivered his Gettysburg Speech.

—Battle of Gettysburg, won by the Union army on Northern soil. Grant captured Vicksburg. Battles of Chickamauga and Lookout Mountain.

—Draft riots in New York City; 1,000 killed.

1864—Grant made Commander-in-Chief of the Union armies. Sherman's march to the sea.

—Lincoln reëlected as President.

1865—General Robert E. Lee, Confederate Commander-in-Chief, surrendered to Grant at Appomattox, April 9th.

—President Lincoln was assassinated on Good Friday, April 14th, at Ford's Theatre, Washington, by the actor John Wilkes Booth. Vice-President Andrew Johnson became the 17th President.

—Slavery was abolished in the United States, by the adoption of the 13th amendment to the Constitution.

1866—The Ku Klux Klan movement commenced in the South, as an answer to Congressional Reconstruction.

1867—Alaska was purchased from Russia.

1868—President Johnson was impeached, tried and acquitted.

—General Ulysses S. Grant was elected as the 18th President.

1869—"Black Friday" on Wall Street, New York City, caused by a corner in gold, September 24th.

1871—The Great Fire in Chicago; 18,000 buildings destroyed, property loss of $196,000,000.

1872—President Grant reëlected.

1873—Financial panic.

1874—"Boss" W. M. Tweed convicted of fraud and sentenced to 12 years in prison.

1876—Centennial Exhibition in Philadelphia.

—Custer's Last Stand against the Sioux Indians, at Little Big Horn, Montana, with death of General Custer and 276 cavalrymen.

—Disputed election of 1876. Governor Samuel J. Tilden, Democrat, won the popular majority. The 19 disputed Electoral College votes were awarded by an Electoral Commission of 8 Republicans and 7 Democrats to Rutherford B. Hayes, Republican, whereupon he was declared elected by 185 electoral votes to 184, as the 19th President.

—The Knights of Labor reached a membership of 150,000.

1877—11 Molly Maguires, Pennsylvania mining labor agitators, hanged.

1880—James A. Garfield, Republican, elected as the 20th President.

1881—President Garfield was shot on July 2nd by a Stalwart Republican fanatic. Chester A. Arthur, the Vice-President, thereupon became the 21st President.

1882—Work on the Panama Canal begun by the French.

1884—Grover Cleveland, Democrat, elected as the 22nd President.

1885—First electric street railway in the United States, at Baltimore.

1886—Haymarket anarchist riots in Chicago, connected with a strike in the McCormick Reaper Works. 7 Policemen killed by bomb. Several anarchists were executed for this, and one committed suicide in jail.

—Statue of Liberty, the gift of France, unveiled on Bedloe's Island in New York harbor.

1888—Benjamin Harrison, Republican, elected as the 23rd President.

1888—Great blizzard in New York City and the eastern United States, March 11–14th. Senator Roscoe Conkling of New York died from exposure.

1890—Ellis Island opened up in New York harbor to receive immigrants.

—Sioux War, the last war against the Indians.

—Sherman Anti-Trust laws passed.

—McKinley Tariff Act enacted.

1892—Homestead strike riots, near Pittsburgh; 10 killed.

—Cleveland defeated Harrison for the Presidency.

1893—World's Fair (Columbian Exposition) at Chicago.

—Severe financial panic.

1894—The Pullman strike. President Cleveland sent United States troops to keep the trains moving. Eugene V. Debs jailed.

—"General" Jacob S. Coxey led an army of 2,000 unemployed from the Middle West to Washington, D. C. He was finally arrested for walking on the grass, by Capital police.

1895—Bloody insurrection in Cuba against Spain.

1896—William B. McKinley, Republican, defeated William J. Bryan, Democrat, for the Presidency, and became 24th President.

—President Cleveland appointed the Venezuela Boundary Commission.

1897—The gold rush to the Klondike, Alaska, began.

1898—The battleship *Maine* was blown up in Havana harbor, with a loss of 260 men.

—Congress declared Cuba independent, April 19th, and declared war against Spain April 21st.

—Admiral Dewey destroyed Spanish fleet in Manila Bay, April 30th. Battles of San Juan and El Caney, July 1–3rd. Admiral Cervera's fleet destroyed in the Battle of Santiago de Cuba, July 3rd.

1898—Preliminaries for peace with Spain signed August 12th.

1899—The Treaty of Paris, ending the Spanish-American War, signed December 10th preceding, was ratified by the United States Senate Feb. 6th.

—Philippine-American War began February 4th.

1900—McKinley reëlected as President.

—Boxer Rebellions in China. The United States acted with the world powers in suppressing it.

1901—William Howard Taft became first civil governor of the Philippine Islands.

—The Supreme Court decided that the Constitution does not follow the flag, in the case of possessions.

—President McKinley assassinated at the Pan-American Exposition, in Buffalo, Sept. 6th. Theodore Roosevelt became the 25th President.

1902—General Leonard Wood, governor of Cuba, resigned in favor of an elected president, Estrada Palma.

—Great anthracite coal strike of 145,000 miners in Pennsylvania, settled by President Roosevelt.

1903—Revolution in Panama; the young republic set up was immediately recognized by the United States.

—First successful heavier-than-air flying machine flight, at Kitty Hawk, North Carolina, by the brothers Wilbur and Orville Wright.

1904—The United States occupied the Panama Canal Zone, and began digging the Panama Canal.

—Construction of the Panama Canal placed in the hands of Colonel George W. Goethals. The zone was made habitable by the sanitation work of Dr. William C. Gorgas.

—Theodore Roosevelt reëlected as President.

—The Russo-Japanese War settled at Portsmouth, N. H., at President Roosevelt's suggestion.

1906—Hepburn Rate Bill passed.

1906—San Francisco earthquake and fire; over 500 lives lost; property damage, $400,000,000.

—Meat packing-houses investigated by the national government, inspired by Upton Sinclair's novel *The Jungle*.

—Pure Food and Drugs Act and Meat Inspection Act passed.

1907—Second Hague Peace Conference met, at the suggestion of President Roosevelt.

1908—William Howard Taft, Republican, elected as the 26th President.

1909—The Payne Tariff Bill passed.

1910—Ex-President Roosevelt returned from his triumphant world tour.

—The muck-raking era in American magazines.

—In the Congressional by-election, the Democrats carried the House of Representatives.

1911—The Progressive movement organized by Senator La Follette, to capture the Republican nomination.

—The United States Supreme Court ordered the Standard Oil Company and the American Tobacco Company to dissolve.

1912—Woodrow Wilson, Democrat, elected as the 27th President, over Taft, Republican candidate, and Theodore Roosevelt, Progressive candidate.

—The steamship *Titanic* was wrecked on her maiden trip from Liverpool toward New York, by an iceberg off The coast of Newfoundland. 1517 lives were lost.

—Embargo on war munitions into Mexico.

1913—The Underwood Tariff Bill enacted, reducing the Wilson-Gorman Tariff Act rates from 39.4 to about 26%.

—The Federal Reserve Act (the Glass-Owen Act) was enacted into law.

1913—The Clayton Anti-Trust Act, which strengthened the 1890 Sherman Anti-Trust Act, was passed.

1914—Exemption of American vessels from Panama Canal tolls was repealed. The canal was opened in August.

—Admiral Fletcher seized Vera Cruz, and held it until Huerta withdrew.

—The World War broke out. Austria declared war on Serbia on July 28th; the other nations speedily were drawn into the conflict.

—President Wilson announced our neutrality on August 4th.

—American Marines seized Haiti, December 13th.

1915—After Germany announced her submarine war zone around the British Isles, Wilson issued his "strict accountability" note to Germany.

—The *Lusitania* sunk by a submarine, with a loss of 1,200 lives, of whom 114 were Americans, on May 7th.

1916—The *Sussex* sunk, with loss of more American lives. Wilson threatened to break off diplomatic relations with Germany if this continued.

—American Marines seized Santo Domingo. They also intervened in Nicaragua, and remained as a "legation guard."

—Woodrow Wilson reëlected as President.

—Pancho Villa raided Columbus, New Mexico, March 9th. Pershing's punitive expedition was in Mexico from April 12th to Nov. 24th.

1917—Germany resumed unrestricted submarine warfare on February 1st. The United States entered the war on April 6th.

—June 26th, the first American soldiers in France.

—The 18th (Prohibition) amendment to the Constitution was submitted to the states. It was ratified by the necessary 26 states by January, 1919.

1918—President Wilson's 14 points of peace announced to Congress, Jan. 8th.

—Upon the collapse of the Central Powers, an armistice ending the World War was signed November 11th.

1919—The Versailles Peace Treaty, signed June 28th, formally terminated the war.

—Revolt in Haiti against American occupation; more than 1,800 Haitians killed by American marines.

1920—The 19th Amendment to the Constitution, giving equal suffrage to women, went into effect.

—Warren Gamaliel Harding, Republican, was elected as the 28th President.

1921—The United States signed separate peace agreements with Germany and Austria, after refusing to join the League of Nations.

—America's Unknown Soldier was buried at Arlington National Cemetery, Nov. 11th.

—Washington Conference against war.

1922—The Fordney-McCumber Tariff Act restored high tariff rates.

1923—On the death of President Harding on a trip to Alaska, Calvin Coolidge, Republican Vice-President, became the 29th President.

1924—Coolidge reëlected as President.

—The Teapot Dome scandal.

—The Allies and Germany accepted the Dawes Reparation plan.

1925—United States marines withdrawn from Nicaragua.

1926—The League of Nations admitted Germany.

1927—The United States intervened in Nicaragua again, the marines remaining until 1933.

—The United States Supreme Court voided the Doheny oil leases; President Coolidge cancelled others connected with the Teapot Dome scandal.

1927—Charles A. Lindbergh flew solo from New York to Paris.

1928—Herbert Clark Hoover, Republican, elected as the 30th President.

1929—The Kellogg-Briand Anti-War Treaty, binding the world's 62 leading nations to renounce war as an instrument of national policy.

—The stock market crash, followed by a long depression.

1930—The London Naval Reduction treaty signed.

1932—Franklin Delano Roosevelt, Democrat, elected as the 31st President.

1933—Bank holidays commenced Feb. 14th, paralyzing the nation's banking as Roosevelt was inaugurated. President Roosevelt took control promptly, his remedies being called the New Deal.

—The Prohibition amendment to the Constitution was repealed.

1934—In Congressional by-elections, the New Deal was upheld.

—Damaging drought in the United States, especially in the Mid-West.

1935—The Boulder Dam, largest in the world, formally opened.

—The United States Supreme Court ruled that vital parts of the New Deal were unconstitutional.

1936—Unemployment still a national problem.

—Reëlection of Franklin Delano Roosevelt.

1939—Second World War broke out in Europe.

1940—Roosevelt reëlected for third term as President.

—United States began gigantic defense program.

CONSTITUTION OF THE UNITED STATES

CONSTITUTION OF THE UNITED STATES

PREAMBLE

We, the people of the United States, in order to form a more perfect Union, establish justice, insure domestic tranquillity, provide for the common defense, promote the general welfare, and secure the blessings of liberty to ourselves and our posterity, do ordain and establish this CONSTITUTION for the United States of America.

ARTICLE I

Section 1—(Legislative power: in whom vested.)

All legislative powers herein granted shall be vested in a Congress of the United States, which shall consist of a Senate and House of Representatives.

Section 2—(House of Representatives, how and by whom chosen. Qualifications of a Representative. Representatives and direct taxes, how apportioned. Enumeration. Vacancies to be filled. Power of choosing officers, and of impeachment.)

1. The House of Representatives shall be composed of members chosen every second year by the people of the several States, and the electors in each State shall have the qualifications requisite for electors of the most numerous branch of the State Legislature.

2. No person shall be a Representative who shall not have attained to the age of twenty-five years and been seven years a citizen of the United States, and who shall not, when elected, be an inhabitant of that State in which he shall be chosen.

3. Representatives and direct taxes shall be apportioned among the several States which may be included within this Union according to their respective numbers, which shall be determined by adding to the whole number of free persons, including those bound to service for a term of years, and excluding Indians not taxed, three-fifths of all

other persons. The actual enumeration shall be made within three years after the first meeting of the Congress of the United States, and within every subsequent term of ten years, in such manner as they shall by law direct. The number of Representatives shall not exceed one for every thirty thousand, but each State shall have at least one Representative; and until such enumeration shall be made, the State of New Hampshire shall be entitled to choose 3; Massachusetts, 8; Rhode Island and Providence Plantations, 1; Connecticut, 5; New York, 6; New Jersey, 4; Pennsylvania, 8; Delaware, 1; Maryland, 6; Virginia, 10; North Carolina, 5; South Carolina, 5, and Georgia, 3.*

4. When vacancies happen in the representation from any State, the Executive Authority thereof shall issue writs of election to fill such vacancies.

5. The House of Representatives shall choose their Speaker and other officers, and shall have the sole power of impeachment.

Section 3—(Senators, how and by whom chosen. How classified. State Executive, when to make temporary appointments, in case, etc. Qualifications of a Senator. President of the Senate, his right to vote. President pro tem., and other officers of the Senate, how chosen. Power to try impeachments. When President is tried, Chief Justice to preside. Sentence.)

1. The Senate of the United States shall be composed of two Senators from each State, chosen by the Legislature thereof, for six years; and each Senator shall have one vote.

2. Immediately after they shall be assembled in consequence of the first election, they shall be divided as equally as may be into three classes. The seats of the Senators of the first class shall be vacated at the expiration of the second year, of the second class at the expiration of the fourth year, and of the third class at the expiration of the sixth year, so that one-third may be chosen every second year; and if vacancies happen by resignation or otherwise, during the recess of the Legislature of any State, the Executive thereof may make temporary appointment until the next meeting of the Legislature, which shall then fill such vacancies.

3. No person shall be a Senator who shall not have attained to the age of thirty years, and been nine years a citizen of the United States,

* See Article XIV, Amendments.

and who shall not, when elected, be an inhabitant of that State for which he shall be chosen.

4. The Vice-President of the United States shall be President of the Senate, but shall have no vote unless they be equally divided.

5. The Senate shall choose their other officers, and also a President pro tempore, in the absence of the Vice-President, or when he shall exercise the office of the President of the United States.

6. The Senate shall have the sole power to try all impeachments. When sitting for that purpose, they shall be on oath or affirmation. When the President of the United States is tried, the Chief Justice shall preside; and no person shall be convicted without the concurrence of two-thirds of the members present.

7. Judgment of cases of impeachment shall not extend further than to removal from office, and disqualification to hold and enjoy any office of honor, trust, or profit under the United States; but the party convicted shall nevertheless be liable and subject to indictment, trial, judgment, and punishment, according to law.

Section 4—(Times, etc., of holding elections, how prescribed. One session in each year.)

1. The times, places and manner of holding elections for Senators and Representatives shall be prescribed in each State by the Legislature thereof; but the Congress may at any time by law make or alter such regulations, except as to places of choosing Senators.

2. The Congress shall assemble at least once in every year, and such meeting shall be on the first Monday in December, unless they shall by law appoint a different day.

Section 5—(Membership, Quorum, Adjournments. Rules. Power to punish or expel. Journal. Time of adjournments, how limited, etc.)

1. Each House shall be the judge of the elections, returns, and qualifications of its own members, and a majority of each shall constitute a quorum to do business; but a smaller number may adjourn from day to day, and may be authorized to compel the attendance of absent members in such manner and under such penalties as each House may provide.

2. Each House may determine the rules of its proceedings, punish its members for disorderly behavior, and with the concurrence of two-thirds expel a member.

3. Each House shall keep a journal of its proceedings, and from time to time publish the same, excepting such parts as may in their judgment require secrecy; and the yeas and nays of the members of either House on any question shall, at the desire of one-fifth of those present, be entered on the journal.

4. Neither House, during the session of Congress shall, without the consent of the other, adjourn for more than three days, nor to any other place than that in which the two Houses shall be sitting.

Section 6—(Compensation. Privileges. Disqualification in certain cases.)

1. The Senators and Representatives shall receive a compensation for their services to be ascertained by law, and paid out of the Treasury of the United States. They shall in all cases, except treason, felony, and breach of the peace, be privileged from arrest during their attendance at the session of their respective Houses, and in going to and returning from the same, and for any speech or debate in either House they shall not be questioned in any other place.

2. No Senator or Representative shall, during the time for which he was elected, be appointed to any civil office under the authority of the United States which shall have been created, or the emoluments whereof shall have been increased during such time; and no person holding any office under the United States shall be a member of either House during his continuance in office.

Section 7—(House to originate all revenue bills. Veto. Bill may be passed by two-thirds of each House, notwithstanding, etc. Bill, not returned in ten days, to become a law. Provisions as to orders, concurrent resolutions, etc.)

1. All bills for raising revenue shall originate in the House of Representatives, but the Senate may propose or concur with amendments, as on other bills.

2. Every bill which shall have passed the House of Representatives and the Senate shall, before it becomes a law, be presented to the President of the United States; if he approve, he shall sign it, but if not, he shall return it, with his objections, to that House in which it shall have originated, who shall enter the objections at large on their journal, and proceed to reconsider it. If after such reconsideration two-thirds of that House shall agree to pass the bill, it shall be sent, together with the objections, to the other House, by which it shall

likewise be reconsidered; and if approved by two-thirds of that House it shall become a law. But in all such cases the votes of both Houses shall be determined by yeas and nays, and the names of the persons voting for and against the bill shall be entered on the journal of each House respectively. If any bills shall not be returned by the President within ten days (Sundays excepted) after it shall have been presented to him, the same shall be a law in like manner as if he had signed it, unless the Congress by their adjournment prevent its return; in which case it shall not be a law.

3. Every order, resolution, or vote to which the concurrence of the Senate and House of Representatives may be necessary (except on a question of adjournment) shall be presented to the President of the United States, and before the same shall take effect shall be approved by him, or being disapproved by him, shall be repassed by two-thirds of the Senate and the House of Representatives, according to the rules and limitations prescribed in the case of a bill.

Section 8—(Powers of Congress.)

1. The Congress shall have power:

To lay and collect taxes, duties, imposts, and excises, to pay the debts and provide for the common defense and general welfare of the United States; but all duties, imposts, and excises shall be uniform throughout the United States.

2. To borrow money on the credit of the United States.

3. To regulate commerce with foreign nations, and among the several States and with the Indian tribes.

4. To establish a uniform rule of naturalization and uniform laws on the subject of bankruptcies throughout the United States.

5. To coin money, regulate the value thereof, and of foreign coin, and fix the standard of weights and measures.

6. To provide for the punishment of counterfeiting the securities and current coin of the United States.

7. To establish post-offices and post-roads.

8. To promote the progress of science and useful arts by securing for limited times to authors and inventors the exclusive rights to their respective writings and discoveries.

9. To constitute tribunals inferior to the Supreme Court.

10. To define and punish piracies and felonies committed on the high seas, and offenses against the law of nations.

11. To declare war, grant letters of marque and reprisal, and make rules concerning captures on land and water.

12. To raise and support armies, but no appropriation of money to that use shall be for a longer term than two years.

13. To provide and maintain a navy.

14. To make rules for the government and regulation of the land and naval forces.

15. To provide for calling forth the militia to execute the laws of the Union, suppress insurrections, and repel invasions.

16. To provide for organizing, arming, and disciplining the militia, and for governing such part of them as may be employed in the service of the United States, reserving to the States respectively the appointment of the officers, and the authority of training the militia according to the discipline prescribed by Congress.

17. To exercise exclusive legislation in all cases whatsoever over such district (not exceeding ten miles square) as may, by cession of particular States and the acceptance of Congress, become the seat of Government of the United States, and to exercise like authority over all places purchased by the consent of the Legislature of the State in which the same shall be, for the erection of forts, magazines, arsenals, drydocks, and other needful buildings.

18. To make all laws which shall be necessary and proper for carrying into execution the foregoing powers and all other powers vested by this Constitution in the Government of the United States, or in any department or officer thereof.

Section 9—Provisions as to migration or importation of certain persons. Habeas corpus. Bills of attainder, etc. Taxes, how apportioned. No export duty. No commercial preference. Money, how drawn from Treasury, etc. No titular nobility. Officers not to receive presents, etc.)

1. The migration or importation of such persons as any of the States now existing shall think proper to admit shall not be prohibited by the Congress prior to the year one thousand eight hundred and eight, but a tax or duty may be imposed on such importations, not exceeding ten dollars for each person.

2. The privilege of the writ of habeas corpus shall not be suspended, unless when in cases of rebellion or invasion the public safety may require it.

3. No bill of attainder or ex post facto law shall be passed.

4. No capitation or other direct tax shall be laid, unless in proportion to the census or enumeration hereinbefore directed to be taken.

5. No tax or duty shall be laid on articles exported from any State.

6. No preference shall be given by any regulation of commerce or revenue to the ports of one State over those of another, nor shall vessels bound to or from one State be obliged to enter, clear, or pay duties to another.

7. No money shall be drawn from the Treasury but in consequence of appropriations made by law; and a regular statement and account of the receipts and expenditures of all public money shall be published from time to time.

8. No title of nobility shall be granted by the United States. And no person holding any office of profit or trust under them shall, without the consent of the Congress, accept of any present, emolument, office, or title of any kind whatever from any king, prince, or foreign state.

Section 10—(States prohibited from the exercise of certain powers.)

1. No State shall enter into any treaty, alliance, or confederation, grant letters of marque and reprisal, coin money, emit bills of credit, make anything but gold and silver coin a tender in payment of debts, pass any bill of attainder, ex post facto law, or law impairing the obligation of contracts, or grant any title of nobility.

2. No State shall, without the consent of the Congress, lay any impost or duties on imports or exports, except what may be absolutely necessary for executing its inspection laws, and the net produce of all duties and imposts, laid by any State on imports or exports, shall be for the use of the Treasury of the United States; and all such laws shall be subject to the revision and control of the Congress.

3. No State shall, without the consent of Congress, lay any duty of tonnage, keep troops or ships of war in time of peace, enter into agreement or compact with another State, or with a foreign power, or engage in war, unless actually invaded, or in such imminent damage as will not admit of delay.

ARTICLE II

Section 1—(President; his term of office. Electors of President; number and how appointed. Electors to vote on same day. Qualification of President. On whom his duties devolve in case of his removal, death, etc. President's compensation. His oath of office.)

1. The Executive power shall be vested in a President of the United States of America. He shall hold his office during the term of four years, and, together with the Vice-President, chosen for the same term, be elected as follows:

2. Each State shall appoint, in such manner as the Legislature thereof may direct, a number of electors equal to the whole number of Senators and Representatives to which the State may be entitled in the Congress; but no Senator or Representative or person holding an office of trust or profit under the United States shall be appointed an elector.

3. The electors shall meet in their respective States and vote by ballot for two persons, of whom one at least shall not be an inhabitant of the same State with themselves. And they shall make a list of all the persons voted for, and of the number of votes for each, which list they shall sign and certify and transmit, sealed, to the seat of the Government of the United States, directed to the President of the Senate. The President of the Senate shall, in the presence of the Senate and House of Representatives, open all the certificates, and the votes shall then be counted. The person having the greatest number of votes shall be the President, if such number be a majority of the whole number of electors appointed, and if there be more than one who have such a majority, and have an equal number of votes, then the House of Representatives shall immediately choose by ballot one of them for President; and if no person have a majority, then from the five highest on the list the said House shall in like manner choose the President. But in choosing the President, the vote shall be taken by States, the representation from each State having one vote. A quorum, for this purpose, shall consist of a member or members from two-thirds of the States, and a majority of all the States shall be necessary to a choice. In every case, after the choice of the President, the person having the greatest number of votes of

the electors shall be the Vice-President. But if there should remain two or more who have equal votes, the Senate shall choose from them by ballot the Vice-President.*

4. The Congress may determine the time of choosing the electors and the day on which they shall give their votes, which day shall be the same throughout the United States.

5. No person except a natural born citizen, or a citizen of the United States, at the time of the adoption of the Constitution, shall be eligible to the office of President; neither shall any person be eligible to that office who shall not have attained to the age of thirty-five years and been fourteen years a resident within the United States.

6. In case of the removal of the President from office, or of his death, resignation, or inability to discharge the powers and duties of the said office, the same shall devolve on the Vice-President, and the Congress may by law provide for the case of removal, death, resignation, or inability, both of the President and Vice-President, declaring what officer shall then act as President, and such officer shall act accordingly until the disability be removed or a President shall be elected.

7. The President shall, at stated times, receive for his services a compensation which shall neither be increased nor diminished during the period for which he shall have been elected, and he shall not receive within that period any other emolument from the United States, or any of them.

8. Before he enter on the execution of his office he shall take the following oath or affirmation:

"I do solemnly swear (or affirm) that I will faithfully execute the office of President of the United States, and will, to the best of my ability, preserve, protect, and defend the Constitution of the United States."

Section 2—(President to be Commander-in-Chief. He may require opinions of Cabinet Officers, etc., may pardon. Treaty-making power. Nomination of certain officers. When President may fill vacancies.)

1. The President shall be Commander-in-Chief of the Army and Navy of the United States, and of the militia of the several States

* This clause is superseded by Article XII, Amendments.

when called into the actual service of the United States; he may require the opinion, in writing, of the principal officer in each of the executive departments upon any subject relating to the duties of their respective offices, and he shall have power to grant reprieves and pardons for offenses against the United States except in cases of impeachment.

2. He shall have power, by and with the advice and consent of the Senate to make treaties, provided two-thirds of the Senators present concur; and he shall nominate and by and with the advice and consent of the Senate shall appoint ambassadors, other public ministers and consuls, judges of the Supreme Court, and all other officers of the United States whose appointments are not herein otherwise provided for, and which shall be established by law; but the Congress may by law vest the appointment of such inferior officers as they think proper in the President alone, in the courts of law, or in the heads of departments.

3. The President shall have power to fill up all vacancies that may happen during the recess of the Senate by granting commissions, which shall expire at the end of their next session.

Section 3—(President shall communicate to Congress. He may convene and adjourn Congress, in case of disagreement, etc. Shall receive ambassadors, execute laws, and commission officers.)

He shall from time to time give to the Congress information of the state of the Union, and recommend to their consideration such measures as he shall judge necessary and expedient; he may, on extraordinary occasions, convene both Houses, or either of them, and in case of disagreement between them with respect to the time of adjournment, he may adjourn them to such time as he shall think proper; he shall receive ambassadors and other public ministers; he shall take care that the laws be faithfully executed, and shall commission all the officers of the United States.

Section 4—(All civil offices forfeited for certain crimes.)

The President, Vice-President, and all civil officers of the United States shall be removed from office on impeachment for and conviction of treason, bribery or other high crimes and misdemeanors.

ARTICLE III

Section 1—(Judicial powers. Tenure. Compensation.)

The judicial power of the United States shall be vested in one Supreme Court, and in such inferior courts as the Congress may from time to time ordain and establish. The judges, both of the Supreme and inferior courts, shall hold their offices during good behavior, and shall at stated times receive for their services a compensation which shall not be diminished during their continuance in office.

Section 2—(Judicial power; to what cases it extends. Original jurisdiction of Supreme Court. Appellate. Trial by jury, etc. Trial, where.)

1. The judicial power shall extend to all cases in law and equity arising under this Constitution, the laws of the United States, and treaties made, or which shall be made, under their authority; to all cases affecting ambassadors, other public ministers and consuls; to all cases of admiralty and maritime jurisdiction; to controversies to which the United States shall be a party; to controversies between two or more States, between a State and citizens of another State, between citizens of different States, between citizens of the same State claiming lands under grants of different States, and between a State or the citizens thereof, and foreign states, citizens, or subjects.

2. In all cases affecting ambassadors, other public ministers, and consuls, and those in which a State shall be party, the Supreme Court shall have original jurisdiction. In all the other cases before mentioned the Supreme Court shall have appellate jurisdiction both as to law and fact, with such exceptions and under such regulations as the Congress shall make.

3. The trial of all crimes, except in cases of impeachment, shall be by jury, and such trial shall be held in the State where the said crimes shall have been committed; but when not committed within any State the trial shall be at such place or places as the Congress may by law have directed.

Section 3—(Treason defined. Proof of. Punishment of.)

1. Treason against the United States shall consist only in levying war against them, or in adhering to their enemies, giving them aid and comfort. No person shall be convicted of treason unless on the

testimony of two witnesses to the same overt act, or on confession in open court.

2. The Congress shall have power to declare the punishment of treason, but no attainder of treason shall work corruption of blood or forfeiture except during the life of the person attained.

ARTICLE IV

Section 1—(Each State to give credit to the public acts, etc., of every other State.)

Full faith and credit shall be given in each State to the public acts, records, and judicial proceedings of every other State. And the Congress may by general laws prescribe the manner in which such acts, records, and proceedings shall be proved, and the effect thereof.

Section 2—(Privileges of citizens of each State. Fugitives from justice to be delivered up. Persons held to service having escaped, to be delivered up.)

1. The citizens of each State shall be entitled to all privileges and immunities of citizens in the several States.

2. A person charged in any State with treason, felony, or other crime, who shall flee from justice, and be found in another State, shall, on demand of the Executive authority of the State from which he fled, be delivered up to be removed to the State having jurisdiction of the crime.

3. No person held to service or labor in one State, under the laws thereof, escaping into another shall in consequence of any law or regulation therein, be discharged from such service or labor, but shall be delivered up on claim of the party to whom such service or labor may be due.

Section 3—(Admission of new States. Power of Congress over territory and other property.)

1. New States may be admitted by the Congress into this Union; but no new States shall be formed or erected within the jurisdiction of any other State, nor any State be formed by the junction of two or more States, or parts of States, without the consent of the Legislatures of the States concerned, as well as of the Congress.

2. The Congress shall have power to dispose of and make all needful rules and regulations respecting the territory or other property

belonging to the United States; and nothing in this Constitution shall be so construed as to prejudice any claims of the United States, or of any particular State.

Section 4—(Republican form of government guaranteed. Each State to be protected.)

The United States shall guarantee to every State in this Union a Republican form of government, and shall protect each of them against invasion, and on application of the Legislature, or of the Executive (when the Legislature cannot be convened) against domestic violence.

ARTICLE V

(Constitution; how amended. Proviso.)

The Congress, whenever two-thirds or both Houses shall deem it necessary, shall propose amendments to this Constitution, or, on the application of the Legislatures of two-thirds of the several States, shall call a convention for proposing amendments which in either case, shall be valid to all intents and purposes, as part of this Constitution, when ratified by the Legislatures of three-fourths of the several States, or by conventions in three-fourths thereof, as the one or the other mode of ratification may be proposed by the Congress, provided that no amendment which may be made prior to the year one thousand eight hundred and eight shall in any manner affect the first and fourth clauses in the Ninth Section of the First Article; and that no State, without its consent, shall be deprived of its equal suffrage in the Senate.

ARTICLE VI

(Certain debts, etc., declared valid. Supremacy of Constitution, treaties, and laws of the United States. Oath to support Constitution, by whom taken. No religious test.)

1. All debts contracted and engagements entered into before the adoption of this Constitution shall be as valid against the United States under this Constitution as under the Confederation.

2. This Constitution and the laws of the United States which shall be made in pursuance thereof and all treaties made, or which shall be made, under the authority of the United States, shall be the supreme law of the land, and the judges in every State shall be bound

thereby, anything in the Constitution or laws of any State to the contrary notwithstanding.

3. The Senators and Representatives before mentioned, and the members of the several State Legislatures, and all Executives and judicial officers, both of the United States and of the several States, shall be bound by oath or affirmation to support this Constitution; but no religious test shall ever be required as a qualification to any office or public trust under the United States.

ARTICLE VII

(What ratification shall establish Constitution.)

The ratification of the Conventions of nine States shall be sufficient for the establishment of this Constitution between the States so ratifying the same.

Done in convention by the unanimous consent of the States present, the 17th day of September, in the year of our Lord one thousand seven hundred and eighty-seven, and of the independence of the United States of America the twelfth.

AMENDMENTS

ARTICLE I

Religious Establishment Prohibited. Freedom of Speech, of the Press, and Right to Petition.

Congress shall make no law respecting an establishment of religion, or prohibiting the free exercise thereof; or abridging the freedom of speech or of the press; or the right of the people peaceably to assemble and to petition the Government for a redress of grievances.

ARTICLE II

Right to Keep and Bear Arms.

A well-regulated militia being necessary to the security of a free State, the right of the people to keep and bear arms shall not be infringed.

ARTICLE III

No Soldier to be Quartered in Any House, Unless, etc.

No soldier shall, in time of peace, be quartered in any house without the consent of the owner, nor in time of war but in a manner to be prescribed by law.

ARTICLE IV

Right of Search and Seizure Regulated.

The right of the people to be secure in their persons, houses, papers, and effects, against unreasonable searches and seizures, shall not be violated, and no warrants shall issue, but upon probable cause, supported by oath or affirmation, and particularly describing the place to be searched, and the persons or things to be seized.

ARTICLE V

Provisions Concerning Prosecution, Trial and Punishment.—Private Property Not to be Taken for Public Use Without Compensation.

No person shall be held to answer for a capital or other infamous crime unless on a presentment or indictment of a Grand Jury, except in cases arising in the land or naval forces, or in the militia, when in actual service, in time of war or public danger; nor shall any person be subject for the same offense to be twice put in jeopardy of life or limb; nor shall be compelled in any criminal case to be a witness against himself, nor be deprived of life, liberty, or property, without due process of law; nor shall private property be taken for public use without just compensation.

ARTICLE VI

Right to Speedy Trial, Witnesses, etc.

In all criminal prosecutions, the accused shall enjoy the right to a speedy and public trial, by an impartial jury of the State and district wherein the crime shall have been committed, which districts shall have been previously ascertained by law, and to be informed of the nature and cause of the accusation; to be confronted with the witnesses against him; to have compulsory process for obtaining witnesses in his favor, and to have the assistance of counsel for his defense.

ARTICLE VII

Right of Trial by Jury.

In suits at common law, where the value in controversy shall exceed twenty dollars, the right of trial by jury shall be preserved, and no fact tried by a jury shall be otherwise re-examined in any court of the United States than according to the rules of the common law.

ARTICLE VIII

Excessive Bail or Fines and Cruel Punishment Prohibited.

Excessive bail shall not be required, nor excessive fines imposed, nor cruel and unusual punishments inflicted.

ARTICLE IX

Rule of Construction of Constitution.

The enumeration in the Constitution of certain rights shall not be construed to deny or disparage others retained by the people.

ARTICLE X

Rights of States Under Constitution.

The powers not delegated to the United States by the Constitution, nor prohibited by it to the States, are reserved to the States respectively, or to the people.

ARTICLE XI

Judicial Powers Construed.

The following amendment was proposed to the Legislatures of the several States by the Third Congress on the 4th of March, 1794, and was declared to have been ratified in a message from the President to Congress, dated Jan. 8, 1798.

The judicial power of the United States shall not be construed to extend to any suit in law or equity, commenced or prosecuted against one of the United States, by citizens of another State, or by citizens or subjects of any foreign state.

ARTICLE XII

Manner of Choosing President and Vice-President.

The following amendment was proposed to the Legislatures of the several States by the Eighth Congress on the 12th of December, 1803, and was declared to have been ratified in a proclamation by the Secretary of State, dated September 25, 1804. It was ratified by 12 of 17 States, and was rejected by Connecticut.

The Electors shall meet in their respective States, and vote by ballot for President and Vice-President, one of whom at least shall not be an inhabitant of the same State with themselves; they shall name in their ballots the person voted for as President, and in distinct ballots the persons voted for as Vice-President; and they shall make distinct list of all persons voted for as President, and of all persons voted for as Vice-President, and of the number of votes for each, which list they shall sign and certify, and transmit, sealed, to the seat of the Government of the United States, directed to the President of the Senate; the President of the Senate shall, in the presence of the Senate and House of Representatives, open all the certificates and the votes shall then be counted; the person having the greatest number of votes for President shall be the President, if such number be a majority of the whole number of Electors appointed; and if no person have such majority, then from the persons having the highest number, not exceeding three, on the list of those voted for as President, the House of Representatives shall choose immediately, by ballot the President. But in choosing the President, the votes shall be taken by States, the representation from each State having one vote; a quorum for this purpose shall consist of a member or members from two-thirds of the States, and a majority of all the States shall be necessary to a choice. And if the House of Representatives shall not choose a President, whenever the right of choice shall devolve upon them, before the fourth day of March next following, then the Vice-President shall act as President, as in the case of the death or other constitutional disability of the President. The person having the greatest number of votes as Vice-President shall be the Vice-President if such number be a majority of the whole number of Electors appointed, and if no person have a majority, then from the two highest numbers on the list the Senate shall choose the Vice-President; a quorum for the purpose shall consist of two-thirds of the whole number of Senators, and a majority of the whole number shall be necessary to a choice. But no person constitutionally ineligible to the office of President shall be eligible to that of Vice-President of the United States.

(The 13th, 14th and 15th Amendments to the Constitution are generally known as the Reconstruction Amendments. They were adopted immediately following the Civil War and were intended to prevent Negro slavery in any form or under other names.)

ARTICLE XIII

Slavery Abolished.

The following amendment was proposed to the Legislatures of the several States by the Thirty-eighth Congress on the 1st of February, 1865, and was declared to have been ratified in a proclamation by the Secretary of State dated December 18, 1865. It finally was ratified by 33 of the 36 States, and was rejected by Delaware (Feb. 8, 1865) (ratified in Feb., 1901) and Mississippi.

President Lincoln signed the joint resolution of Congress proposing the 13th amendment, although such resolutions (proposing amendments) are not submitted to the President. The U. S. Supreme Court decided, in 1798, that the President has nothing to do with the proposing of amendments to the Constitution, or their adoption.

1. Neither slavery nor involuntary servitude, except as a punishment for crime whereof the party shall have been duly convicted, shall exist within the United States, or any place subject to their jurisdiction.

2. Congress shall have power to enforce this article by appropriate legislation.

ARTICLE XIV

Citizenship Rights Not to be Abridged.

The following amendment was proposed to the Legislatures of the several States by the Thirty-ninth Congress on the 13th of June, 1866, and was declared to have been ratified in a proclamation by the Secretary of State, dated July 28, 1868. The amendment got the support of 23 Northern States; it was rejected by Delaware (Feb. 7, 1867) (ratified in Feb. 1901); Kentucky, Maryland, and 10 Southern States. California took no action. Subsequently it was ratified by the 10 Southern States.

The 14th amendment was adopted only by virtue of ratification subsequent to earlier rejections. Newly constituted legislatures in both North Carolina and South Carolina, respectively, on July 4 and 9, 1868, ratified the proposed amendment, although earlier legislatures had rejected the proposal. The Secretary of State issued a proclamation which, though doubtful as to the effect of attempted withdrawals by New York and New Jersey, entertained no doubt as to the validity of the ratification by North and South Carolina. The following day, July 21, 1868, Congress passed a resolution which declared the 14th amendment to be a part of the Constitution and directed the Secretary of State so to promulgate it. The Secretary waited, however, until the newly constituted legislature of Georgia had ratified the amendment, subsequent to an earlier rejection, before the promulgation of the ratification of the new amendment.

1. All persons born or naturalized in the United States, and subject to the jurisdiction thereof, are citizens of the United States and of the State wherein they reside. No State shall make or enforce any law which shall abridge the privileges or immunities of citizens of the United States, nor shall any State deprive any person of life, liberty, or property without due process of law, nor deny to any person within its jurisdiction the equal protection of the laws.

Apportionment of Representatives in Congress.

2. Representatives shall be apportioned among the several States according to their respective numbers counting the whole number of persons in each State excluding Indians not taxed. But when the right to vote at any election for the choice of Electors for President and Vice-President of the United States, Representatives in Congress, the executive and judicial officers of a State, or the members of the Legislature thereof, is denied to any of the male inhabitants of such State, being twenty-one years of age, and citizens of the United States, or in any way abridged, except for participation in rebellion, or other crime, the basis of representation therein shall be reduced in the proportion which the number of such male citizens shall bear to the whole number of male citizens twenty-one years of age in such State.

Power of Congress to Remove Disabilities of United States Officials for Rebellion.

3. No person shall be a Senator or Representative in Congress, or Elector of President and Vice-President or holding any office, civil or military, under the United States, or under any State, who, having previously taken an oath, as a member of Congress, or as an officer

of the United States, or as a member of any State Legislature or as an executive or judicial officer of any State, to support the Constitution of the United States, shall have engaged in insurrection or rebellion against the same, or given aid and comfort to the enemies thereof. But Congress may, by a vote of two-thirds of each House, remove such disability.

What Public Debts Are Valid.

4. The validity of the public debt of the United States, authorized by law, including debts incurred for payment of pensions and bounties for services in suppressing insurrection and rebellion, shall not be questioned. But neither the United States nor any State shall assume or pay any debt or obligation incurred in aid of insurrection or rebellion against the United States, or any claim for the loss or emancipation of any slave; but all such debts, obligations, and claims shall be held illegal and void.

5. The Congress shall have power to enforce by appropriate legislation the provisions of this article.

ARTICLE XV

Equal Rights for White and Colored Citizens.

The following amendment was proposed to the Legislatures of the several States by the Fortieth Congress on the 26th of February, 1869, and was declared to have been ratified in a proclamation by the Secretary of State, dated March 30, 1870. It was ratified by 31 of the 37 States, and was rejected by California, Delaware (March 18, 1869) (ratified in Feb., 1901) and Kentucky. New York rescinded its ratification Jan. 5, 1870. New Jersey rejected it in 1870, but ratified it in 1871.

1. The right of the citizens of the United States to vote shall not be denied or abridged by the United States or by any State on account of race, color, or previous condition of servitude.

2. The Congress shall have power to enforce the provisions of this article by appropriate legislation.

ARTICLE XVI

Income Taxes Authorized.

The following amendment was proposed to the Legislatures of the several States by the Sixty-first Congress on the 12th day of July, 1909, and was declared to have been ratified in a proclamation by the Secretary of State, dated February 25, 1913. The amendment was ratified by 42 of the 48 States, and was rejected by Connecticut, Rhode Island, and Utah.

The Congress shall have power to lay and collect taxes on incomes, from whatever sources derived, without apportionment among the several States, and without regard to any census or enumeration.

ARTICLE XVII

United States Senators to be Elected by Direct Popular Vote.

The following amendment was proposed to the Legislatures of the several States by the Sixty-second Congress on the 16th day of May, 1912, and was declared to have been ratified in a proclamation by the Secretary of State, dated May 31, 1913. The amendment was adopted by 37 of the 48 States, but was rejected by Utah.

1. The Senate of the United States shall be composed of two Senators from each State, elected by the people thereof, for six years; and each Senator shall have one vote. The electors in each State shall have the qualifications requisite for electors of the most numerous branch of the State Legislatures.

2. When vacancies happen in the representation of any State in the Senate, the executive authority of such State shall issuc writs of election to fill such vacancies: Provided, That the Legislature of any State may empower the Executive thereof to make temporary appointment until the people fill the vacancies by election as the Legislature may direct.

3. This amendment shall not be so construed as to affect the election or term of any Senator chosen before it becomes valid as part of the Constitution.

ARTICLE XVIII

Liquor Prohibition Amendment.

The following amendment was proposed to the Legislatures of the several States by the Sixty-fifth Congress, December 18, 1917: and on January 29, 1919, the United States Secretary of State proclaimed its adoption by 36 States, and declared it in effect on January 16, 1920.

The total vote in the Senates of the various States was, 1,310 for, 237 against—84.6% dry. In the lower houses of the States the vote was, 3,782 for, 1,035 against—78.5% dry.

The amendment ultimately was adopted by all the States except Connecticut and Rhode Island.

1. After one year from the ratification of this article the manufacture, sale, or transportation of intoxicating liquors within, the importation thereof into, or the exportation thereof from the United States and all territory subject to the jurisdiction thereof for beverage purposes is hereby prohibited.

2. The Congress and the several States shall have concurrent power to enforce this article by appropriate legislation.

3. This article shall be inoperative unless it shall have been ratified as an amendment to the Constitution by the Legislatures of the several States, as provided in the Constitution, within seven years from the date of the submission hereof to the States by the Congress.

ARTICLE XIX

Giving Nation-Wide Suffrage to Women.

The following amendment was proposed to the Legislatures of the several States by the Sixty-fifth Congress having been adopted by the House of Representatives, May 21, 1919, and by the Senate, June 4, 1919. On August 26, 1920, the United States Secretary of State proclaimed it in effect, having been adopted (June 10, 1919–August 18, 1920) by three-quarters of the States. In West Virginia, despite Senate rules of procedure which forbade reconsideration of a measure during the session in which it was defeated, the Senate ratified the proposed 19th amendment, subsequent to a rejection in the same session. The amendment was rejected by Alabama, Maryland, and Virginia.

1. The right of citizens of the United States to vote shall not be denied or abridged by the United States or by any State on account of sex.

2. Congress shall have power, by appropriate legislation, to enforce the provisions of this article.

ARTICLE XX

Terms of President and Vice-President to begin on Jan. 20; those of Senators and Representatives, on Jan. 3.

The following amendment was proposed to the Legislatures of the several States by the Seventy-second Congress, in March, 1932, a joint resolution to that effect having been adopted, first by the House, and then, on March 2, by the Senate. On Feb. 6, 1933, the Secretary of State proclaimed it in effect, 39 of the 48 States having ratified. By Oct. 15, 1933, it had been ratified by all of the 48 States.

Section 1. The terms of the President and Vice-President shall end at noon on the 20th day of January, and the terms of Senators and Representatives at noon on the 3rd day of January, of the years in which such terms would have ended if this article had not been ratified; and the terms of their successors shall then begin.

Section 2. The Congress shall assemble at least once in every year, and such meeting shall begin at noon on the 3rd day of January, unless they shall by law appoint a different day.

Section 3. If, at the time fixed for the beginning of the term of the President, the President elect shall have died, the Vice-President elect shall become President. If a President shall not have been chosen before the time fixed for the beginning of his term, or if the President elect shall have failed to qualify, then the Vice-President elect shall act as President until a President shall have qualified; and the Congress may by law provide for the case wherein neither a President elect nor a Vice-President elect shall have qualified, declaring who shall then act as President, or the manner in which one who is to act shall be selected, and such person shall act accordingly until a President or Vice-President shall have qualified.

Section 4. The Congress may by law provide for the case of the death of any of the persons from whom the House of Representatives may choose a President whenever the right of choice shall have devolved upon them, and for the case of the death of any of the persons from whom the Senate may choose a Vice-President whenever the right of choice shall have devolved upon them.

Section 5. Sections 1 and 2 shall take effect on the 15th day of October following the ratification of this article (Oct., 1933).

Section 6. This article shall be inoperative unless it shall have been ratified as an amendment to the Constitution by the legislatures of three-fourths of the several States within seven years from the date of its submission.

ARTICLE XXI

Repeal of the Eighteenth (Prohibition) Amendment by Conventions in the States.

The following proposed amendment to the Constitution, embodied in a joint resolution of the Seventy-second Congress (Senate, Feb. 16, 1933, by 63 to 23; House, Feb. 20, 1933, by 289 to 121), was transmitted to the Secretary of State on Feb. 21 and he at once sent to the Governors of the States copies of the resolution. The amendment went into effect Dec. 5, 1933, having been adopted by 36 of the 48 States—three-quarters of the entire number. The amendment is:

Section 1. The eighteenth article of amendment to the Constitution of the United States is hereby repealed.

Section 2. The transportation or importation into any State, Territory, or Possession of the United States for delivery or use therein of intoxicating liquors, in violation of the laws thereof, is hereby prohibited.

Section 3. This article shall be inoperative unless it shall have been ratified as an amendment to the Constitution by conventions in the several States, as provided in the Constitution, within seven years from the date of the submission hereof to the States by the Congress.

DECLARATION OF INDEPENDENCE

DECLARATION OF INDEPENDENCE

(Unanimously Adopted July 4, 1776.)

When in the Course of human events, it becomes necessary for one people to dissolve the political bands which have connected them with another, and to assume among the powers of the earth, the separate and equal station to which the Laws of Nature and of Nature's God entitle them, a decent respect to the opinions of mankind requires that they should declare the causes which impel them to the separation.

We hold these truths to be self-evident, that all men are created equal, that they are endowed by their Creator with certain unalienable Rights, that among these are Life, Liberty and the pursuit of Happiness. That to secure these rights, Governments are instituted among Men, deriving their just powers from the consent of the governed. That whenever any Form of Government becomes destructive of these ends, it is the Right of the People to alter or to abolish it, and to institute new Government, laying its foundation on such principles and organizing its powers in such form, as to them shall seem most likely to effect their Safety and Happiness. Prudence, indeed, will dictate that Governments long established should not be changed for light and transient causes; and accordingly all experience hath shewn, that mankind are more disposed to suffer, while evils are sufferable, than to right themselves by abolishing the forms to which they are accustomed. But when a long train of abuses and usurpations, pursuing invariably the same object evinces a design to reduce them under absolute Despotism, it is their right, it is their duty to throw off such Government, and to provide new Guards for their future security. Such has been the patient sufferance of these Colonies; and such is now the necessity which constrains them to alter their former Systems of Government. The history of the present King of Great Britain is a history of repeated injuries and usurpations, all having in direct object the establishment of an absolute Tyranny over these States. To prove this, let Facts be submitted to a candid world.

He has refused his Assent to Laws, the most wholesome and necessary for the public good.

He has forbidden his Governors to pass Laws of immediate and pressing importance, unless suspended in their operation till his Assent should be obtained, and when so suspended, he has utterly neglected to attend to them.

He has refused to pass other Laws for the accommodation of large districts of people, unless those people would relinquish the right of Representation in the Legislature, a right inestimable to them and formidable to tyrants only.

He has called together legislative bodies at places unusual, uncomfortable, and distant from the depository of their public Records, for the sole purpose of fatiguing them into compliance with his measures.

He has dissolved Representative Houses repeatedly, for opposing with manly firmness his invasions on the rights of the people.

He has refused for a long time, after such dissolutions, to cause others to be elected; whereby the Legislative powers, incapable of Annihilation, have returned to the People at large for their exercise; the State remaining in the meantime exposed to all the dangers of invasion from without, and convulsions within.

He has endeavoured to prevent the population of these States; for that purpose obstructing the Laws for Naturalization of Foreigners; refusing to pass others to encourage their migrations hither, and raising the conditions of new Appropriations of Lands.

He has obstructed the Administration of Justice, by refusing his Assent to Laws for establishing Judiciary powers.

He has made Judges dependent on his Will alone, for the tenure of their offices, and the amount and payment of their salaries.

He has erected a multitude of New Offices, and sent hither swarms of Officers to harass our people and eat out their substance.

He has kept among us, in times of peace, Standing Armies, without the Consent of our legislatures.

He has affected to render the Military independent of and superior to the Civil power.

He has combined with others to subject us to a jurisdiction foreign to our constitution and unacknowledged by our laws; giving his Assent to their Acts of pretended Legislation: For quartering large bodies of armed troops among us: For protecting them by a mock Trial from punishment for any Murders which they should commit on the Inhabitants of these States: For cutting off our Trade with all parts of the world: For imposing Taxes on us without our Consent: For depriving us in many cases of the benefits of Trial by Jury: For transporting us beyond Seas to be tried for pretended offenses: For abolishing the free System of English Laws in a neighbouring Province, establishing therein an Arbitrary government, and enlarging its Boundaries so as to render it at once an example and fit instrument for introducing the same absolute rule into these Colonies: For taking away our Charters, abolishing our most valuable Laws and altering fundamentally the Forms of our Governments: For suspending our own Legislatures, and declaring themselves invested with power to legislate for us in all cases whatsoever.

He has abdicated Government here by declaring us out of his Protection and waging War against us.

He has plundered our seas, ravaged our Coasts, burnt our towns, and destroyed the lives of our people.

He is at this time transporting large Armies of foreign Mercenaries to complete the works of death, desolation and tyranny, already begun with circumstances of cruelty and perfidy scarcely paralleled in the most barbarous ages, and totally unworthy the Head of a civilized nation.

He has constrained our fellow Citizens taken Captive on the high Seas to bear Arms against their Country, to become the executioners ot their friends and Brethren, or to fall themselves by their Hands.

He has excited domestic insurrections amongst us, and has endeavoured to bring on the inhabitants of our frontiers, the merciless Indian Savages, whose known rule of warfare is an undistinguished destruction of all ages, sexes and conditions. In every stage of these Oppressions We have Petitioned for Redress in the most humble terms. Our repeated Petitions have been answered only by repeated injury. A Prince, whose character is thus marked by every act which

SIGNERS OF THE DECLARATION OF INDEPENDENCE

NAME.	DELEGATE FROM.	OCCUPATION.	DATE OF BIRTH.	DATE OF DEATH.
Adams, John	Mass.	Lawyer	Oct. 30, 1735	July 4, 1826
Adams, Samuel	Mass.	Merchant	Sept. 27, 1722	Oct. 2, 1803
Bartlett, Josiah	N. H.	Dr. Judge	Nov. 21, 1729	May 19, 1795
Braxton, Carter	Va.	Planter	Sept. 10, 1736	Oct. 10, 1797
Carroll, Charles	Md.	Lawyer	Sept. 20, 1737	Nov. 14, 1832
Chase, Samuel	Md.	Lawyer	April 17, 1741	June 19, 1811
Clark, Abraham	N. J.	Lawyer	Feb. 15, 1726	Sept. 15, 1794
Clymer, George	Pa.	Merchant	Jan. 24, 1739	Jan. 23, 1813
Ellery, William	R. I.	Lawyer	Dec. 22, 1727	Feb. 15, 1820
Floyd, William	N. Y.	Farmer	Dec. 17, 1734	Aug. 4, 1821
Franklin, Benjamin	Pa.	Printer	Jan. 17, 1706	April 17, 1790
Gerry, Elbridge	Mass.	Merchant	July 17, 1744	Nov. 23, 1814
Gwinnett, Button	Ga.	Merchant	April 10, 1735	May 27, 1777
Hall, Lyman	Ga.	Physician	April 12, 1724	Oct. 19, 1790
Hancock, John	Mass.	Merchant	Jan. 12, 1737	Oct. 8, 1793
Harrison, Benjamin	Va.	Planter	1726	April, 1791
Hart, John	N. J.	Farmer	1708	 1780
Hewes, Joseph	N. C.	Lawyer	1730	Nov. 10, 1779
Heyward, Thomas, Jr.	S. C.	Lawyer	1746	Mar. 6, 1809
Hooper, William	N. C.	Lawyer	June 17, 1742	Oct., 1790
Hopkins, Stephen	R. I.	Farmer	Mar. 7, 1707	July 13, 1785
Hopkinson, Francis	N. J.	Lawyer	Sept. 21, 1737	May 9, 1791
Huntington, Samuel	Conn.	Lawyer	July 3, 1731	Jan. 5, 1796
Jefferson, Thomas	Va.	Lawyer	April 2, 1743	July 4, 1826
Lee, Richard Henry	Va.	Lawyer	Jan. 20, 1732	June 19, 1794
Lee, Francis Lightfoot	Va.	Farmer	Oct. 14, 1734	April 3, 1797
Lewis, Francis	N. Y.	Merchant	March, 1713	Dec. 19, 1803
Livingston. Philip	N. Y.	Merchant	Jan. 15, 1716	June 12, 1778

NAME.	DELEGATE FROM.	OCCUPATION.	DATE OF BIRTH.	DATE OF DEATH.
Lynch, Thomas, Jr.	S. C.	Lawyer	Aug. 5, 1749	(at sea) 1779
McKean, Thomas	Del.	Lawyer	Mar. 19, 1734	June 24, 1817
Middleton, Arthur	S. C.	Lawyer	June 26, 1742	Jan. 1, 1787
Morris, Lewis	N. Y.	Farmer	1726	Jan. 22, 1798
Morris, Robert	Pa.	Banker	Jan. 20, 1734	May 8, 1806
Morton, John	Pa.	Surveyor	1724	April, 1777
Nelson, Thomas, Jr.	Va.	Statesman	Dec. 26, 1738	Jan. 4, 1789
Paca, William	Md.	Lawyer	Oct. 31, 1740	 1799
Paine, Robert Treat	Mass.	Lawyer	Mar. 11, 1731	May 11, 1814
Penn, John	N. C.	Lawyer	May 17, 1741	Sept., 1788
Read, George	Del.	Lawyer	Sept. 17, 1733	Sept. 21, 1798
Rodney, Caesar	Del.	General	Oct. 7, 1728	June 29, 1784
Ross, George	Pa.	Lawyer	1730	July, 1779
Rush, Benjamin	Pa.	Physician	Dec. 24, 1745	April 19, 1813
Rutledge, Edward	S. C.	Lawyer	Nov. 23, 1749	Jan. 23, 1800
Sherman, Roger	Conn.	Shoemaker	April 19, 1721	July 23, 1793
Smith, James	Pa.	Lawyer	(About) 1720	July 11, 1806
Stockton, Richard	N. J.	Lawyer	Oct. 1, 1730	Feb. 28, 1781
Stone, Thomas	Md.	Lawyer	1743	Oct. 5, 1787
Taylor, George	Pa.	Physician	1716	Feb. 23, 1781
Thornton, Matthew	N. H.	Physician	Mar. 17, 1714	June 24, 1803
Walton, George	Ga.	Lawyer	1740	Feb. 2, 1804
Whipple, William	N. H.	Sailor	Jan. 14, 1730	Nov. 28, 1785
Williams, William	Conn.	Statesman	April 18, 1731	Aug. 2, 1811
Wilson, James	Pa.	Lawyer	Sept. 14, 1742	Aug. 28, 1798
Witherspoon, John	N. J.	Minister	Feb. 5, 1722	Sept. 15, 1794
Wolcott, Oliver	Conn.	Physician	Nov. 26, 1726	Dec. 1, 1797
Wythe, George	Va.	Lawyer	1726	June 8, 1806

may define a Tyrant, is unfit to be the ruler of a free people. Nor have We been wanting in attentions to our British brethren. We have warned them from time to time of attempts by their legislature to extend an unwarrantable jurisdiction over us. We have reminded them of the circumstances of our emigration and settlement here. We have appealed to their native justice and magnanimity, and we have conjured them by the ties of our common kindred to disavow these usurpations, which would inevitably interrupt our connections and correspondence. They too have been deaf to the voice of justice and of consanguinity. We must, therefore, acquiesce in the necessity, which denounces our Separation, and hold them, as we hold the rest of mankind, Enemies in War, in Peace Friends.

We, Therefore, the Representatives of the United States of America, in General Congress, Assembled, appealing to the Supreme Judge of the world for the rectitude of our intentions, do, in the Name, and by authority of the good People of these Colonies, solemnly publish and declare, That these United Colonies are, and of Right ought to be Free and Independent States; that they are Absolved from all Allegiance to the British Crown, and that all political connection between them and the State of Great Britain is and ought to be totally dissolved; and that as Free and Independent States, they have full Power to levy War, conclude Peace, contract Alliances, establish Commerce, and to do all other Acts and Things which Independent States may of right do. And for the support of this Declaration, with a firm reliance on the protection of Divine Providence, we mutually pledge to each other our Lives, our Fortunes, and our sacred Honor.

THE MONROE DOCTRINE

THE MONROE DOCTRINE

The pertinent parts of the Doctrine as announced by President Monroe in his message to Congress (December 2, 1823), are these:

. . . "the occasion has been judged proper for asserting, as a principle in which the rights and interests of the United States are involved, that the American continents, by the free and independent condition which they have assumed and maintain, are henceforth not to be considered as subjects for future colonization by any European powers.

. . . "It is only when our rights are invaded or seriously menaced that we resent injuries or make preparation for our defense. With the movements in this hemisphere we are of necessity more immediately connected, and by causes which must be obvious to all enlightened and impartial observers. The political system of the allied powers is essentially different in this respect from that of America. This difference proceeds from that which exists in their respective Governments; and to the defense of our own, which has been achieved by the loss of so much blood and treasure, and matured by the wisdom of their most enlightened citizens, and under which we have enjoyed unexampled felicity, this whole nation is devoted.

"We owe it, therefore, to candor and to the amicable relations existing between the United States and those powers to declare that we should consider any attempt on their part to extend their system to any portion of this hemisphere as dangerous to our peace and safety. With the existing colonies or dependencies of any European power we have not interfered and shall not interfere.

"But with the Governments who have declared their independence and maintained it, and whose independence we have, on great consideration and on just principles, acknowledged, we could not view any interposition for the purpose of oppressing them, or controlling in any other manner their destiny, by any European power in any other light than as the manifestation of an unfriendly disposition toward the United States.

"It is still the true policy of the United States to leave the parties to themselves, in the hope that other powers will pursue the same course."